ADVANCES IN
BUSINESS MARKETING
AND PURCHASING

Volume 5 • 1992

MAPPING HOW
INDUSTRY BUYS

Advances in Business Marketing and Purchasing, Volume 5

EDITORIAL BOARD

ADVANCES IN BUSINESS MARKETING AND PURCHASING

MAPPING HOW INDUSTRY BUYS

Editor: ARCH G. WOODSIDE
A.B. Freeman School of Business
Tulane University

VOLUME 5 • 1992

 JAI PRESS INC.

Greenwich, Connecticut　　　　　　　　*London, England*

CONTENTS

LIST OF CONTRIBUTORS

Michael J. Baker

Department of Marketing
University of Strathclyde
Scotland

Wouter Faes

School of Economics
University of Gent
Belgium

Dr. T. Ireneo

School of Economics
University of Gent
Belgium

Anita M. Kennedy

Department of Marketing
University of Strathclyde
Scotland

Kristian Möller

Marketing Department
Helsinki School of Economics
State College—Finland

Orla Nielsen

Institute of Marketing
Copenhagen School of Economics
  and Business Administration
Denmark

Stephen T. Parkinson

Management Centre
University of Bradford
United Kingdom

Jacques de Rijcke

Economische Wetenschappen
Rijksuniversiteit-Gent
Belgium

vii

Daniel L. Sherrell

Marketing Department
College of Business Administration
Louisiana State University

Jan B. Vollering

Graduate School of Marketing
Erasmus University
The Netherlands

Arch G. Woodside

Freeman School of Business
Tulane University

DEDICATION

This volume of the *Advances in Business Marketing and Purchasing* series is dedicated to the Professional Development (Pro-D) Committees of all chapters of the National Association of Purchasing Management in the United States and similar committees in other countries that are working to improve the knowledge, insights, and skills of purchasing professional. In particular, *Volume 5* is dedicated to H. Ervin Lewis, CPM, the Purchasing Manager at Wellman Inc., South Carolina, and a highly active member in the Purchasing Management Association of Carolinas-Virginia, a chapter of N.A.P.M. Erv Lewis encouraged the research project that resulted in the in-depth case studies on purchasing strategies reported in this volume. The support of PMAC-V and the insights and encouragement of Erv Lewis to complete this project is deeply appreciated.

PREFACE

The importance of effective industrial purchasing strategies in achieving acceptable returns on investments within the firm has been confirmed in several empirical studies. The key finding of these studies is that an effective purchasing strategy has a greater impact on return on investment (ROI) than any other single strategic activity within the firm. While an effective marketing strategy (e.g., product planning and customer segmentation), has the greater impact on increasing sales and market share, ROI is more sensitive to specific measures that increase the effectiveness of purchasing activity (see Buzzell, Gale, and Sultan 1975; Woodside and Samuel 1981).

Industrial purchasing activity accounts for 40 to 70% of the purchasing dollar in most firms in the United States, United Kingdom, Denmark, and other highly industrialized nations. A 1% reduction in the total cost of purchases converts to an average increase in ROI of 4%. The recognition of the potential ROI impact and the sheer dollar volume of purchasing activity are the primary reasons that purchasing strategies are receiving more attention from senior management and academic scholars in the 1980s versus the 1970s.

One result of this increase in attention has been an upward shift in the organizational position/authority of purchasing within the firm. In the early 1980s, the senior purchasing officer was included as a full member of the senior executive committees in large multiplant corporations for the first time.

A second result of the increase in attention directed to purchasing is an increase in the amount of empirical scholarly research being devoted to purchasing. Research on purchasing strategies has become more scientific and less speculative in the 1980s than previous decades. Thus, both the quantity and quality of research on purchasing has increased.

Empirical and scientific research on purchasing strategies includes the planning and execution of studies based on theory and tested by analyzing primary data—data collected specifically for the planned study. Thus, the publication of hard evidence that purchasing strategy usually has the largest impact on ROI, and the sheer size of industrial purchasing as a share of sales, are resulting in a revolution in purchasing philosophy and corporate management culture.

The 1950s and 1960s marked the decades of adoption of the marketing concept by senior management in large corporations; the position of Executive or Senior Vice President for Marketing was introduced in the mid-1960s for the first time in most corporations, for example, AT&T (see Guiltinan and Paul 1985). The 1970s and 1980s have proven to be the decades of adoption of a strategic purchasing concept by senior management: the purchasing strategist is a full partner with the marketing strategist in developing and implementing actions to achieve sales and ROI objectives.

The relationship between evidence, attention, and action is summarized in Figure 1. Without the initial research and reporting on the impact of purchasing on ROI and the recognition of the large purchasing/sales ratios involved, the attention and actions of senior management would not have followed.

Hard Evidence:	Attention:	Actions:
Purchasing Most Affects →	by Senior Management →	Reorganize, Record
ROI and Is Large	& Research	

Figure 1.   Causes of the Strategic Purchasing Concept

This volume is one result of the adoption of the strategic purchasing concept. Recognizing the importance of industrial purchasing in reaching a firm's profit objectives, a small group of industrial marketing professors from several countries joined together as a research team. They applied the same research method in conducting research on strategies in industrial purchasing. The research team named itself the Industrial Buying Behavior (IBB) Group.

Research on strategies used in industrial purchasing that includes primary data collections is a relatively recent phenomenon compared to research on marketing strategies. Therefore, the IBB Group team decided to set one central objective. The goal was to describe in detail the emerging purchasing strategies for major purchases in industrial firms. The emerging purchasing strategies include the streams of behavior, decisions, and interactions of people involved in the purchasing process. Decision systems analysis (DSA) was the primary data collection method selected by the research team (see Hulbert [1981] for a description of DSA). The results of DSA include detailed flow diagrams of the streams of behavior, decisions, and interactions for specific purchasing strategies, along with diagnostic commentaries by members of the research team. The method, flow diagrams, and commentaries are reported in-depth in this book.

The central purpose of the research effort reported here is to increase understanding of how industrial purchasing strategies actually work. The secondary purpose is to provide diagnostic insights on how industrial purchasing and marketing strategies might be improved. The ultimate aim of the IBB Group is to contribute to the building of a behavioral theory of industrial purchasing strategy which includes a description of what is and recommendations on what should be. The reader is provided with insights on how purchasing behaviors, decisions, and interactions of people combine and flow through time. Theoretical propositions are developed from the descriptions, as well as insights to help shape future research and to form a behavioral theory of purchasing strategies.

The research support provided by Deans James W. McFarland and John M. Trapani of Tulane University helped substantially in completing the research project resulting in *Volume 5*. This support is very much appreciated. The editorial assistance work of Emily Charles and Deborah Loze is acknowledged with gratitude. The plan and work related to this volume benefitted from the research encouragement and financial support provided by Malcolm S. Woldenberg and his family; their support is appreciated.

The really useful training yields a comprehension of a few general principles [propositions] with a thorough grounding in the way they apply to a variety of concrete details.

—Alfred North Whitehead 1861-1947.

Arch G. Woodside
Series Editor

REFERENCES

Buzzell, R.D., B.T. Gale, and R.G.M. Sultan. (1975). "Market Share—A Key to Profitability." *Harvard Business Review* 53(January-February): 97-106.

Guiltinan and Paul. (1985).

Hulbert, J.M. (1953). "Descriptive Models of Marketing Decisions." In *Marketing Decisions Models*, edited by R.L. Schultz and A.A. Zoltners. New York: North-Holland.

Woodside, A.G., and D.M. Samuel. (1981). "Observations of Centralized Corporate Procurement." *Industrial Marketing Management* 10:191-195.

EMERGING STRATEGIES FOR INDUSTRIAL PURCHASING

Arch G. Woodside

"A pattern in a stream of decisions" is the operating definition of "strategy" used in this book. This definition was developed to operationalize the concept of strategy, namely to provide a tangible basis on which to conduct research into how strategy occurs in industrial purchasing. The central focus here is on realized purchasing strategies: the actual stream of decisions, behaviors, and interaction of people involved in buying.

Realized strategies may be based on emergent or deliberate strategies or a blend of these. Deliberate strategies are streams of decisions realized as intended (as planned). Emergent strategies are patterns realized despite, or in the absence of, intentions (see Mintzberg and Waters 1985).

The objectives of this book are (1) to increase understanding of realized strategies for industrial purchasing in several national environments, (2) to provide structure (diagrams, models, and theory) of realized strategies, and (3) to compare realized strategy to normative (i.e., textbook recommended) strategy for insight into ways to improve industrial purchasing and marketing.

Advances in Business Marketing and Purchasing, Volume 5, pages 1-19.
Copyright © 1992 by JAI Press Inc.
ISBN: 1-55938-364-X

TWO RESEARCH APPROACHES

Two research approaches appear to have been taken most often in the study of industrial purchasing strategies: surveys on how industry buys and case studies describing the streams of behaviors, interactions, and decisions occurring in buying.

Surveys

Large-scale surveys (with sample sizes greater than 2,000) on how industry buys (e.g., "How Industry Buys/1970" 1969) were beneficial in focusing the attention of business strategists and academic scholars on the scarcity of empirical evidence available on how buying actually occurs in industry. The key finding in these studies was that no more than one-half of product or vendor selection decisions are made by the purchasing department; other departments, notably design and development engineering, production engineering, and research, often dominate project initiation and specification of purchasing processes.

Before the survey studies on how industry buys, most publications on industrial purchasing strategies were based on personal insights and speculations of the authors. These publications often provided recommendations and checklists of questions to consider and rules-of-thumb to follow. While such recommendations may be useful, no evidence was provided concerning what questions and rules-of-thumb were actually used by purchasing strategists or whether or not the recommendations were adopted.

Thus, the studies on how industry buys were valuable in calling the attention of both strategists and scholars to the need for empirical research on purchasing decisions, behavior, and interactions of the people involved in the purchasing process. Only a handful of researchers were concerned with documenting the purchasing process before the large-scale survey studies on how industry buys (e.g., Robinson, Faris, and Wind 1967).

The important positive function of calling attention to the need for empirical research on purchasing strategies compensates for the shortcomings of the how industry buys surveys. The shortcomings of these studies were severe: low response rates to the mail surveys used to collect data (less than 30% response); responses from only one person per firm, causing a biased view of who was actually involved in the buying process; focusing only on the issue of who was involved, and not on what decision rules were used, how conflicts were resolved, or whether or not specific buying activities were actually performed. Furthermore, neither pre-tests of the survey form nor post-checks on who actually completed the surveys were performed.

Survey research on how industry buys continues. Attempts have been made to improve survey research procedures since the early studies and to relate empirical studies of how industry buys to theories on these buying processes. The size of the surveys have been reduced substantially and questions on how decisions are made have been included for different purchasing problems—new-task versus straight rebuy situations (e.g., Doyle, Woodside, and Mitchell 1979; Bellizzi 1979; Dempsey 1978). Valuable information on how industry buys is being provided by such survey studies.

Case Studies

The first systematic attempts to build a theory of purchasing strategy based on reality, an application of theory-in-use, was the work of Howard and Moore (1963) and Strauss (1962). Howard and Moore (1963) suggested that the basic unit of analysis for theory development was the decision process actually used in purchasing. The following conclusions can be drawn based on Howard and Moore:

1. Reality-based theory of purchasing strategy is needed to provide structure, a complete picture of what is occurring in buying behavior.
2. Actual decision processes are composed of a finite series of steps in the form of highly simplified rules (i.e., heuristics for making choices).
3. It is possible to accurately describe important and complex buying processes with relatively simple nonoptimizing models; these models represent fairly rational behavior.

Howard and Moore provided the first purchasing strategy buyflows: diagrams of the decisions (heuristics, choices, and rationales), interactions of people, and observed behavior occurring in industrial purchasing. (See Moore [1969a, 1969b] for further reports on this work.)

Strauss (1962) called attention to interactions among several people and departments related to buying—buyer, specifying engineer, using department—within the industrial firm. He found that the buyer's work behavior is influenced strongly by "lateral negotiations" with people in other departments. "The ambitious buyer skillfully uses formal and informal techniques to influence the terms of the requisitions that he receives. Thus, he introduces a two-way work flow [decision buyflow] and in this way raises his own status."

Even though Strauss did not use the term, his work was the first to demonstrate the importance of informally formed buying centers. These centers consist of two or more persons employed by the firm who interact in making buying decisions. Thus, interaction between people is one of three key dimensions of purchasing strategies. The other two dimensions include decisions (heuristics, choices, and rationales) and observable behaviors (e.g., purchase requisitions, request for quotes, vendor quotes, purchase orders, vendor evaluation reports, value analysis of competing materials or components).

The best known inductive (observation to theory) case approach in determining the decisions, behaviors, and interactions of people in firms is the work of Cyert and March (1963). While their behavioral theory of the firm is not built on strategies for industrial purchasing, they do demonstrate that complex organizational problems are solved in practice by dividing the problems into a series of subproblems and applying simple decision rules. The most important insight provided by Cyert and March is that attempts to optimize solutions within departments (e.g., purchasing, engineering, and user departments), often result in suboptimizing solutions for the entire firm. For example, what is best for specifying engineering may be not considering a new material and supplier because of the risks of product failure (even though testing indicates successful product performance); the specifying engineer may view any new material or vendor as too risky, given that current suppliers of known materials are providing a satisfactory product. The direct rewards experienced for approving a new material may be perceived as small, even nonexistent, by the specifying engineer. Furthermore, the risk of reprimand if product failure occurs is great.

THE BASIC FRAMEWORK FOR CASE RESEARCH ON STRATEGIES FOR INDUSTRIAL PURCHASING

The Buygrid Model (Robinson, Faris, and Wind 1967) is a useful basic framework for examining strategies used in industrial purchasing (see Table 1).

Table 1. The Buygrid Analytic Framework for Industrial Buying Situations

	Buyclasses		
Buyphases	*New Task*	*Modified Rebuy*	*Straight Rebuy*
1. Anticipation or Recognition of a Problem (Need) and a General Solution			
2. Determination of Characteristics and Quantity of Needed Item			
3. Description of Characteristics and Quantity of Needed Item			
4. Search for and Qualfication of Potential Sources			
5. Acquisition and Analysis of Proposals			
6. Evaluation of Proposals and Selection of Supplier(s)			
7. Selection of an Order Routine			
8. Performance Feedback and Evaluation			

Notes: 1. The most complex buying situations occur in the upper left portion of the Buygrid matrix, when the largest number of decision makers and buying influences are involved. Thus, a New Task in its initial phase of problem recognition generally represents the greatest difficulty for management.
2. Clearly, a New Task may entail policy questions and special studies, whereas a Modified Rebuy may be more routine, and a Straight Rebuy essentially automatic.
3. As Buyphases are completed, moving from phase 1 through phase 8, the process of "creeping commitment" occurs, and there is diminishing likelihood of new vendors gaining access to the buying situation.

Source: From Robinson, Faris, and Wind (1967).

Most industrial buying strategies are in one of three classes: new task, modified rebuys, or straight rebuys. These three buyclasses vary in complexity, length of time, buying center member participation, dollar volume, and amount of previous buying experience. New task buying decisions tend to be complex, extended in time, involving four or more departments and persons, high in dollar volume, and involve serious consideration of vendors never before used by the firm. Modified rebuys usually involve changes in written specifications on production materials or component parts. Current vendors are usually awarded the contracts in modified rebuys, but not necessarily. Straight rebuys involve no changes in product specifications or vendors, but may involve changes in delivery dates, share of requirements allocated by in-suppliers, and some price negotiation.

How an industrial purchasing case situation is classified within a particular buyclass depends primarily on the perceived importance of the purchase. Negotiations with vendors for annual plant purchase agreements (PPAs) involving materials purchased for several years may have more characteristics in common with a new task buying situation than a straight rebuy.

Marketing managers apparently have little difficulty identifying the BUYCLASS situations facing their customers. In one study (Doyle, Woodside, and Michell 1979), industrial marketing managers with customers in new task/modified rebuy situations reported substantially different buying decision processes than those managers with customers in straight rebuy situations. The results of this study are summarized in Table 2.

Note in Table 2 that several buying decision process variables varied substantially between the two categories of BUYCLASSES (e.g., length of time taken in the decision process, number of persons in the buying center, and sources of contact for the marketers).

In Table 1, eight BUYPHASES are listed. BUYPHASES are the steps taken during the buying process. Each buyphase is a decision subroutine. Two important theory-in-use propositions should be noted about the eight BUYPHASES. First, some steps are skipped because of previous experience. For example, Step 4 (Search for and Qualification of Potential Sources) is skipped in buying situations identified as straight rebuys and usually in modified rebuys. Second, completion of one step is not necessary before another step is taken; the eight buyphases often occur simultaneously. Feedback loops among the buyphases often occur, and each step may appear several times in actual buying strategies.

For large-scale new task buyclass problems, these two theory-in-use principles have been well documented by Witte (1972) and others (Cyert, Simon, and Trow 1956; Vyas and Woodside 1986). The results of these studies refute the basic "phase theorem" that buying decision processes follow one specific pattern from (1) problem identification, (2) obtaining necessary information, (3) production of possible solutions, (4) evaluation of such solutions, (5) selection of a strategy for performance, and (6) actual performance of an action or actions.

Witte (1972) best summarizes tests of the phase theorem. Although the phase theorem was not supported in its full meaning, the following propositions were confirmed: (1) complex, innovative decision making is a multi-operational, multi-temporal process; (2) a complex decision-making process does not have only one final decision, but consists of a plurality of subdecisions—most of these choices occur at the end of the total process; (3) the theorem's claim of information-gathering, alternative-developing, and alternative-evaluating operations can be

Table 2. Summary of Findings of Organizational Buying Process for
Two Buying Class Groups

	Buyclass	
Process Variable	*New-Task/Modified Rebuy (n = 7)*	*Straight Rebuy (n = 7)*
Length of time	Seven months to five years	One week to seven months
Number in buying center	Three to six members	Two to three members
Source of contact of suppliers	Purchasing agent, plant or project manager, engineer	Purchasing agent
Initiating need to buy	Manager, other suppliers, engineers	Purchasing agent, user
Concession limits	Price, product, performance, delivery, guarantee	Delivery, price, terms of payment
Composition of buying party	Fluctuates	PA and fluctuates
Reasons for supplier contact by customers	Modifications desired, incapable suppliers, dissatisfaction	Depletion of stocks, dissatisfaction
Postpurchase evaluation procedure	Informal, sometimes informal	Informal

Source: Doyle, Woodside, and Mitchell (1979).

discerned in any decision-making processes. However, these steps do not culminate in distinct phases in time, but are distributed over the total duration of the process.

AN EARLY EXAMPLE OF THE CASE APPROACH TO RESEARCH IN STRATEGIES FOR INDUSTRIAL PURCHASING

The stream of behavior and the people/departments involved in buying a special industrial drill are summarized in Figure 1; people are shown as nodes and behavior is shown as connecting lines. Note in Figure 1 that the same buying problem can be in any of the three buyclasses: new task, modified rebuy, or straight rebuy for this specific purchase. The planner node (node 5 in the figure), is a critical turning point in this stream of decisions and behaviors. If the planner's search reveals no previous purchases of the specified special drill, a new task buying strategy emerges. If the planner's search does reveal previous purchase experience, a modified rebuy or straight rebuy decision stream is entered

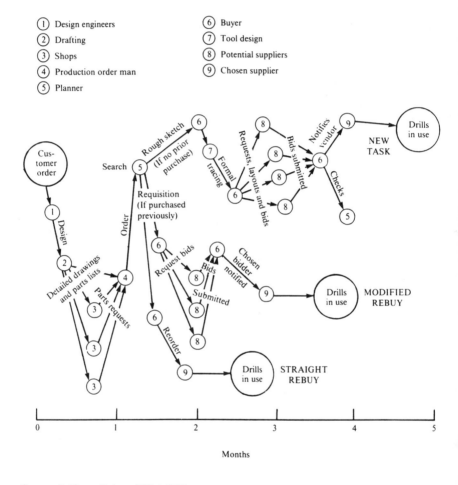

Figure 1.   Decision Network Diagram of the Buying Situations: Special Drill

Whether or not the modified rebuy or straight rebuy decision stream is entered is important to both the buyer and current suppliers. In Figure 1 bids are requested only in the modified rebuy and new task decision stream. Entering a straight rebuy decision stream is good for Supplier 9, less work for the buyer, and involves less time putting the drill into use (2.8 months versus 3.8 months). Shown in Figure 1 are the rationales—explanations for the turning points. For example, why does a buying decision become a modified rebuy versus a straight rebuy? Explanations, rationales, for the selection of one decision stream versus another can be divided into two parts: (1) decision attributes for making a choice and (2) heuristics, the rules-of-thumb or company purchasing policies, which dictate the method of applying the decision attributes. "Requests bids if three or more qualified suppliers are available and substantial cost savings can be achieved by bidding, reorder from the first qualified recalled otherwise" might be the operating rationale for selecting the modified rebuy versus straight rebuy stream. Rationales can be included in diagraming purchasing strategies. Determining the rationales—decision attributes and heuristics—used in actual purchasing strategies is crucial in understanding why specific behavioral streams are selected.

The Creeping Commitment Proposition

The decision streams in Figure 1 illustrate a third proposition of theory-in-use in industrial purchasing strategies, the creeping commitment hypothesis: decision making actually involves a sequence of incremental choices, each of which eliminates certain alternative solutions from further consideration.

> As each successive decision is made, the number of possible alternatives is reduced. Eventually, the bulk of initial alternatives has been eliminated and only a few alternative solutions to the problem are feasible (Robinson, Faris, and Wind 1967, p. 19).

Creeping Commitment versus Revised Phase Theorem

The creeping commitment and revised phase theorem propositions taken together present an apparent paradox. The revised phase theorem states that problem definition, searching for and gathering information, alternative evaluation, and making choices occur in all time intervals during a decision stream; the creeping commitment proposition involves the elimination of specific behavior/decision streams and the increasing likelihood of following remaining or emerging behavior/decision streams. How can commitment creep toward one stream when all things remain possible according to the phase theorem?

This paradox is resolved by viewing the creeping commitment proposition at a micro-analysis level, with the emphasis on the elimination of specific alternative solutions during the buying process— commitment creeps, in that eliminated solutions rarely receive a second consideration. All of the decision steps in the phase theorem are likely to occur in several time periods for important buying problems. Thus, "no one solution is guaranteed" is a corollary to the revised phase theorem. "Once a vendor or product design is eliminated no opportunity to rebid is given" is an example of creeping commitment. Both propositions are likely to be observed in important buying problems, for example, annual plant purchase agreements.

RATIONALE FOR CASE RESEARCH ON STRATEGIES FOR INDUSTRIAL PURCHASING

Peter's (1981) dictum in marketing applies equally well for industrial purchasing: "we clearly need to know *what* behaviors people perform before we can explain *why* they perform them. Not only has little study been devoted to overt behavior, but little attention has been given to delineating the basic sequence of behaviors people must perform to purchase a product or other sequences or behavior of interest in marketing" (p. 143).

The prime reason for case research on strategies used in industrial purchasing is to increase the understanding of how and why buying processes occur. What heuristics and buying criteria are used and when are they used? What are the contents, conflicts, and outcomes of interactions of people in the buying center and between members of the buying center and vendors? What are the actions and sequences of actions in the streams of behavior in real-life industrial purchasing strategies?

The case approach involves ethnographic research methods: a long period of intimate study and residence in a well-defined community (the firm), employing a wide range of observational techniques. These include prolonged face-to-face contact with members of local groups, direct participation in some of the groups' activities, and an emphasis on intensive work with informants rather than the use of documentary or survey data (Conklin 1978). The end results are (1) detailed descriptions of actual streams of behaviors, interactions, and decisions; (2) theory-in-use propositions (e.g., the revised phase theorem), suitable for testing using other research methods; and (3) post hoc, prescriptive, insights on how the effectiveness of the observed strategies might be improved.

The case approach is best viewed as a complement to the more widely used "empirical positivist" research methods. The empirical positivist approach involves deductive reasoning—a formal statement of hypotheses before data collection and tests of the hypothesis using classical statistics, for example, analysis of variance and multiple regression analysis. Testing the validity of a theory (and competing theories) is the purpose of empirical positivism. Tests of validity of theory usually include measures of association (e.g., correlation coefficients) between independent and dependent variables.

Developing theory is the ultimate goal of the case approach and other descriptive research methods. The term "validity" in the case approach refers to accuracy of the observations/recordings of streams of behaviors. Validity is achieved through several methods: using different observers, different research methods (observation, interviews, document analysis), and observing/recording multiple time periods and multiple cases.

The case approach is "direct" research having the seven properties outlined by Mintzberg (1979), applied to research on industrial purchasing strategies.

1. Much of the data collection is purely descriptive, "as purely descriptive as we have been able to make it" (Mintzberg 1979, p. 583). Such an approach provides insights, and raises serious doubts about a good deal of accepted wisdom on the execution of strategies, for example, strategy formation is better understood as a discontinuous, adaptive process rather than a formally planned one.

2. The research relies on simple—in a sense, inelegant— methodologies. Depth is preferred over width in the case approach. Small samples and detailed descriptions are the usual result. For new task buying the case researcher would prefer to interview and observe 4 persons in each of 10 firms than 40 persons from 40 different firms.

3. The research is as purely inductive as possible. It includes two steps: (1) detective work to accurately report strategies used in industrial buying, and (2) some creative leaps taken in summarizing the observed streams of behaviors, interactions, and decisions. Detective work in case research involves relying on multiple sources of information—asking the same questions independently to several persons working in several departments who were involved in the buying process, direct observation, and document analysis—and resolving conflicts in data whenever possible. Sherlock Holmes is the role-model of the case researcher.

4. The research is systematic in nature. Data are collected on the sequence of steps taken (and in most cases retaken) during the buying process. The number of contacts—face-to-face, telephone, and correspondence—between persons is recorded, and the content of these interactions is analyzed. "Hard" data does exist, and is collected in case research on industrial purchasing strategies.

The studies by Pettigrew (1973, 1975) are examples of the best systematic case research. Pettigrew provided detailed evidence that middle managers may act as gatekeepers between senior and junior management concerning information on vendor evaluation. Pettigrew analyzed the number of contacts as well as the contents of written communications between middle and junior management with competing vendors over several months.

5. The research is measured in real organizational terms. Doing case research involves getting out into the field (i.e., inside real organizations). Establishing the validity of an interview or observation datum requires a second source confirming the first datum point; preferably. The second piece of information should be collected from a different information source. Thus, interview data are validated by direct observation and/or written documents. Case researchers tend to believe it only if they can see it *and* read it, or interview two persons about it.

6. The research, by its intensive nature, ensures that systematic data are supported by anecdotal data. "Theory building seems to require rich description, the richness that comes from anecdote. We uncover all kinds of relationships in our "hard" data, but it is only through the use of this "soft" data that we are able to explain them, and explanation is, of course, the purpose of [case] research" (Mintzberg 1979, p. 587.)

7. The research seeks to synthesize, to integrate diverse elements into configurations or ideal types. These configurations are summary

patterns, typologies, of what usually occurs in the main streams of behavior, interactions, decisions. Such typologies are presented in this book at three levels of detail.

Level 1:   within the firm for a given material or component part at a specific buyclasss (e.g., new task)

Level 2:   across firms showing details of actual purchasing strategies for all three buyclasses

Level 3:   a summary across firms and buyclasses.

Level 3 is the most general typology. An example of a Level 3 typology is from Vyas and Woodside (1986) presented in Figure 2.

The stream of behaviors, interactions, and decisions is divided into five stages in Figure 2. Two or more persons are involved in each stage; one to three decisions (heuristics, rationales, and choices) are included in each stage; and one to three behaviors are described briefly in each stage. A great deal of information is provided in Figure 2, but for rich detail and insight typologies at Levels 1 and 2 must be examined. Several Level 1 and 2 typologies are included in the papers in this book.

TYPOLOGIES AND TAXONOMIES

Typologies differ from taxonomies. While both involve creative leaps from data, typologies are attempts to classify and summarize descriptions of reality, descriptions made from induction. Taxonomies are attempts to classify and summarize predictions of reality, predictions made from deduction. A useful taxonomy of strategies in industrial buying behavior has been provided by Sheth (1973) and is summarized in Figure 3. This model has been constructed by deduction: the insights and literature review (see Sheth 1977) by Sheth.

Sheth's deductive model is a Level 3 type model which shows that purchasing strategy consists of four parts:

1.   expectations of the participants in the buying center,
2.   an industrial buying process,
3.   conflict resolution, and
4.   situational factors.

This deductive model is useful in suggesting specific hypotheses to be tested (e.g., the presence or absence of specific conditions for

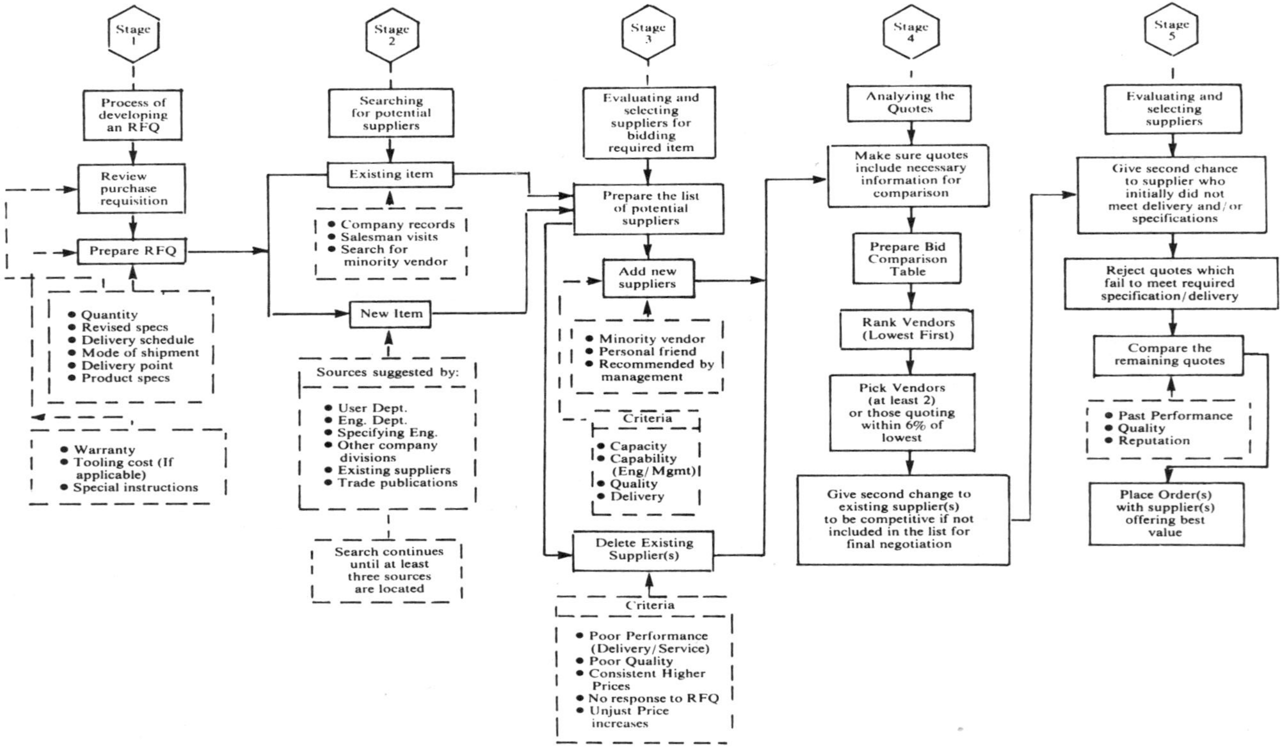

Figure 2. Major Steps Observed in the Purchase Decision Process for Packaging

Source: Vyas and Woodside (1986, p. 50).

14

autonomous versus joint decisions, the particular mechanisms used to resolve conflicts among the participants in the buying center).

Similar to the typology presented in Figure 2, the taxonomy in Figure 3 summarizes out much detail. Deductive research using Figure 3 would involve testing specific hypotheses (e.g., conflict is a common consequence within the buying center because of the differing goals and perceptions of the persons/departments who are members of the buying center). The IBB Group advocates further development of inductive models parallel to the testing of Sheth's and others (e.g., Webster and Wind 1972) deductive models. Both approaches provide useful information for understanding and predicting strategies used in industrial buying behavior.

PLAN OF THE VOLUME

Following this introductory paper, general, Level 3, inductive models of industrial purchasing are described in the paper by Woodside and Möller. The general inductive modelling approach is compared with a general normative model of how industrial purchasing strategy *should be* executed.

In the paper by Woodside and Sherrell, a case study is presented to illustrate a new replacement-part buying situation for disc refinery plates.

The next paper, Tufted Carpets Limited, by Parkinson and Baker is a case study which presents a purchasing situation for a promising new material in the carpet manufacturing industry—needled woven polypropylene.

Another paper by Parkinson and Baker provides insight into the buyflow process for three individual companies engaged in purchasing the same piece of equipment, a JCB 110B crawler-loader machine.

A complex purchasing situation for a Danish contracting firm is presented in the first paper by Nielsen. The situation involves a modified rebuy purchasing process for a production materials component, steel casting.

In another paper by Nielsen, the purchasing process for a component needed in the manufacturing of a new product is observed for the ABNEL Company, a large, Danish electronics company.

The paper by Vollering presents the case of the Delsola Cosmetics Company, which seeks a restyling of its present shampoo product

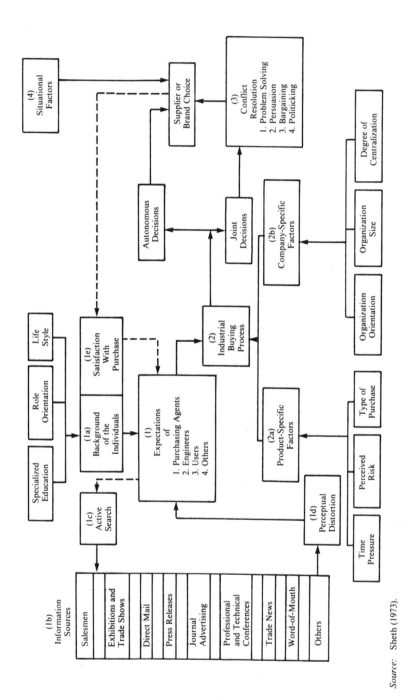

Figure 3. An Integrative Model of Industrial Buyer Behavior

Source: Sheth (1973).

16

packaging to enhance marketing efforts. The restyling involves a rather complex problem solving process.

The case study presented in a second paper by Vollering illustrates a highly challenging purchase decision involving gum rosin, a gelling agent used in the production of printing ink. Research and development both internal and external to the firm prove to play an influential role in the purchasing process.

The paper by Faes and de Rijcke includes a case study that presents the most complex of all purchasing situations. The pharmaceutical company in the case faces a new buy situation for a chemical raw material needed in the production of an important new drug. The case is complicated by the fact that the raw material needed is not immediately available on the market.

The paper by Faes and Ireneo describes the purchasing process for a Belgian manufacturer of engineering plastics. The process is complex, and reflects the importance of involving the purchasing department from an early stage in determining new material specifications.

The results of a case history analysis of the J. Hampden & Company Ltd.'s decision to purchase steel plate is presented in a paper by Kennedy. A flow-chart method is used to document the many activities, events, and people involved in the course of the purchasing process.

The final paper by Woodside includes a summary of the theoretical propositions and structures on what the IBB Group has learned about strategies in-use in industrial buying behavior. Suggestions for future research projects are also included.

A UNIQUE CONTRIBUTION

Comparative analyses of industrial purchasing strategies within several industrialized nations are included in this book. While research on international marketing and purchasing strategies has been reported elsewhere (Cunningham 1983; Hakansson 1984; Turnbull 1981) and is reviewed briefly in the present book, the focus by the IBB Group has been on inductive modelling within manufacturing firms located in several industrialized nations. Some of these inductive models do include strategies in-use that involve international purchasing. However, comparisons of industrial purchasing strategies among the countries studied are emphasized, rather than focusing only on international buying and marketing strategies.

REFERENCES

Bellizzi, J.A. (1979). "Product Type and the Relative Influence of Buyers in Commercial Construction," *Industrial Marketing Management*, 8(1979), 213-220.

Conklin, H. (1978). "Ethnography." Pp. 115-208 in *International Encyclopedia of Social Sciences*, Vol. 5, edited by D.L. Sills. New York: Free Press.

Cunningham, M.T. (1983). "International Marketing and Purchasing of Industrial Goods—Features of a European Research Project." *European Journal of Marketing*, 14: 322-338.

Cyert, R.M., and J.G. March. (1963). *A Behavioral Theory of the Firm*. Englewood Cliffs, NJ: Prentice-Hall.

Cyert, R.M., H.A. Simon, and D.B. Trow. (1956). "Observation of a Business Decision." *Journal of Business* 29(October): 237-238.

Dempsey, W.A. (1978). "Vendor Selection and the Buying Process." *Industrial Marketing Management*, 7: 257-267.

Doyle, P., A.G. Woodside, and P. Mitchell. (1979). "Organizations Buying in New-Task and Rebuy Situations." *Industrial Marketing Management* 8.

"How Industry Buys/1970." (1969). New York: Scientific American.

Howard, J.A., and C.G. Moore. "A Descriptive Model of the Purchasing Function." Unpublished monograph, Graduate School of Business, University of Pittsburgh.

Mintzberg, H. (1979). "An Emerging Study of 'Direct' Research." *Administrative Science Quarterly* 24(December): 582-589.

Mintzberg, H., and J.A. Waters. (1985). "Of Strategies, Deliberate and Emergent." *Strategic Management Journal* 6: 257-272.

Moore, C.G. (1969b). "A Descriptive Model of the Industrial Purchasing Process: The Supplier Selection Routine." In *Management Action: Models of Administrative Decisions*, edited by C.E. Weber and G. Peters. Scranton, PA: International Textbook.

Moore, C.G. (1969b). "Simulating Actual Decision-Making Process in Organizations: A Progress Report." In *Management Action: Models of Administrative Decisions*, edited by C.E. Weber and G. Peters. Scranton, PA: International Textbook.

Peter, J.P. (1981). "Construct Validity: A Review of Basic Issues and Marketing Practices." *Journal of Marketing Research* 18(May): 133-145.

Pettigrew, A. (1973). *The Politics of Organizational Decision Making*. London: Tavistock.

Pettigrew, A. (1975). "The Industrial Purchasing Decision as a Political Process." *European Journal of Marketing* 9(March): 4-19.

Robinson, P.J., C.W. Faris, and Y. Wind. (1967). *Industrial Buying and Creative Marketing*. Boston: Allyn & Bacon.

Sheth, J.N. (1973). "A Model of Industrial Buyer Behavior." *Journal of Marketing* 37: 50-56.

Sheth, J.N. (1977). "Recent Developments in Organizational Buying Behavior." In *Consumer and Industrial Buying Behavior*, edited by A.G. Woodside, J.N. Sheth, and P.D. Bennett. New York: Elsevier North-Holland.

Strauss, R.G. (1962). "Tactics of Lateral Relationship: The Purchasing Agent." *Administrative Science Quarterly* 24(December): 539-550.

Turnbull, P.W. and M.T. Cunningham, eds. (1981). *International Marketing and Purchasing*. Hong Kong: The Macmillan Press Ltd.

Vyas, N. and A.G. Woodside. (1967). "An Inductive Model of Industrial Supplier Choice Processes." *Journal of Marketing*. Boston: Allyn & Bacon.

Vyas, N. and A.G. Woodside. (1986). "Micro Analysis of Supplier Choice Strategies: Industrial Packaging Materials." In *Industrial Marketing*, edited by K. Backhaus and D.T. Wilson. Berlin: Springer-Verlag.

Webster, F.E., Jr., and Y. Wind. (1972). *Organizational Buying Behavior*. Englewood Cliffs, NJ: Prentice-Hall.

Witte E. (1972). "Field Research on Complex Decision-Making Processes—The Phase Theorem." *International Studies of Management and Organization* 2(Summer): 156-182.

MIDDLE RANGE THEORIES
OF INDUSTRIAL PURCHASING
STRATEGIES

Arch G. Woodside and Kristian Möller

ABSTRACT

In this paper descriptions of real-life industrial purchasing strategies are compared to prescriptions for improving industrial purchasing strategies. As an introduction to middle range theory, the paper presents the primary parties, including their interactions, involved specifically in the development of annual plant purchasing agreements (PPAs). Thus, the theory is not necessarily meant to relate to all organizational buying decisions. Thorough explanation is provided regarding strategy behind the many phases and subphases of the purchasing process. In this way, the reader will become familiar with the emergence of common decision problems, heuristics, and conflict situations throughout the course of the often lengthy purchasing process. Providing an explanation of the structure of PPA decision processes will prove most useful in practice. Comparing descriptions of *what is* to prescriptions of *what should be* is helpful for suggesting improvements in PPA strategies that may be possible to achieve.

Advances in Business Marketing and Purchasing, Volume 5, pages 21-59.
ISBN: 1-55938-364-X

Both descriptive and prescriptive theories of industrial purchasing strategies are "theories of the middle range" (Merton 1957). Middle range theories have neither too few nor too many boundary determining criteria. The theories and descriptions presented in this chapter are bounded to include the following characteristics (criteria):

- "important" purchases involving purchasing managers, buyers, and persons from other departments usually within a single manufacturing plant;
- "important" purchases that include plant purchase agreements (PPAs) of raw materials, components parts, and nonproduction items; and capital products, such as complete turn-key operations (buying a manufacturing plant);
- manufacturing plants located in industrialized nations (Belgium, Denmark, Finland, the Netherlands, the United Kingdom and the United States).

A PPA is an agreement, usually not legally binding, between two manufacturing firms, confirming that one firm will buy a specified product at a specified quantity and price, during a certain time period, from the other firm. This time period is usually one year, or six months, with a time often specified in the agreement during which the price may be changed due to cost changes, for example, "during the six months of the agreement either the buyer or seller may request a price change plus or minus 6%, such a change will be subject to negotiation at that time." PPAs are useful for sales forecasting for the industrial marketer, and commodity requirements planning for the industrial purchaser. PPAs may best be viewed as written understandings of a purchasing-marketing relationship between two manufacturing firms. PPAs are a strong form of commitment indicating a continuing relationship; gaining one annual PPA often results in gaining a second PPA in the following year.

Thus, the theory and research reported here is not intended to cover all organizational or industrial buying strategies; some strategies are excluded (e.g., straight rebuys within a time specified in a purchase contract). The aim is to provide wholistic views—including flow diagrams—of the streams of decisions, behaviors, and interactions of people involved in certain types of real-life industrial strategies. Such theories of the middle range provide several connected propositions about how important industrial purchasing strategies occur through time. Fragments of theories may be studied within the middle range theories but the focus is on providing complete, accurate, pictures of entire strategies. No attempt is made to build a global model of buying behavior by studying how the industrial purchasing strategies examined here relate to organizational buying by governments, hospitals, and educational institutions. Extensive comparisons are not made relating industrial buying and consumer buying models (cf. Howard and Sheth 1969; Hansen 1972; Engel, Blackwell, and Miniard 1986), even though such comparisons are useful for understanding both industrial and consumer buying behavior (cf. Wind 1978).

PHASES IN INDUSTRIAL PURCHASING STRATEGIES

While the research reported here confirms Witte's (1972) observation that the phase theorem (decisions are made in a prespecified sequence of steps) does not hold true in real-life, the persons involved in industrial purchasing strategies are able to identify phases in purchasing decisions. These phases often include "do-loops" (several executions of the same step with each loop executed for a different element, e.g., product trials of three competing vendors' samples), rest periods, and re-starts between phases. Each phase may be considered to be a fragment of the middle range theory of industrial purchasing strategy.

Eight phases that often occur in PPA's and other important industrial purchasing strategies are as follows.

1. Purchase initiation: the act of stimulating the purchasing process with information.
2. Evaluative criteria formation: assessment and development of evaluative criteria for supplier and product evaluation.
3. Information search: the acquisition of information from internal and external sources for defining suppliers to receive RFQs, and the supplier finally chosen.
4. Supplier definition of requests for quotations (RFQs): the decision of supplier (bidding) policy, the choice of suppliers requested for a quotation, and the acquiring of quotation.
5. Evaluation of quotations: the act of evaluating the suppliers based on their quotations and other available product and company information.

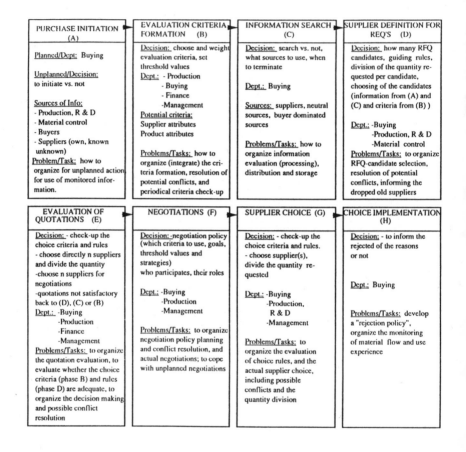

Source: Möller (1983).

Note: The departments referred to are probable examples, the number and names of departments participating in the material buying proess varies from one organization to another, and from one type of production material to another.

Figure 1.

6. Negotiations: the act of negotiating with the suppliers chosen in quotation evaluation for concessions concerning choice criteria.
7. Supplier choice: deciding which suppliers to award a contract, also determining the order quantity.
8. Choice implementation: the act of (a) handling the rejected bidders, (b) arranging logistical supply routines, and (c) arranging the monitoring and feedback of the suppliers' performance.

Each phase will be described in terms of the decision problems and tasks involved. This discussion is primarily based on the "MATBUY-model" developed by Möller (1981, 1983) and summarized in Figure 1.

Purchase Initiation

The input act of stimulating the purchasing process with information. For established stable materials, this is a routine process of initiating the negotiations for renewing the annual supply contracts. In many cases, however, dynamism or turbulence exists both in the supply markets (e.g., in product development, price stability, supplier power structure, supply capacity) and within the buying company (e.g., in the end-product development, production process development, warehousing system, buying policy). Because of these exogenous and/or endogenous factors, the initiation may lead to a search for potential new suppliers, or to starting negotiations with the established suppliers within the contract period.

This kind of dynamic initiation process implies that the actors of the buying organization perceive (1) a current or potential worsening of the supplier and/or product attributes, (2) a potential way to gain better attributes (e.g., by engaging new suppliers), or (3) an endogenous necessity to redefine the purchasing criteria. The dynamic initiation process (versus the passive process of reviewing old contracts) may occur either in a planned or unplanned mode, depending on such factors as whether the impulse is endogenous and the degree of sophistication of the buying organization. The definition of purchase initiation illustrates that, in the case of dynamic supply markets and/or company products or buying policy, this stage may develop into a complex subprocess involving not only the input component (Farley, Hulbert, and Weinstein 1980), but also communication, decision making, and conflict resolution.

The potential complexity of purchase initiation has been described above. Customarily, buying organizations strive for simplicity in order to avoid costs imbedded in the complex decision situation. In dynamic contexts, one may have to develop a more complex initiation to be able to achieve substantial potential gains and avoid unnecessary costs. This usually involves strategic materials, which are either of crucial technical importance to the end-product, or representing a considerable share of costs, or both.

Evaluative Criteria Formation

In static, established supply markets, a buying organization usually has a defined set of both product and supplier evaluation criteria. In the dynamic case, a company must perpetually redefine these criteria. In this volume, criteria are conceptualized with attribute theory concepts as recommended by Wilson (1977). Ordinarily the criteria are composed of supplier attributes such as ability to supply (quantity plus schedule), dependability, terms of payment, technical and other services, marketing personnel, and communications. Product-related attributes such as technical characteristics and price are also included. Numerous supplier evaluation or choice criteria studies have been done, including Lehmann and O'Shaughnessy (1974), Kelly and Coaker (1976), Kiser and Rao (1977), and Möller and Leino (1980).

The specific values believed by a buyer to hold true of supplies and product attributes comprise the definition of supplier alternatives. For example, a buyer may believe that Supplier A will provide a product that meets the specifications in the RFQ, but will be unable to deliver in the time specified unless a premium price is paid by the buyer. Theoretically and pragmatically, attributes used by the buyer play a central role, as they form the basis of buyers' material need. The buying goals of the company can also be expressed using these attributes, and these goals in turn are used as choice criteria. More formally, the criteria can be expressed as a criteria set C, which contains a number of subcriteria: $x_i : c = \{x_1,...,x_m\}$, where x_i indicates the ith subgoal and $i = 1,...,m$. Lower case x's indicate the subcriteria or elements of c, (instead of c's, which are used in the set theory notation) because x's will also be used to denote supplier alternatives.

The attributes are usually not of equal importance. To reflect varying levels of importance, the criteria may be assigned weights (w_i), which reflect their relative importance to the buying company. Frequently, certain attributes must pass a specific threshold value before they are determined to be acceptable. Minimum or maximum threshold values are often assigned subjectively by the buyer to the respective choice criteria. Typical threshold criteria are price and technical product specifications.

In summary, the buying organization compiles a list of product and supplier attributes to be used as evaluative criteria. Moreover, the criteria may be assigned importance weights and/or minimum and maximum threshold values. The relative importance and threshold values do not necessarily have to be stated in explicit figures. These concepts have, however, been found to be valid in a group of Finnish companies studied by Möller and Allos (1983).

Assessing criteria attributes and their relative importance and thresholds is an interdepartmental decision-making situation; thus, conflict may develop, calling for conflict resolution behavior. Typical departments involved in evaluation criteria formation are R&D, production, quality control, and buying. Evaluation criteria formation should actually be viewed as continuous information processing of the attributes of the needed material and the information available on potential supplier alternatives. The process is further complicated by a changing environment, which results in uncertainty in criteria formation. In rapidly changing buying periods, the threshold values of technical specifications and price may be difficult to define even for a year.

The previous discussion includes one set of evaluative criteria. Buying organizations frequently use two or even three different criteria sets: those used to define acceptable suppliers (who will receive requests for quotations—RFQs), and those used in negotiations and final supplier choice. These criteria sets generally have many attributes in common. The sets are dynamically evolutive, that is, their make-ups are time and process dependent. In the following section, the process of forming evaluative criteria is considered to be integrated with the supplier definition, evaluation of quotations, negotiations, and supplier choice subprocesses.

Information Search

Evaluative criteria formation and information search subprocesses are actually dynamically interactive and may occur simultaneously. That is, the formation of evaluation criteria presumes information about product and supplier attributes. As the criteria become more structured (as in static circumstances), they guide the information search, which may eventually further affect the criteria, and so on. The information search includes items defined by the evaluative criteria, including supplier and product attributes, as well as the more general supply market information, and trends in the development of the buying firm's production technology and end-products. This monitoring task is generally the responsibility of the buying department, although R&D and quality control may also provide information on technical questions and the product quality of present suppliers. External sources can be classified as buyer-dominated, supplier-dominated, and neutral sources. The first group includes other buying companies and their possible associations, and the second includes supplier companies. The neutral group includes trade journals, trade fairs, research organizations, and professional seminars. The evaluation of the perceived importance of different information sources and information items, as well as the effect of sales personnel and industrial advertising on buying, forms a well developed research tradition. Relevant studies include Patti (1977), Dempsey (1978), and *Liiketaloustieteellinen Tutkimuslaitos* (Möller and Leino 1980).

In a stable buying context, the information search is usually of limited importance and represents a routinized organizational effort. If, however, a company is not satisfied with its current suppliers, search becomes more crucial. One decision problem related to search is whether or not to begin the search, and if the search is begun, how long to continue it. These decisions are usually determined by such policy directives as "we must have at least n suppliers," or "we must have one supplier in country x and one in y." Also, decisions are related to the issues discussed in the section on purchase initiation.

Together, purchase initiation, evaluative criteria formation, and information search form the pre-request quotation process, which provides the basis on which to determine those suppliers selected to receive RFQs.

Supplier Definition of RFQs

To begin the RFQ process, the buyer must determine his supplier policy, including such information as: how many suppliers are to submit quotations, how the established criteria are used (are there specific restrictions concerning the country of origin or other geographic area of suppliers, size of suppliers, other customers of suppliers?), and how to divide the total quantity between the suppliers to be sent RFQs. These supplier or buying policy criteria represent a set of policy related norms that are superior to supplier and product attribute-specific goals. These criteria guide the determination of relative importance and the threshold values of evaluative criteria. Furthermore, they provide independent rules for various tradeoff decisions, such as choosing between price and quality, or risk and gain. One example of a risk and gain dilemma is the choice between one customized supplier and a multiple supplier situation. Typically, simple heuristics such as "at least two to three suppliers situated in regions A and B" are used. The supplier policy decision usually involves several departments, including buying, R&D, production, and sometimes top management. Such interaction between departments may lead to conflict situations requiring conflict resolution.

Formally, suppliers can be defined with the aid of attributes. A supplier is a set X containing attributes $x_{oi} : X_i = \{x_{ok} ,..., x_{on}\}$, where $0 = 1 ,..., r$, and denotes the supplier, $i = 1 ,... n$, and denotes the attribute. When each attribute making up a supplier (suppliers can possess a varying number of attributes) has been assigned a value, the supplier is completely specified. The concept "supplier attribute" is used in an extensive sense, as it covers both objective and perceived supplier and product attributes.

When the company has defined the suppliers and determined supplier policy, it can then choose the suppliers to be sent an RFQ. This decision can be made by first processing the information available on suppliers from the purchase initiation process and information search according to the evaluative criteria. This processing should indicate a group of suppliers acceptable according to the criteria. Second, the suppliers to be sent RFQs are chosen using rules defined in the supplier policy decision.

There may be fewer acceptable or available suppliers than the number recommended by the company's supplier policy. In this case, there are three alternative solutions: (1) if the information search for new suppliers can be extended (and there is time for it), the company may continue the search; (2) the company may again consider the threshold levels of evaluative criteria, whether or not they can be lowered; or (3) if solutions (1) and (2) do not solve the problem, the company must simply accept the situation for the time being. This last possibility may lead the company to a make-or-buy situation. Another policy would be to support new suppliers entering the field.

The evaluation process can be carried out by both the buying (supplying commercial information) and R&D departments (supplying technical information). The final choice decision is often made by a committee or the purchasing manager. This stage may also develop into a conflict situation. The potential for conflict depends upon the amount of agreement concerning initiating the process, developing evaluative criteria, and supplier policy. If intra- and interdepartmental disputes were not resolved during these previous processes, they often resurface during the RFQ supplier selection.

The probability of conflict is increased if vendors who have not previously been suppliers are included in the set of approved vendors, and some members of the buying center perceive substantial risk in using these new vendors. This situation often occurs with perceptions of new supplier alternatives, because the available information on suppliers not previously used is often incomplete and possibly unreliable. The seriousness of perceived supplier uncertainty is stressed in cases of both financially and technically important products, since the negative consequences of unsatisfactory solutions are great. Accepting only old or well-known suppliers for RFQs and collecting more information (going back to the information search stage) are risk-avoiding strategies often used by buyers.

Preparing, sending, and acquiring RFQs completes the supplier definition. Decision implementation can be routinized, as the content of the RFQs is determined by the evaluative criteria formation, and the quantities (and other specification combinations) to be quoted in the supplier policy decision stage.

Evaluation of Quotations

The evaluation is again an information processing task in which suppliers and their bids are compared according to the established criteria. As mentioned in the section on evaluative criteria formation, the criteria and especially their threshold values and importance weights may change at this stage (compared to supplier definition). Moreover, the manner in which the criteria are applied (i.e., choice or judgmental rules are applied to the data to produce a preference order of suppliers), may also change from the way criteria were applied in the supplier definition. These rules are essential in decision making, which completes quotation evaluation. This may result in three potential outcomes.

1. Of the bidding suppliers, *n* are chosen directly, and the quantity demanded is divided among them.
2. Negotiations are initiated with the *n* suppliers, or with some subgroup *n-m* of them (some can be chosen directly).
3. The quotations are found unacceptable.

Concerning the first outcome, decisions must be made as to whether or not negotiations would be worthwhile, how to choose suppliers (which will be discussed in the choice stage), and finally, how to divide the quantity among the chosen suppliers. One way to answer whether or not negotiations would be worthwhile involves calculating the probability and values of price reductions or other concessions due to negotiations, versus the costs of negotiating. The quantity decision is guided by such heuristics as supplier relations, prices, and policy to keep at least *n* suppliers.

Concerning the second possible outcome, the primary issue is that of the negotiation policy; this issue is dealt with in the next subprocess. The third possible outcome is improbable, as the bidding suppliers have been prechecked in the supplier definition subprocess. If it does occur, the options open for the buyer are discussed in connection with supplier definition.

Organizing for the evaluation of quotations, including the potential redefinition of supplier policy rules and supplier choice, usually involves several departments, such as buying, R&D, and/or production. The decision group may be the same as the group involved in the supplier definition process. The probability of top management participation is increased, as this stage (the first outcome above) includes the possibility of final choice. Group decision making again implies interdepartmental communication and potential for conflict, requiring conflict resolution.

Negotiations

The decision on negotiation policy is a prerequisite for actual negotiations. Information and guiding rules for policy formulation are provided by the importance weights of the criteria, differences in quotations on the criteria, and supplier policy heuristics. An example of a frequent negotiation policy is "playing" suppliers against each other in order to reach a lower price level or other concessions.

Another aspect of negotiation decision concerns organizing actual discussion (decision implementation, Farley et al. [1980]). This involves such issues as determining who will participate in the negotiations and what kind of roles they will play, as well as who has the final decision-making power. Both the negotiation policy and participation questions may also involve multiple departments and potential for conflict. This is improbable in static buying situations, however, as the negotiations become a matter of standardized routine. Companies with an active buying policy (using, for example, target prices below the average market level) often strive to maintain dynamism in negotiations.

Supplier Choice

The final choice stage is similar in principle to the evaluation of quotations subprocess. First, the results of supplier negotiations are evaluated by comparing the submitted bids according to the evaluative criteria. These criteria may, however, have changed during the negotiations. For example, the number of criteria may have been reduced and the threshold levels changed. In the supplier choice, a final preference of remaining supplier candidates must be determined. This decision is made when the decision-making group applies the choice or judgmental rules to the processed negotiation information. The judgmental rules have been mentioned briefly in the supplier definition, evaluation of quotations, and negotiations subprocesses. As these rules form a decisive component of any decision, they are elaborated upon here.

The decision maker's choice heuristics usually include one of three main types of judgmental rules (models) or some combination of these: (1) compensatory models, (2) satisficing models, and (3) lexicographic models.

A decision maker following a linear compensatory rule assigns an importance weight to each attribute, and then evaluates the alternatives (supplier candidates, quotations, or negotiations results, etc.) according to the amount of each attribute they possess. The final preference is determined by adding the weighted attribute scores.

The satisficing judgmental rules can be classified as conjunctive or disjunctive models. In the conjunctive model, the decision maker requires each supplier to exceed certain minimum levels (thresholds) for each attribute. That is, the conjunctive process basically dichotomizes the suppliers into unacceptable and acceptable categories, without determining a complete preference order. A preference order can be achieved if the buyer gradually strengthens attribute requirements (such as price) until only one supplier quotation remains acceptable.

The disjunctive heuristics describe a choice or evaluation situation in which the decision maker is very interested in one supplier attribute with "top" values (such as a certain quality specification). According to this model, those suppliers which do not meet the required minimum value on the specified attribute are classified as unacceptable. This process is also only a dichotomizing one.

The lexicographic choice rule assumes that decision makers evaluate alternative suppliers by comparing them first on the most important attribute and, if there is a significant difference between them, choosing the best supplier. If there are ties, the decision maker will not discriminate between the leading two or more supplier candidates. He will simply perform a comparison on the next most important attribute, and continue that process until a preference is determined. For mathematical modeling of the rules, see Green and Wind (1973).

The principal choice models presented were discussed as "single" models. It seems evident that decision makers may use more complex sequential or hierarchical choice processes constituting a number of models (choice rules). So far, choice models in organizational buying have received little empirical investigation. Some evidence supports the idea of a supplier screening phase followed by an evaluative screening phase leading to choice (Crow, Olshavsky, and Summers 1980; Möller and Allos 1983; Vyas and Woodside 1984). From consumer choice research and a few organizational buying studies, it is evident that the first stage is characterized by satisficing rules, and the second by either lexicographic or compensatory rules (Russ 1971; Stiles 1974; Wright 1975; Wright and Barbour 1977; Park 1974; Pras 1973; Möller 1977; Crow, Olshavsky, and Summers 1980). An exploratory attempt to integrate the choice rules and principal stages of production material buying is ventured. Discussion will be limited to supplier definition, evaluation of quotations, negotiations, and choice stages.

In supplier definition, the decision problem is usually of a discriminating nature: how to dichotomize the known supplier candidates into acceptable (receiving RFQs) and unacceptable suppliers. The conjunctive heuristics seem to be most appropriate for this situation.

The decision-making style and rewarding policy of the buying company can have a considerable impact on the judgmental heuristics adopted. If the basic recommendation is to avoid mistakes in choosing a group of acceptable suppliers, this leads to very strict threshold values on attributes, and the use of a conjunctive rule. In the opposite situation, the company policy would support finding new supplier candidates with top values on a few critical criteria. This would increase the buyers' tendency to apply disjunctive heuristics. Using the first policy, there is the risk of losing good potential suppliers because of minor difficulties in some attributes (criteria); the second policy might lead to accepting some actually unacceptable supplier candidates. In general, one of the satisficing rules, or a combination of them, is most often applied to the supplier evaluation situation by the decision makers.

The evaluation of quotations subprocess contains such decision problems as whether or not to initiate negotiations, or to make a final choice among the bidding suppliers. The latter is valid for choice rule discussion. This can be achieved with both a compensatory and lexicographic model, or with a conjunctive model via the strengthening of attribute requirements (or with a combination of these). It is argued that the nature of the evaluation situation—defined by such characteristics as the number of bidders, the number of attributes (and the similarity level of the relative importance), the differences between the suppliers, newness of the situation, technical and/or commercial importance of the situation, and time-pressure—influences the choice model used. Several propositions follow:

Proposition 1.   If there are many suppliers and many attributes, the propensity to use two-phased heuristics, with a satisficing rule as a first-stage restriction method, is increased.

Proposition 2.   If there are many attributes and relatively many competitive supplier candidates, the propensity to use a compensatory or lexicographic rule for preference ordering (after a possible rejection phase) is increased. This proposition is enhanced if there is no time-pressure and the buying situation is relatively new and important.

Proposition 3.   If there are relatively few attributes and/or suppliers, the propensity to apply a conjunctive rule to preference ordering is increased. This possibility is supported by clear differences between the suppliers, time pressure, and familiarity of the situation.

In the negotiations stage, the concern is usually for achieving better terms in one or more attributes, such as price, quality, or terms of delivery. The process generally involves playing two or more suppliers against each other. This suggests that a sequential use of the conjunctive rule, where the buyer continuously strengthens the threshold values, would be appropriate. Concerning the final supplier choice, the preference ordering task has already been discussed in connection with the evaluation of quotations with the suggestive hypothesis given. The supplier choice subprocess completes the politically important part of the production material buying process. It may be followed by a carefully planned purchase implementation stage.

Choice Decision Implementation

The handling of rejected bidders involves the decision whether or not to inform bidders of the reasons they have been rejected. Generally, this concerns all companies rejected, either in the supplier evaluation for RFQs, evaluation of quotations, negotiations, or supplier choice stages. In many cases, the suppliers which are dropped are aware of these reasons. When this is not the case, a possible decision heuristic is to try to evaluate the effect of disclosing/not disclosing the raison d'être of the rejection (or reduction of quantity ordered) to the supplier.

The technical arrangement of logistical supply routines is the scope of this paper. However, the logistic process is connected to the monitoring of both the supplier performance (delivery dates, quantities) and product performance (quality specifications). The organization for supply monitoring often consists of reception control, quality control, and performance control of the production materials taken care of by the quality control and production departments. The extent and degree of routinization of these performance monitoring points are generally a function of the technical complexity and importance of the materials. Monitoring provides feedback information, which is primarily used in the evaluative criteria formation and information search stages. If, however, the performance values monitored show a significant discrepancy from those agreed upon in the final purchase contract— or otherwise produce signals of problems—the initiation stage should be activated.

Summary of the Phases in Industrial Purchasing Strategies

The phases that occur often in industrial purchasing strategies for
PPAs have been defined and discussed fairly extensively. The IBB
research team is well aware of the fact that companies actually strive
to simplify and routinize their purchasing. This model of the phases
of industrial purchasing strategies is an attempt to conceptually cover
all the principal decision problems and conflict situations within each
substage, which can potentially emerge into a new and dynamic
purchasing situation. For describing a static, well conceptualized
material buying, only a reduced version of the model is needed. Table
1 is a summary of the decision knots or problems contained in the eight
buying phases. These decisions form the chain of focal areas for
planning buying.

As locations for multiperson and often interdepartmental interaction,
the decision knots are potential conflict areas in the buying organization.
A common set of factors covering all decisive and politically interesting
decision areas includes supplier attributes, choice criteria (defined using
attributes, importance weights and threshold values) and the choice
rules. These can be used to conceptualize (and quantify) both the
research and planning of the crucial evaluative criteria formation,
supplier definition for RFQs, evaluation of quotations, negotiations,
and supplier choice stages. Together, the attribute/choice criteria and
judgmental rule conceptualizations form strong integrative elements
relating the subprocesses by focusing on the underlying information
processing activity.

A DESCRIPTIVE MODEL OF THE STREAM OF DECISIONS—BEHAVIORS—INTERACTIONS OF BUYING CENTER PARTICIPANTS

Detailing the eight major phases that often occur in industrial
purchasing strategies is useful for understanding the major chunks of
decisions-behaviors-interactions that may be observed in practice.
However, the flow among the phases and loops (returns) back-and-forth
between phases, can only be learned by detailing the actual streams of
decisions-behaviors-interactions that occur in industrial purchasing
strategies. Detailed flow-diagrams describing actual strategy streams are
provided from research using decision systems analysis (DSA). The

Table 1. Summary of Decision Problems in Material Buying

Stage	Decision Problems
Purchase Initiation	• To initiate/not initiate the process
Evaluative Criteria Formation	• To decide on which attributes to use in evaluation, how to weight these, and what threshold values to adopt
Information Search	• To search or not • What sources to use • When to terminate the search
Supplier Definition for RFQ's	• Supplier policy decisions: how many potentials should be included, what are the restriction rules guiding the process, how to divide the quantity between the potentials • Which to choose
Evaluation of Quotations	• Are the evaluative criteria still valid, what judgemental rule(s) to use • To negotiate or make a terminal choice • Which suppliers to choose for negotiations
Negotiations	• Negotiation policy decisions: which attributes are used, what are the threshold values and goals, and what strategy(ies) is (are) adopted • Who should participate, their status and roles
Supplier Choice	• Evaluation and possible redefinition of the choice criteria (attributes) and decision rules (formed in Evaluative Criteria Formation) • Whom to give contract and (if more than one chosen) how to divide the quantity requested
Choice Implementation	• To inform the rejected or not

Source: Möller (1981).

methodology of DSA is provided in the paper by Woodside and Sherrell (this volume, pp. 67-71).

In this section, a composite stream of industrial purchasing strategy is provided. The aim is to provide an understanding of how the phases actually occur and are linked together. A summary of this composite stream is provided in Figure 2 for developing RFQs and Figure 3 for bid evaluations and final supplier selection.

Two points should be emphasized. First, the descriptive model summarized in Figures 2 and 3 is not intended to be an exact replica of the patterns of all industrial purchasing strategies. Instead, this model provides a general description of the decisions, behaviors, and interactions which occur often (cf. Vyas and Woodside 1984; Woodside and Sherrell 1980; Möller 1983; Nielsen 1981; Vollering 1982). Second, the model is descriptive, not normative; "what is" is summarized, not "what should be."

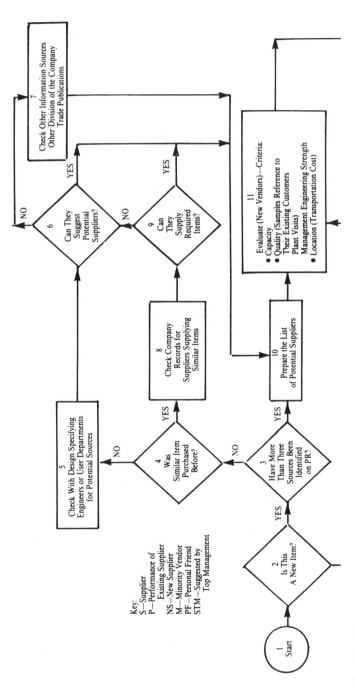

38

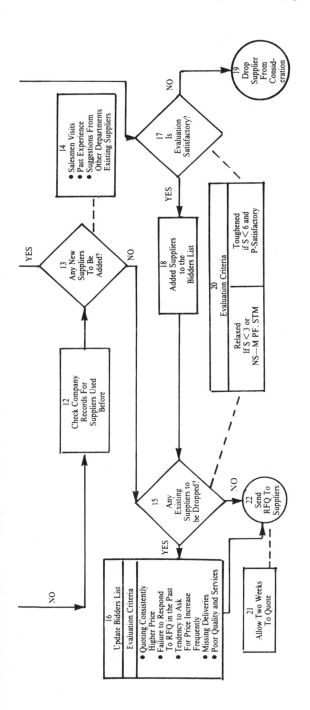

Figure 2. Devloping Requests for Quotations

Source: Vyas and Woodside (1984, p. 35).

39

Developing Requests for Quotations (RFQs)

The start of the buying strategy is shown in Figure 2 as a circle with the number "1." A plant purchasing agreement (PPA) is an agreement, usually not legally binding, between two manufacturing firms, confirming that one firm will buy a specified product at a specified quantity and price, during a certain time period, from the other firm. An actual buying strategy for a PPA may be initiated three to four months before current annual PPAs are scheduled to expire. Each diamond, circle, and box following the starting circle in Figure 2 includes a number for reference. In diamond 2, a purchasing agent or senior buyer is likely to first ask if the product or service to be purchased under a PPA is a new item. If not, then "external memory" (Bettman 1979) in the form of company records (box 12) is examined to locate possible suppliers. If the item is new for the firm, then the buyer checks to see if three sources have been listed by the requesting department (e.g., production), on the purchase requisition (diamond 3 in Figure 2). Identifying and contacting at least three potential sources for a PPA is a goal of the buyer, whether or not contracts with three or fewer suppliers will be awarded.

Thus, the buyer attempts to identify the buying problem as a new task, modified rebuy, or straight rebuy (not the buyer's terminology but ours) early in the buying process. Different heuristics, behaviors, and buying center memberships will occur depending on how the decision is defined. Diamond 2 is an important early decision in the buying strategy.

The buyers interviewed in the United Kingdom, Denmark, Finland, the Netherlands, Belgium, and the United States during the data collection stage of the IBB project were usually not concerned with doing a thorough search to find all suppliers with a given profile. Search for potential suppliers was usually terminated after a few potential suppliers (3 to 6) were found. A major exception to this rule was search for potential vendors for corporate purchase agreements (CPAs) (cf., Woodside and Sammuel 1981). CPAs are similar to PPAs, except that CPAs cover the buying requirements for two or more plant locations of large manufacturing corporations (e.g., General Motors, G.T.E., and I.B.M).

Buyers prefer not to have to seek information from design and specifying engineers or user departments for potential sources (box 5 in Figure 2). Whenever possible, buyers want to develop the reputation of being the experts on supplier availability and capability. Also, some buyers want to avoid the risk of ridicule from members of the engineering and other departments, "Don't you know the supply industry?" (cf. Strauss 1962; Wind 1966; Vyas 1981).

For new items to be purchased, a list of potential suppliers is prepared following an initial search (box 10). These potential suppliers are evaluated (box 11) using primarily conjunctive heuristics, for example, if the vendor's product quality was not judged to be satisfactory, the vendor was eliminated from further consideration. Three qualifying criteria are used most often.

1. *Capacity*—becomes a deciding factor for uninterrupted shipment when purchase quantity is large.
2. *Location*—with increasing transportation cost, buyers often prefer suppliers with mining, manufacturing, and major storage facilities nearby.
3. *Quantity*—when the item was technically complex (e.g., electric cable, fuel oil, chemical acids, castings), approval from other departments (engineering, quality control) was required.

Disagreements among the buying center members on qualifying decisions are often resolved by mutual discussions (face-to-face interactions). A typical remark made by a purchasing manager concerning vendor evaluations (diamond 17) follows:

> We have to deal with many departments within the company. If differences arise, I voice my opinion. We discuss it, see each other's point of view, and try to decide what is best for the company. We try not to get personalities involved. I have been in purchasing for over 25 years and this approach has always worked (Vyas and Woodside 1984, p. 34).

When a vendor is approved for addition to the bidders' list (box 18), this is an important accomplishment. Buyers and the other members of the buying center are biased to avoid risk by using known vendors (e.g., current suppliers), whenever possible. In practice, new vendors often must fulfill three requirements to be added to the approved bidders' list: (1) higher performance/quality, (2) ability to meet delivery requirements, and (3) the potential for significant cost savings. Even if strong proof was available to support a new vendor's ability to meet these requirements, the new vendor was still unlikely to receive a substantial share of the available purchase requirements of the buying firm (see Figure 3 for details). Buyers often believe that they are fulfilling their responsibility to new vendors if, following a positive evaluation, a new vendor is added to the bidders' list. Thus new vendors must work harder than existing suppliers to overcome the power of precedence, and the buyers' strong preference for existing suppliers to avoid perceived risk. An operating heuristic for both developing bidders' lists and evaluating bids received is: "Don't change what's working. Avoid the risk."

Industrial buyers appear to be willing to use about three criteria in deciding whether or not a specific vendor should be approved to receive an RFQ. The use of about three criteria occurs later in the decision process in deciding on the final selection of suppliers, and also for deciding on how the required volume should be split among multiple suppliers. This heuristic of using three (or so) criteria may be explained theoretically by what Haines (1974) has called "the principle of information-processing parsimony." According to this principle, because of man's limited cognitive capacity, human decision makers will adopt heuristics that permit them "to process as little data as is necessary in order to make rational decisions" (Haines 1974, p. 96; Payne 1976; Wright 1975). Reliance on the three (or so) most important criteria would be an example of such a strategy of information simplification.

Note in box 20 that the evaluation criteria in box 16 are tightened or relaxed depending on the number approved for the bidder's list. If the number of vendors is greater than six, buyers often increase minimum performance levels in order to reduce the number of bidders to six. This heuristic was followed especially if more than 10 vendors were on the bidders' list. One buyer gave the following description concerning the dynamic nature of deciding how many vendors to include on the bidders' list.

> There are no restrictions on the maximum number of suppliers (on a bidders list). Usually it depends on the amount of work one is willing to put in, the dollar volume, and the critical nature of the item purchased. The higher the dollar volume and more important an item, the larger the number of suppliers preferred on the bidders list. Normally you don't gain much in having more than ten (Vyas and Woodside 1984, p. 34).

If the number of suppliers is less than three, and no other potential suppliers meet the minimum requirements, the acceptance level of some criteria might be lowered. The same action occurs when a new supplier is recommended by someone in top management. This is not to say that a vendor recommended to receive an RFQ would always receive an RFQ or a purchase contract; the vendor favored by senior management is most likely only to receive special consideration in the bidders' list decision. However, anecdotal evidence shows that sometimes the preference of senior management for a certain vendor is enough for the preferred vendor to receive a purchase contract, even when lower management prefers other vendors following a formal evaluation process (cf. Pettigrew 1975; Hill and Hillier 1977).

Bid Evaluations and Final Supplier Selection

After RFQs have been sent to the approved vendors and the quotes have been received (sometimes with one or two telephone prompts to late vendors), the bid evaluation process starts. The initial question asked most often concerns how many bids have been received (see diamond 4 in Figure 3a). Buying strategies usually become less complex if only one approved vendor submits a bid. Several members of the buying center are notified that a bid has been received. If the quote includes the specifications as stated in the RFQ and the quoted price "seems reasonable" (see boxes 12 and 13 in Figure 2), the order is placed. Some attempt is made by the buyer to negotiate with the one vendor submitting a bid (box 8 and 9) before a meeting of the buying center is held (box 11).

The bid evaluation procedure when two or more bids are received starts with box 16 in Figure 3a. The prices that vendors submit are converted to a common base, F.O.B. destination. Also, the quoted price is modified upward if the price is not firm during the period called for in the RFQ. These actions reflect the use of a modified compensatory decision process with quoted price used as a base which is subject to adjustment.

Diamond 27 is a question that is more important than might be expected, "Do all quotes meet [product and performance] specs?" Because all of the vendors submitting bids have been approved by the buying center—sanctioned as capable of meeting the specifications listed in the RFQs—and the approved vendors have had the opportunity to review the specs and discuss them with members of the buying center, these vendors might be expected to submit bids which include specs matching those listed in the RFQ. However, approved vendors often substitute items and processes listed in an RFQ with other items and processes because of costs, vendor manufacturing capability, and belief in the superior performance of the substitution versus the RFQ requirement. Failure to meet the specs called for in RFQs is the most frequent reason that the approved vendor with the lowest bid does not receive a contract (Kelly and Coaker 1976; Dickson 1966). Vendors often fail to meet the specs called for, but still submit a bid, that is, 20 to 50 percent of the submitted bids, depending on whether or not the specs in the RFQ are stringent.

The preparation of specs by material (e.g., aluminum tubing only), versus by performance (e.g., pressure capability), restricts some vendors from being approved for the bidders' list. However, even if a vendor is approved for the bidders' list, a bid submission that meets the specs required in the RFQ is not guaranteed. Boxes 29 and 31 are applications of conjunctive and modified compensatory heuristics for evaluating and adjusting the specs in the quotes received.

The final supplier selection process is summarized in Figure 3b. The remaining vendors are ranked by modified, quoted, price (box 33). If three or more vendors remain, only those vendors having prices within 6 percent of the lowest quoted (and modified) price are evaluated further (box 34). Several subroutine decision processes are now entered into by the buyer and other members of the buying center.

The delivery schedule quoted in each bid is now reviewed. Given that a quoting vendor is within 6 percent of the lowest bid and the vendor's delivery schedule is unacceptable, the vendor is given a chance to improve the delivery schedule quoted (box 36).

A bias toward having two or possibly three supply sources for strategic items exists among U.S. industrial buyers. This bias was also observed in the firms studied in the United Kingdom, Denmark, the Netherlands, Belgium, and Finland. The buyers believe that having a second supply source serves as an inexpensive insurance policy for continuity of supply and helps to stimulate competition. The criteria considered for having multiple sources were having (a) enough volume of business to keep two or more suppliers interested, (b) no change in price-volume relationship, (c) tooling cost, if applicable, not prohibitive of multiple sources, and (d) the need to develop a new source (e.g., minority vendor). (The felt need to develop a minority vendor (e.g., black-owned vendor enterprise), was expressed by U.S. buyers only.)

The adoption of just-in-time (JIT) production may reduce the bias among European and American industrial buyers for multiple sourcing;

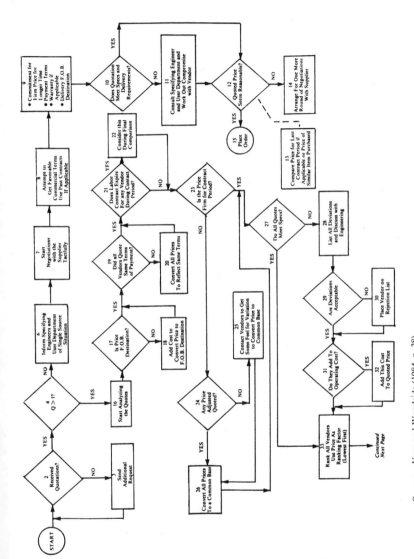

Source: Vyas and Woodside (1984, p. 38).

Figure 3a. Bid Evaluations and Final Selection

45

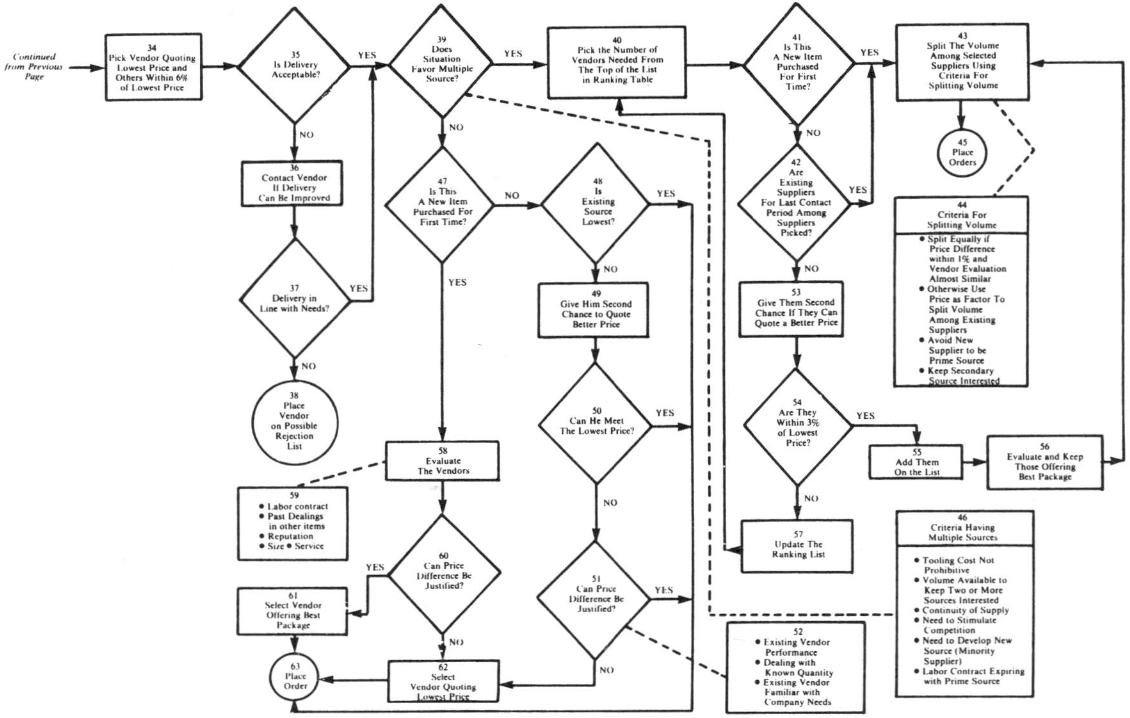

Figure 3b. Bid Evaluations and Final Selection

Source: Vyas and Woodside (1984, p. 39).

however, the use of JIT systems is not widespread outside of Japan (Walleigh 1986). JIT systems require even closer cooperation between supplier and buying manufacturing firms than that found by the IMP group (Hakansson 1982; Cunningham 1979) and this research group's study of international marketing and purchasing among five European countries.

When the buyer decides to use multiple sources, the required number of selected vendors are chosen from the top of the vendor ranking list, and the volume is split among them according to the following rules.

1. Split the volume equally if the price difference is within 1%; the rationale is that contract execution among the sources thus remains simple.
2. If the price difference is more than 1%, split the volume using price as the deciding criterion, providing there are no appreciable differences in other characteristics; if other differences exist, they should be weighed against price.
3. When the volume is to be split between an existing and a new supplier (no prior experience in dealing with vendor), do not permit a new supplier to be a prime source; a prime source supplies more than 50% of a company's requirements for a given PPA.

If the buyer rejects the lowest bid that meets the minimum company requirements, the purchasing department must often submit a written explanation for accepting a higher price bid to satisfy company auditors. The auditing of purchasing activities is widespread in large industrial firms in the United Kingdom, United States, and the Netherlands; auditing activity is found to a lesser extent in Belgium, Denmark, and Finland.

Buyers most often use compensatory decision rules only during the final evaluation and selection process. In all of the cases examined involving multiple sourcing, the buyer had the authority to decide how the required volume was to be split among two or more suppliers. The heuristics involved in these splitting decisions were complex and compensatory but were clearly specified by the buyers as a combination of simple rules, for example, new suppliers never receive more than 50% of the available business.

The bias against new suppliers was widespread. For example, one buyer reported the following. "I will not consider a new vendor unless he quoted a 10 percent lower price compared to the price quoted by our established prime source. The product from the new vendor requires special monitoring for several months, which is expensive and time consuming."

When new suppliers quote prices substantially lower than those of current suppliers, several buyers often use these quotations to bargain with current suppliers (see boxes 40, 41, 42, 53, and 54). In other words, they will give existing vendors the opportunity to match the lower price quoted by the new vendor. Other buyers feel that giving a second chance to existing suppliers is unethical and unjust to new vendors (elimination of this behavior is recommended by the associations of purchasing managers in the United States and the United Kingdom., e.g., National Association of Purchasing Management in the United States). However, the actual experience of buyers allowing existing suppliers a second chance to bid showed that using this heuristic usually led to success in obtaining lower prices from existing vendors.

National regulations in the United States and the United Kingdom outlaw giving second chances to existing suppliers to prevent contract awards to new vendors, but this heuristic is probably widespread in practice. For example, the General Accounting Office (the GAO is the U.S. Congress investigative arm) found that the Immigration and Naturalization Service had violated federal regulations and wasted taxpayers money in awarding a $61.3 million computer contract to I.B.M. in 1984. Violations included a late-night meeting held between Immigration and I.B.M. officials after the company and a competing firm submitted their "best and final offers," the GAO reported.

> In the meeting, 12 days before the contract was awarded, I.B.M.'s "final" offer
> was reduced by $3.3 million, making it $2,713 lower than the comparable offer
> from Electronic Data Systems [the new vendor], the GAO reported (Associated
> Press 1986).

Other violations of the Immigration Department included accepting changes proposed by I.B.M. in the specs called for in the RFQ for the computer system nine days after the contract was awarded, which quadrupled the Immigration Department's computing capacity and increased the cost of the product to $100 million. A vendor's attempt to negotiate changes after contract agreement has been reached between the vendor and customer is known as low-balling (cf. Motes and Woodside 1979; Cialdini 1985).

Example of a Final Contract Award Strategy

Here is a "protocol" of one buyer applying a splitting heuristic. A protocol is the buyer's response when asked to think aloud while making a decision (cf. Crow, Olshavsky, and Summers 1980).

> Let's see. For this item the specifications are quite important. Supplier X and Y both meet the specifications. In the past we have done business with both. However, if one of them was a new supplier, the choice will be to give smaller volume, say 25 to 50%, to this new supplier and treat him as a secondary source. On-time delivery record for both X and Y is pretty good, although X had some problems, but those are straightened out now. Both are known for their quality. Neither of these have labor contracts negotiations in 1980. However, if any one of them had labor contracts in 1980, I would be quite hesitant to give him a major share of the business. What's next? Yes, supplier X was our prime source in 1979. He is aware of our revised specifications and worked closely with our requirements and idiosyncracies. But look here—he is about 4.3% higher in price compared to Y. I would like to see X as our prime supplier for this year too, but not at his high price . . . I will have to split the business 60-40 between Y and X (X getting 40% because of his higher price) (Vyas and Woodside 1984, p. 40).

Prescriptive Theories of Industrial Purchasing Strategies

Most textbooks on industrial purchasing strategies are prescriptive in perspective, that is, the focus is on how purchasing should be done rather than how purchasing is done in practice.

Some understanding of prescription and description is provided in these books: Heinritz, Farrell, and Smith (1986), Van Weele (1984), Lee and Dobler (1984), and Ammer (1980). However, most of the material presented in these books tell how decisions-behaviors-interactions should be, rather than "telling it like it is." For example, "New products must be brought into the value engineering program only through the purchasing department. However, department heads and other personnel who become acquainted with new products by way of exhibits or reading can submit them to the [value engineering] committee through the [committee] chairman" (Heinritz et al. 1986, p. 288). A telling weakness of these books is their lack of evidence on how often and how many industrial organizations follow the prescriptive advice.

Two books that might be useful as textbooks, providing extensive commentaries on industrial purchasing strategies in-use, are studies by Hill and Hillier (1977) and Corey (1978). Hill and Hillier (1977) provide the most complete survey of the empirical research literature up to 1977 on industrial purchasing strategies in-use. Unfortunately, no detailed studies on the streams of industrial buying strategies are included in Hill and Hillier (1977), for example, the research on real-life industrial purchasing strategies reported by Wind (1966) and Moore (1969) is not described.

Corey (1978) provides extensive and insightful descriptions of industrial purchasing strategies in six major U.S. firms representing five different industries: General Motors, I.B.M., Raytheon Company, PPG Industries, General Foods Corporation, and Heinz USA. Corey provides a detailed view of how top management relates procurement to other business functions. In Corey (1978) prescription follows description. No attempt is made by Corey to build a model of industrial purchasing strategies in-use; the focus is on situational insight via case analyses of purchasing strategies in-use in the six firms. A very poor review of "the literature of procurement" is included as an appendix in Corey (1978); eleven references from the literature are included.

Kudrna (1975) and Van Weele (1984) provide detailed prescriptions on how industrial purchasing strategies should occur. For example, Kudrna considers the question of how senior management should decide whether or not to use centralized versus decentralized buying in a company with multiple production facilities. Decision trees similar to flow diagrams of the streams of actual behaviors-decisions-interactions of people are provided. Figure 4 is one recommended decision tree from Kudrna (1975) on the centralized-decentralized decision.

Note in Figure 4 that Kudrna (1975) recommends seven "considerations in determining whether a centralized or decentralized organization offers the greatest benefits with respect to specific commodities" (p. 141):

1. Is the dollar volume high?
2. Is a long period of training required to become proficient in procurement of the commodity?
3. Is there a wide geographical separation between engineering and departments?
4. Are there a limited number of suppliers capable of producing this requirement?
5. Are these vendors capable of supplying more than one operating site?

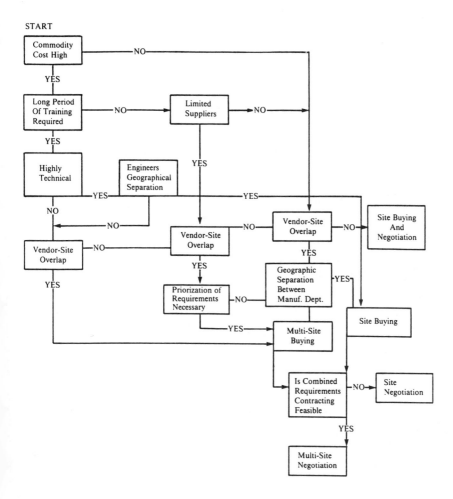

Source: Kudrna (1975, p. 142).

Figure 4.   Centralized-Decentralized Decision Tree

6. Is it necessary to set priorities for site demands with these vendors to assure supply?
7. Is there a wide geographical separation between manufacturing operations?

Kudrna (1975) provides several applications of this recommended decision stream. An important lesson to learn from studying Figure 4 is that specific decision nodes, "considerations," relate to some, but not necessarily all, other decision nodes. For example, if the cost of the commodity being considered is not high, the technical level of the product is not a consideration but vendor overlap is a consideration. "Vendor overlap" refers to the situation in which the same vendor supplies more than one manufacturing site of the company buying the commodity. Specific decision streams are recommended on the basis of specific decision characteristics related to buying a commodity.

Kudrna (1975) does not provide evidence that using the recommended decision trees actually improves purchasing strategies; nor is evidence provided that such decision trees correspond to reality in any purchasing organizations. However, some similarities do exist between the recommended decision trees and the descriptions of centralized versus decentralized purchasing strategies provided by Corey (1978) and Woodside and Sammuel (1981). The biggest difference between the prescription Kudrna recommends and the description Corey, and Woodside and Sammuel provide is that the perceived potential money savings is an overriding consideration in centralized versus decentralized decision processes.

Prescriptive models of industrial purchasing strategies usually include compensatory vendor and buyer evaluations. For example, Jain and Laric (1979) include a compensatory decision rule on how to evaluate a buyer's strength. Buyers' strengths are determined by looking at several characteristics and comparing them to those of other buyers in the industry. These characteristics could include (a) size of organization (as compared to industry average), (b) purchasing volume in the past, (c) size of future, expected orders, (d) credit standing, and (e) dependence on the seller.

Buyers and other members of the buying center would use these characteristics to rate the buying department using, for example, a belief scale of 1 to 10. Importance weights are assigned to each characteristic; the organization's size might be assigned a weight of 3. Each characteristic's belief score is multiplied by its importance weight, and the weighted scores are summed. An example is provided in Table 2. Thus a low score on one characteristic, for example, dependence of seller has a belief score of 2 (reverse scored, the higher the value the less the dependence) can be compensated by a high score on another characteristic, for example, the organization's size is valued at 9 in Table 2.

Attempts to learn how purchasing executives rate vendor attributes on importance scales and how they rate specific vendors on vendor attributes have been reported (e.g., Dempsey 1978; Moriarty 1983).

Table 2. Sample Measurement of Buyer's Strengths

Strength Criteria	Scale Value (*between 1-10*)	Weights	Total Score
a. Organization's Size	9	3	27
b. Past Purchases' Volume	7	2	14
c. Size of Future Orders	9	4	36
d. Credit Standing	6	7	42
e. Dependence On Seller	2	5	10
			Total 129

Notes: Total possible score = 210.

Percentage score $\dfrac{129}{210} \times 100 = 61.4$.

Source: Jain and Laric (1979, p. 3).

Such research reports are useful in suggesting what information sources may be used by buyers but research is needed on what information sources are actually used, when and how these information sources are used.

In reality, buyers and other members of the buying centers studied rarely used numerical compensatory decision rules in vendor evaluations or in evaluating their own strengths and weaknesses. Research using rating questionnaires and compensatory decision models may be predictive of buying outcomes and useful in prescribing buying improvement, but are unlikely to reflect actual buying behavior or increase understanding of the actual industrial purchasing strategies.

SUMMARY

A general, descriptive, middle range theory of industrial purchasing strategy was presented in this paper. The theory relates to important industrial purchasing decisions (e.g., annual plant purchasing agreements), not all organizational buying decisions. The descriptive middle range theory is intended as a broad view of how industrial purchasing strategies emerge through time; the model includes eight phases and streams of decisions, behaviors, and interactions between people through time. The model is not intended to be accurate at the micro-level, that is, within the firm for every material or component part purchased for a given buyclass. The model is intended to provide structure and understanding of the decision process, interactions of the

Table 3. Importance of Information Sources (Mean Ratings)[a]

Variables	Capital Equipment, New Task Purchasing Equipment		Component Material Modified Rebuy Problem		Influences		
	Electric Utilities	Electronics Manufacturers	Electric Utilities	Electronics Manufacturers	Industry	Problem	Interaction
Purchasing records	5.74 (1.25)	5.72 (1.26)	5.91 (1.08)	6.24 (0.96)		x	
Personal calls of salesmen	5.08 (1.28)	4.81 (1.44)	5.23 (1.32)	4.66 (1.33)	x		
Other departments	4.67 (1.50)	4.84 (1.27)	4.72 (1.45)	4.70 (1.33)			
Visiting vendor's plant	4.25 (1.66)	5.72 (1.26)	3.62 (1.64)	5.00 (1.55)	x	x	
Catalogs	4.51 (1.50)	4.07 (1.32)	5.14 (1.31)	4.44 (1.27)	x	x	
Purchasing directories	3.70 (1.42)	4.48 (1.29)	3.87 (1.59)	4.94 (1.33)	x	x	
Credit and financial reports	4.25 (1.34)	4.58 (1.37)	3.75 (1.54)	4.17 (1.52)	x	x	

(continued)

54

Table 3. Continued

Variables	Capital Equipment, New Task Purchasing Equipment		Component Material Modified Rebuy Problem		Influences		
	Electric Utilities	Electronics Manufacturers	Electric Utilities	Electronics Manufacturers	Industry	Problem	Interaction
Telephone calls of salesmen	3.83 (1.48)	4.00 (1.49)	4.44 (1.36)	4.08 (1.63)		x	
Outside purchasing managers	3.82 (1.58)	3.88 (1.59)	3.93 (1.60)	3.86 (1.59)			
Journal articles	3.65 (1.35)	3.73 (1.29)	3.65 (1.28)	3.44 (1.46)			
Journal advertisements	3.33 (1.44)	3.52 (1.41)	3.41 (1.41)	3.30 (1.42)			
Trade shows and conventions	3.44 (1.53)	3.48 (1.36)	3.41 (1.39)	3.00 (1.41)			
Telephone directories	2.92 (1.57)	3.31 (1.51)	3.07 (1.68)	3.90 (1.68)	x	x	
Local purchasing chapter	3.03 (1.62)	3.04 (1.43)	3.09 (1.64)	3.15 (1.59)			
Mail advertisements	2.95 (1.41)	3.00 (1.29)	3.07 (1.28)	2.91 (1.29)			

Note: [a] Rating scale ranged from 1 (of no importance) to 7 (of extreme importance). Standard deviations are within parentheses.

Sources: Dempsey (1978, p. 263).

buying center members, and the behaviors performed in real-life industrial purchasing strategies.

The guiding principle in developing descriptive theories of industrial purchasing strategies has been expressed well by Moore (1969), "valid description must precede proposed prescription if the latter is to provide much in the way of practical application" (p. 76). The middle range theory of outlining how industrial purchasing strategies occur is a modest attempt to provide a few propositions (e.g., the actual heuristics used by members of the buying center within each phase of the buying strategy). The theory is based on direct observations of the behaviors of members of the buying center, analysis of written records, interviews, and protocols collected from several points through time.

Some prescriptive comments are included in this paper concerning the widespread tendency of buyers to give current suppliers a second chance to offer a more competitive bid after a new, approved vendor has submitted a more attractive bid and all the "final" bids have been received. The value and limitations of building prescriptive theory on industrial purchasing strategies were reviewed. While valuable in providing useful principles on how industrial purchasing strategies should be executed, the major problem with prescriptive theory is the lack of current knowledge on whether or not the prescriptions are being followed and, more generally, how and why industrial purchasing strategies actually emerge. To some general extent, a deductive theory always precedes an inductive, descriptive theory (cf. Armstrong 1985). Thus, boundaries for research on industrial purchasing strategies have been outlined in this paper. The boundaries are included in a series of hypotheses: (1) industrial buyers can easily identify phases in decisions they make; (2) some of these phases are repeated before final vendor choices and product quality and quantity decisions are made; (3) while complex from a total perspective, members in the buying center break up the purchasing process into a series of simple decisions; (4) search is limited to finding a limited number of qualified suppliers, for example, up to six; (5) buyers prefer to receive at least 3 bids for important purchase problems such as PPAs; and (6) heuristics may change during the buying process depending on situational variables, for example, if senior management requests that consideration be given to adding a specific vendor to the approved list of vendors to receive RFQs.

REFERENCES

Ammer, D.S. (1980). *Materials Management and Purchasing*, 4th ed., Homewood, IL: Richard D. Irwin.

Associated Press. (1986). "Immigration Office Violated Bid Rules for IBM, Report Says." New Orleans: *The Times-Picayune*, March 29.

Armstrong, J.S. (1985). *Long Range Forecasting*, 2nd ed. New York: Wiley.

Bettman, J.R. (1979). *An Information Processing Perspective Theory of Consumer Choice*. Reading, MA: Addison-Wesley.

Cialdini, R.B. (1985). *Influence*. New York: Morrow.

Corey, E.R. (1978). *Procurement Management*. Boston, MA: CBI Publishing.

Crow, L.E., R.W. Olshavsky, and J.O. Summers. "Industrial Buyer's Choice Strategies: A Protocol Analysis." *Journal of Marketing Research* 17(February): 34-44.

Cunningham, M.T. (1979). "International Marketing and Purchasing of Industrial Goods—Features of a European Research Project." *European Journal of Marketing* 14: 322-338.

Dempsey, W.A. (1978). "Vendor Selection and the Buying Process." *Industrial Marketing Management* 7(August): 257-268.

Dickson, G.W. "An Analysis of Vendor Selection Systems and Decisions." *Journal of Purchasing* 2(February): 5-17.

Engel, J.F., R.D. Blackwell, and P.W. Miniard. (1986). *Consumer Behavior*, 5th ed. Chicago: Dryden.

Farley, J.U., J.M. Hulbert, and D. Weinstein. (1980). "Price Setting and Volume Planning by Two European Industrial Companies: A Study and Comparison of Decision Processes." *Journal of Marketing* 44(Winter): 46-54.

Green, P.E. and Y. Wind. *Multiattribute Decisions in Marketing: A Measurement Approach*. Hinsdale, IL: Dryden Press.

Hakansson, H. (1982). *International Marketing and Purchasing of Industrial Goods*. Chichester: Wiley.

Haines, G.H., Jr. (1974). "Process Models of Consumer Decision Making." Pp. 89-107 in *Buyer/Consumer Information Processing*, edited by G.D. Hughes and M.L. Ray. Chapel Hill: University of North Carolina Press.

Hansen, F. (1972). *Consumer Choice Behavior*. New York: Free Press.

Heinritz, S.F., P.V. Farrell, and C.L. Smith. *Purchasing: Principles and Applications*. Englewood Cliffs, NJ: Prentice-Hall.

Hill, R.W., and T.J. Hillier. (1977). *Organizational Buying Behavior*. London: Macmillan.

Howard, J.A., and J.N. Sheth. (1969). *The Theory of Buyer Behavior*. New York: Wiley.

Jain, S., and M.V. Laric. (1979). "A Model for Purchasing Strategy." *Journal of Purchasing and Materials Management* 15(Fall 1979): 2-7.

Kelly, P., and J.W. Coaker. (1976). "Can We Generalise about Choice Criteria for Industrial Purchasing Decisions." *Proceedings*, American Marketing Association, Chicago.

Kiser, G.E., and C.P. Rao. (1977). "Important Vendor Factors in Industrial and Hospital Organizations: A Comparison." *Industrial Marketing Management* 6(August): 54-68.

Kudrna, D.A. (1975). *Purchasing Manager's Decision Handbook.* Boston, MA: Cahners.

Lee, L., Jr. and D.W. Dobler. (1984). *Purchasing and Materials Management,* 4th ed. New York: McGraw-Hill.

Lehmann, D., and J. O'Shaughnessy. (1974). "Difference in Attribute Importance for Different Industrial Products." *Journal of Marketing,* 38(April): 36-42.

Merton, R.K. (1957). *Social Theory and Social Structure,* 2nd ed. Glencoe, IL: Free Press.

Möller, K. (1977). *Monidimensioiset Valintamallit Kuluttajan Merkinvalintakayttay-tymisen Tutkimuksessa.* Helsinki: Helsinki School of Economics.

Möller, K. (1983). *Research Paradigms in Analysing Organizational Buying Process.* Helsinki: Helsinki School of Economics.

Möller, K. (1983). *Industrial Buying Behavior of Production Materials: A Conceptual Model and Analysis.* Helsinki: Helsinki School of Economics Publications.

Möller, K., and J. Allos. (1983). *Buying of Production Materials: An Intensive Study in Three Finnish Corporations.* Helsinki: Helsinki School of Economics.

Motes, W.H., and A.G. Woodside. (1979). "Inducing Consumer Compliance Using Low-Balling." *Journal of Advertising Research* 19(April): 219-221.

Nielsen, O. (1981). "Introducing a New Purchasing Strategy in a Firm Producing to Order: A Case of Steel Casting." *Proceedings,* edited by A. Mitchell. Ann Arbor, MI: Association for Consumer Research.

Payne, J.W. (1976). "Heuristic Search Processes in Decision Making." Pp. 321-327 in *Proceedings, Association for Consumer Research Sixth Annual Conference.* Chicago: Association for Consumer Research.

Park, C.W. (1974). "An Exploration of the Consumer's Judgmental Rules." Unpublished doctoral dissertation, University of Illinois, Champaign-Urbana.

Patti, C.H. (1977). "Buyer Information Sources in the Capital Equipment Industry." *Industrial Marketing Management* 6(August).

Pettigrew, A. (1975). "The Industrial Purchasing Decision as a Political Process." *European Journal of Marketing* 9(March): 4-19.

Pras, B. (1973). "Predictive Qualities of Linear and Nonlinear Evaluation Process Models." Unpublished doctoral dissertation, Indiana University, Bloomington.

Russ, F.R. (1971). "Evaluation Process Models and Prediction of Preferences." Pp. 212-216 in *Proceedings,* edited by D. Gardner. Chicago: Association for Consumer Research.

Stiles, G.W. (1974). "Determinants of the Industrial Buyer's Level of Information Processing: Organizations, Situations, and Individual Differences." In *Buyer/Consumer Information Processing,* edited by D. Hughes and M. Ray. Chapel Hill: University of North Carolina.

Strauss, G. (1962). "Tactics of Lateral Relationships: The Purchasing Agent." *Administrative Science Quarterly* 24(December): 539-550.

Van Weele, A.J. (1984). *Purchasing Control.* Amsterdam: Wolters-Noordhoff.

Vollering, J.B. (1982). "A Methodology for Analysing Interaction Processes of Buying and Selling Organizations." Working paper, Graduate School of Management, Delft, Holland.

Vyas, N.M. (1981). "Observation of Industrial Purchasing Decisions on Supplier Choices for Long-Term Contracts in Naturalistic Settings." Unpublished doctoral dissertation, University of South Carolina.

Vyas, N., and A.G. Woodside. (1984). "An Inductive Model of Industrial Supplier Choice Processes." *Journal of Marketing* 48(Winter): 000-000.

Walleigh, R.C. (1986). "What's Your Excuse for Not Using JIT?" *Harvard Business Review* 86(March-April): 38-54.

Wilson, D.T. (1977). "Dyadic Interactions." *Consumer and Industrial Buying Behavior*, edited by A.G. Woodside, J. N. Sheth, and P. D. Bennett. New York: Elsevier North-Holland.

Wind, Y. (1966). "Industrial Buying Behavior: Source Loyalty in the Purchase of Industrial Components." Unpublished doctoral dissertation, Stanford University, Palo Alto, CA.

Wind, Y. (1978). "Organizational Buying Center: A Research Agenda." Pp. 67-76 in *Organizational Buying Behavior*, edited by T.V. Bonoma and G. Zaltman. Chicago: American Marketing Association.

Witte, E. (1972). "Field Research on Complex Decision-Making Processes—The Phase Theorem." *International Studies of Management and Organization* 2(Summer): 156-182.

Woodside, A.G., and D.M. Sammuel. (1981). "Observation of Centralized Corporate Procurement." *Industrial Marketing Management* 10(August): 191-205.

Woodside, A.G., and D.C. Sherrell. "New Replacement Part Buying." *Industrial Marketing Management* 9(1980): 123-132.

Wright, P. (1974). "The Harassed Decision Maker: Time Pressures, Distractions, and the Use of Evidence." *Journal of Applied Psychology* 59(1974): 555-561.

Wright, P. (1975). "Consumer Choice Strategies: Simplifying vs. Optimising." *Journal of Marketing Research* 12(February): 33-42.

Wright, P., and F. Barbour. (1977). "Phased Decision Strategies: Sequels to an Initial Screening." Pp. 304-369 in *Multiple Criteria Decision Making: TIMS Studies in the Management Sciences*, edited by M.K. Starr and M. Zeleny. New York: Elsevier North-Holland.

DISC REFINERY PLATES:
NEW REPLACEMENT PART BUYING

Arch G. Woodside and Daniel L. Sherrell

ABSTRACT

This case describes a modified rebuy purchasing situation for industrial equipment in the paper manufacturing industry. Information for the case was drawn from an analysis of written call reports by and interviews with sales representatives at 26 paper mills located in 8 of the United States. The results indicate that it is in fact possible to make several generalizations on industrial buying behavior for the paper manufacturing industry. Buying behavior for the equipment part discussed in the case, disc refinery plates, describes five decision stages and five overlapping buying centers. Each major focal point of the purchase phase is categorized by at least one major decision. A clear understanding of the structure of the purchasing decision process common among firms in the paper manufacturing industry will provide one with the insight necessary to establish and maintain a lucrative, long-term relationship with a client. It will also help one procure the most favorable terms for the company order split, which is a common purchasing practice for the industry.

Advances in Business Marketing and Purchasing, Volume 5, pages 61-77.
ISBN: 1-55938-364-X

INTRODUCTION

The purpose of this case study is to report the results of an empirical study to describe the buying centers for equipment parts within a specific industry. The study reported is an examination of the applicability of viewing organizational buying as a problem-solving process spread over time and among multiple individuals and departments. The testing of specific hypotheses was not intended in the study but the findings discussed from prior research were used to develop several questions to direct the investigation.

RESEARCH QUESTION

The following basic research question was posed based on the literature reported on organizational buying behavior: What can be generalized across buying firms of industrial equipment parts about buying centers and buying stages in the problem-solving process? This question was developed from recognizing the difficulty of generalizing research findings on organizational buying behavior.

The results of the empirical study to be presented are limited to the buying behavior in 26 paper mill plants located in 8 U.S. states. The study is further limited to the purchases of disc refinery plates, which are replacement parts in paper mill machinery used to refine pulp fibers in the process of manufacturing paper. Thus, a limited attempt is made to generalize buying behavior activities within these constraints.

A second research question is: How does the buying behavior for this group of firms compare to the buying behavior of organizations reported in other studies? How does reaching valid conclusions on buying behavior for this group of firms compare to the buying behavior of organizations reported in other studies? Reaching valid conclusions on buying behavior that hold for more than one industry requires cross-industry research using more than one data collection method and contacts with several persons per firm.

METHOD

The method of data collection and analysis included content analysis of sales representatives' written call reports, interviews with four sales representatives, and telephone or personal interviews with persons in six paper mill plants. Call reports of sales representatives on persons in the paper mill plants provided an unobtrusive method of measuring the sales representative's reported contacts with persons in the paper mills and the sales representative's perception of buying behavior. Interviews with the four sales representatives who called on the 26 paper mills were made to learn additional insights on their perceptions of the persons involved directly in the buying process at each paper mill. These interviews were conducted in the presence of the sales manager of one firm marketing disc refinery plates to the paper mills.

Telephone or personal interviews were conducted with persons in six paper mills in an attempt to confirm personal contacts between the sales representatives and paper mill personnel mentioned in the call reports. Two persons were contacted in each paper mill who were mentioned in the call reports. Each person contacted was asked several open-ended questions on the buying process for disc refinery plates for the paper mill. A total of 76 call reports were analyzed, one to three call reports per paper mill. Each paper mill is a current buyer, or actively considering the purchase of, disc refinery plates from the manufacturing firm cooperating in the study. The call reports were provided by the sales reps. A content analysis form shown in Figure 1 was developed after studying the call reports and reviewing relevant literature suggesting research using content analysis of call reports. Each call report included the names, organizational positions, and departments of persons contacted in each paper mill. The content analysis form shown as Figure 1 was completed for each call report. The 13 categories of information shown in Figure 1 from number of persons contacted to whether or not the paper mill was a new account suggest the content of the interactions between sales representatives and persons involved in buying in the paper mills.

FINDINGS

Problem Solving Stages

As suggested by Hill and Hiller (1977) in other organizational contexts, the buying behavior process for disc refinery plates is a decision process of several related focal points with each focal point categorized by at least one major decision. However, each major decision might best be referred to as a decision area because it is

---

Sales Rep.   ———   Call Report No. ———
Customer Firm   ———   Evaluator   ———

A. No. of Personnel Contacted
B. No. of Departments Contacted
C. No. of Products (Systems) Discussed
D. Specific Requests   Rep: Customer:
    A. No.
    B. Type
E. Call Completed with Person Scheduled: Yes ———   No ———
    —If not, why not?
F. Suggestions for Marketing Strategy
G. Competitors Mentioned:
H. Problems Mentioned: Rep: Customer:
    A. No.
    B. Type
I. Report on Product Use
    A. No.
    B. Outcome
J. Orders Placed
    A. No.
    B. Size $ amount ———   or units ———
    C. Products
K. Changes Noted in Customer Organization and/or Managers:
L. Assessment of Future Sales and Service Potential:
    A. No. or assessments
    B. Postitive or negative
M. New Account   Yes ———   No ———

Figure 1.   Content Analysis Form for Sales Representative Call Reports

composed of a number of subsidiary decisions. The decision processes for buying disc refinery plates included some idiosyncratic problem formulations, search activities, and negotiations with suppliers among the 26 paper mills studied. However, five focal points appear to direct the buying activities and negotiations with suppliers for nearly all 26 firms. The decision processes may be described in more detail than the five focal points to differentiate the buying processes among the firms.

The content analysis and interviews with persons in the six paper mill plants and four sales representatives highlighted the same general question of concern in buying disc refinery plates: Is a new plate available which provides higher performance and/or lower purchasing and operating costs than the plate in current use? This was the general focus of over 70 percent of the activities and time of (1) persons involved in the buying process in the paper mills and (2) interactions of sales representatives and persons involved in the buying process in the mills. A total of 30 percent of the activities and time related to buying plates in the paper mills concerned material handling problems, performance problems, and straight rebuy behavior. The question of general focus in buying disc refinery plates is indicative of a modified rebuy situation. All 26 paper mills had prior experience with the product class (disc refinery plates). New physical specifications in the facing on the plates and metal alloys to produce the plates were being considered by the mills. A total of 19 of the 26 mills were current or recent former customers of the plate manufacturer cooperating in the study.

The purchase decision phases (focal points) are represented by the following five questions:

1. Information search and problem formulation: Does the new product offer a substantial potential advantage relative to current purchases?
2. Product performance evaluation: Do product trial results meet company performance requirements?
3. Product/seller "package" negotiations: Are potential product and supplier capabilities an "optimum" use of company resources?
4. "Package" performance monitoring: Does package performance continue to meet company requirements and expectations?
5. Long-term relationship: Should the paper mill "secure" this source of supply?

Phase One

Information search and problem recognition occurred jointly in time, with the sales representative being reported most often by persons involved in buying in the paper mills as the major source of information about the availability of new plates. Advertising in industrial magazines and informal communications by telephone with persons in other paper mills (in some instances, competing mills) were reported as secondary information sources. Interest in new plate specifications by persons in the paper mills depended most on the level of dissatisfaction with performance of the plates in current use. Poor quality in paper fiber production maintenance problems of the plates were reported as major causes of dissatisfaction. Costs associated with buying or using the plates were less often reported as causing dissatisfaction by persons in the paper mills possibly due to the early recognition of these costs. Dissatisfaction with disc refinery plates in current use most often resulted in complaints to current suppliers, and not in search among new suppliers or for new plate specifications. However, such dissatisfaction increased the amount of time in interaction between buyers and sales reps. Substantially greater attention was given to the topic of new plate specifications in those paper mills where dissatisfaction was expressed. Both the majority of persons interviewed in the paper mills and the sales representatives reported that contact by the sales people initiated information search and problem formulation more often than contact by persons in the paper mills. The majority of decision phases concerning the general focus of buying new disc refinery plates was initiated by contact by the sales representatives and not from dissatisfaction with plates in current use.

Phase Two

The second phase in the decision process for persons in the buying process focused on a trial use of a new set of plates provided by the manufacturer. The performance of the sales representatives was judged to be unsuccessful if the first decision phase did not result in an agreement for a trial use of a set of new plates. Buying behavior related to the general focus of modified rebuys ended if a trial was not agreed to by persons in the mill. The standard operating procedure for the trial specified payment by the paper mill for the set of plates used in the trial if the trial was successful. If the trial was unsuccessful, the plates would be returned to the manufacturer. A trial would include two weeks to two months operating time for all but special alloy plates. A serious problem for the manufacturer and the sales representatives was getting the trial to occur after a trial agreement had been reached and the trial set of plates had been received. An actual trial involved greater coordination and supervision activities among persons in the paper mills than using a new set of plates with the same specifications as the old set. Consequently, trials were often delayed until the mill manager would order the trial to start. The sales representatives would sometimes telephone or visit the paper mills to "check" if the trial had started.

Phase Three

A successful trial outcome with a new set of plates usually resulted in a formal request for product price quotes and manufacturer delivery capabilities by management in the paper mill to the sales rep. Price quotes were always discussed informally and in general terms between the buyer and the sales representative before trial. After the trial, prices were discussed in situation-specific terms based on the performance characteristics of the trial and in comparison with the purchase and operating costs of the plates in current use. The quotation marks are placed around "optimum" in the focal point question of the third decision phase to refer to the use of the word by persons involved in buying in the paper mill. "Optimum" use of company resources actually referred to local optimality for the paper mill, that is, optimum refers to the best decision choice (disc refinery plate or supplier choice) among those chosen as alternatives for evaluation for a given paper mill operation. An attempt to search for and evaluate several alternative specifications of new plates at one time was not reported by persons interviewed in the six mills nor by the sales representatives.

The set of trial plates was "accepted" and payment was sent to the manufacturer if the trial results produced (1) substantial improvements in performance at the same or lower initial operating costs, or (2) the same level of performance at substantially lower initial operating costs compared with plates in use before the trial. The first type of result was the type preferred by nearly all mill managers in the paper mills. The mill manager's general focus with machinery equipment most often was directed toward increasing performance (i.e., increasing paper production) at the same or lower costs. Personal pride in being able to increase paper production in a given time period (per week, month, and year) was specifically mentioned by three mill managers interviewed as their major concern with the performance of operating parts.

Phase Four

A successful trial of a new set of disc refinery plates did not guarantee an order for several additional sets of the plates, as indicated by the call reports analysis, and interviews with the sales representatives and purchasing agents at the paper mills. The placing of an order after a successful trial was most likely if the plate manufacturer was a current supplier of the paper mill. Placing an order with a new supplier after a successful trial was complicated by two factors: (1) additional bookkeeping required in purchasing, material handling, and accounting; and (2) the need felt by the purchasing agent and the mill manager in some cases to explain the reason for the change to the previous suppliers. The prevention of an order for a new plate or reducing the size of the initial order after a successful trial was reported in four mills in the call reports. The need felt by the purchasing agent, mill manager, or machine superintendent to maintain stable relationships with existing suppliers was reported by the sales representatives as the primary reason for preventing, delaying, and reducing the size of an order for a new plate after a successful trial among new customers.

The refinery of the wood fiber using plates from the first order was often viewed as an extension of the trial of the test plates by the mill managers and purchasing agents. Thus, the central focus of phase four was "package" performance monitoring to answer the following question: Does package performance continue to meet company requirements and expectations? The package was the set of plates from the new order following the trial. Trial included operation with plates from the first order in all cases involving a new supplier. In such cases the question most often raised by purchasing agents and previous suppliers was whether or not the trial plates were "extra clean" and impossible to supply on a routine order basis. Extra clean plates might be produced with special care in the manufacturing process and special selection by the supplier.

Phase Five

Successful operation with the new plates from the first order led to a long-term relationship between the paper mill and the supplier. Orders occurred two to ten times per year depending on the type of paper being manufactured and the operating characteristics of the plates.

Should the firm (paper mill) "secure" this source of supply (disc manufacturer)? This question was the focal point of phase five following the successful refinery operation of the sets of ordered plates. A secured supplier was one who received a minimum proportion of the plate orders required for a specific paper production. All persons interviewed in all six paper mills and the four sales representatives reported the standard operating procedure of ordering from two or three suppliers for plates specified for paper production, when possible. The reasons for this buying procedure included (1) decreasing the possibility of delivery problems of the required plates by using a second supplier if the first supplier was unable to deliver, (2) maintaining current prices by increasing each supplier's concern with competitive reactions to price changes, and (3) learning information on new disc refinery plates and operations.

Orders between suppliers were split 60-40, 70-20, or 80-20. Orders of 50-50 were uncommon for disc plates. The purchasing agents and mill managers offered several explanations for this practice. They reported that special concessions on delivery dates, acceptance of large orders of plates in high demand, and return policies of poor quality plates were more likely to be agreed to by a supplier selected as the primary supplier of a specific plate. The potential of receiving larger orders in the future was made known to the secondary supplier by the purchasing agent or mill manager if the purchasing or performance relationship deteriorated with the primary but not the secondary supplier. "It keeps them (suppliers) on their toes," was stated by one purchasing agent.

The possibility existed for changing a 60-40 order split between two suppliers to an 80-20 split. In one case reported by a sales rep, a computer terminal operator and records clerk in purchasing changed the order split from 60-40 to 80-20 in favor of the sales representative's firm. The sales representative and records clerk discussed hunting experiences during the sales representative's visits to the mill. At one point, the records clerk asked the sales representative if he wanted the plate orders increased to a 90-10 split. This offer was refused gently according to the sales representative. The new 80-20 versus the old 60-40 split produced complaints from the secondary supplier, orders from purchasing management in the form of 60-40 splits, and continued actual orders using an 80-20 split by the records clerk. The sales representative reported that purchasing management would be likely to investigate the causes of a change from a 60-40 to a 90-10 split but not to an 80-20 split. The conclusion suggested to this case incident by the sales representative was that "It's important to get to know everyone at the mill. You never know who can help you or hurt you." All four sales representatives mentioned the occurrence of similar cases as the change in order splits between suppliers. However, no pattern of such behavior is apparent. Such changes were not actively reported by the sales representatives with persons in the paper mills. Such special relationships were not reported in the call reports and the sales representatives reported verbally that such cases were unlikely to occur in most paper mills.

Summary of Problem Solving for Buying Disc Refinery Plates

Table 1 and Figure 2 are attempts to summarize the flow of activities, decisions, and people involved in the buying process for disc refinery plates. They do not do justice to the variety of behaviors reported in the call reports and from interviews with the four sales representatives and persons in the six paper mills. However, the activity sequence and decision phases described were found consistently using the two different research methods. Activities and decisions unique to each of the 26 paper mills included in the study could be reported but they would not refute the sequences of activities and decisions described. Adding additional sequences of activities and decisions limits the generalization of the findings among the 26 mills, while such additions increase the usefulness for understanding the behavior of any one firm. Table 1 and Figure 2 are frames of reference for adding more specific activities and decisions for the study of specific disc refinery plate purchases in paper mills.

A favorable response of a purchase decision phase leads to a new activity, as shown in Figure 2. An unfavorable outcome leads to "continue with current supplier" or currently used plates, or to "adjust relationship or terminate" following an unfavorable outcome to package performance monitoring (phase four). Such an adjustment might occur if the mill foreman, quality control engineer, and purchasing manager could be convinced that the unfavorable use of the plates ordered (in phase four) was an unusual event and this event would not be repeated with a second order. This adjustment was likely to occur since the initial order was often viewed as a continuation of the trial and the persons in the paper mill had an investment in time and effort to reach valid conclusions about the use of the new plates. The decision process appeared to be a never-ending search. Buying disc refinery plates was oriented toward an implicit faith that some new plate might provide a major breakthrough in performance and dramatically lower costs of operation compared to the plates in current use. Since an infinite number of plate facings might be developed by engineers of the plate manufacturer for a specified paper production, the modified rebuy of possibly improved plates was the central focus of persons involved in buying in the paper mills. The sales representatives played the role of urging the search to continue and directing the search toward particular plants.

Humans

Table 1. Activity Sequence of Industrial Buying Behavior by Decision Phase and Buying Center

Activity Sequence	Purchase Decision Phase	Buying Center Description
1. Initial Contact by Manufacturing Representative	1. *Information Search and Problem Formulation* [Does new product offer substantial potential advantage relative to current purchases?]	1. *Buying Center A* —mill manager —purchasing agent —machine foreman —machine operators
2. Product Design and Installation for Trail	2. *Product Performance Evaluation* [Do product trial results meet company performance requirements?]	2. *Buying Center B* —machine foreman —quality control —purchasing agent
3. Request for Product Price Quotes and Seller Delivery Capability	3. *Product/Seller "Package" Negotiations* [Are potential product and supplier capabilities an "optimum" use of company resources?]	3. *Buying Center C* —mill manager —purchasing agent —machine foreman
4. Product Delivery, Installation, and Use	4. *"Package Performance Monitoring* [Does package performance continue to meet company requirements and expectations?]	4. *Buying Center D* —purchasing agent —machine foreman —quality control
5. Negotiation of a Requirements Contract (establishment of a straight rebuy situation)	5. *Long-term Relationship Establishment* [Should the firm "secure" this source of supply?]	5. *Buying Center E* —purchasing agent —mill foreman

The Buying Centers for the Decision Phases

The concept of a buying center of different persons involved in the purchasing process was supported by the content analysis of the 76 call reports and interviews with the sales representatives and persons involved in buying in the paper mills. Also, the hypothesis developed by Hill and Hiller (1977) that multiple buying centers occur for different stages in the decision process was supported. Five buying centers are described in Table 1, one for each of the major decision phases.

Persons are listed in Table 1 according to job title and only persons having major direct involvement are included. "Major direct

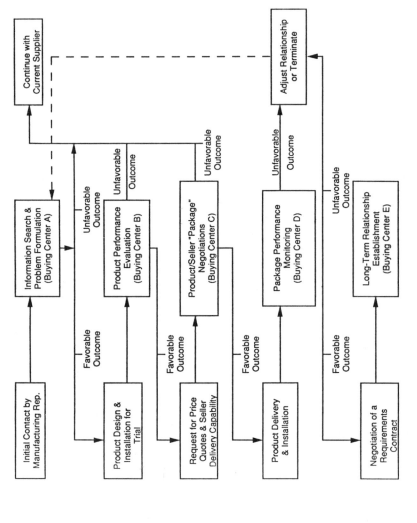

Figure 2. Flow Diagram of Industrial Buying Behavior For Paper Mill Disc Refinery Plates

72

involvement" was limited to respondents in the personal interviews as persons who met face-to-face with a sales representative before a long-term relationship (phase five) was established or whose opinion or approval was nearly always sought for a particular decision in the buying process. The interviews with persons in the six paper mills confirmed the findings from the content analysis of the call reports and reports from the sales representatives that the sales representatives met face-to-face at least once with all levels of management directly involved in purchasing disc refinery plates. Management included machine foreman, purchasing managers (agents), quality control managers (engineers), mill foremen, and mill managers (superintendants). Machine operators were also contacted directly by the sales representatives.

Top management's ("mill manager" or "mill superintendant") approval (ratification) was needed in phase one in the purchase decision process before a final agreement for a trial occurred. First, the purchasing agent and the machine foremen usually needed to agree that a trial of a new plate should be recommended. Several two-person and three-person meetings were reported before a trial was agreed upon. Such meetings often included the following parties meeting in the following order:

1. purchasing agent and sales representative;
2. sales representative, machine foreman, and machine operator;
3. sales representative, purchasing agent, and machine foreman;
4. purchasing agent, machine foreman, and mill manager.

Both the purchasing agent and machine foreman played multiple roles in phase one of the buying process. Both collected information on plate specifications and the advantages of new plates from the sales representative. The machine foreman collected information on use from the machine operator and his own inspection of the disc refinery operation. Purchasing agents and machine foremen acted as gatekeepers of information reaching the mill manager. The mill manager acted as ultimate decider in the decision to order a trial use of the new plates.

A second buying center was formed for phase two in the decision process (product performance evaluation). Membership in this second group (Buying Center B) overlapped with the first buying center. However, the roles played by participants changed. For phase two, both the machine foreman and the purchasing agent evaluated the performance in using the new plates versus the standard plates. A plant engineer (quality control) inspected the fiber quality produced using the new plates and met face-to-face with the machine foreman and the purchasing agent to discuss the findings of his analysis. The sales representative usually attempted to meet at least once with the engineer and machine foreman during the trial to discuss the progress of the trial and to recommend adjustments in refinery operations if needed.

The machine foreman and the quality control engineer usually agreed with each other on the results of the trial. From the interviews with individuals in the paper mills and the sales representatives, a range of 2 to 5 meetings were reported between a machine foreman and a quality control engineer for evaluating a trial of a new plate. Each of these meetings would be brief with most being under 10 minutes. A substantial minority of purchasing agents were reported by the sales representatives to meet with the machine foreman and engineer, jointly and separately. This interaction was confirmed in eight call reports and by interviews with four purchasing agents in four different paper mills. The role of these active purchasing agents during the trial was to ensure that an evaluation was completed and to help resolve conflicts between the machine foreman and engineer if conflicts occurred. Serious conflicts concerning the trial (cause for delays, evaluating results) were less often reported when the purchasing agent was involved actively in the trial. A problem-solving approach to conflict resolution was reported and observed in the call reports most often for conflicts during trial in Buying Center B. The active purchasing agent often referred to the machine foreman and engineer's areas of expertise using questions directed toward each during 2-person and 3-person group meetings. This approach also served the psychosocial needs of the foreman and engineer to contribute to the evaluation and have their specialized knowledge recognized. With less active purchasing agents, the sales representative often served the function of coordinating the trial of the new plate. The sales representative would meet with the machine foreman and quality control engineer to learn if delays were occurring, to "check" (request) if the engineer had met with the foreman to discuss the performance of the new plate, and to suggest points of comparison between the new and regularly used plates.

The vice-president of marketing of the cooperating plate manufacturer reported that the sales representatives needed to vary the amount of their involvement with the buying center during the trial according to the involvement displayed by the purchasing agent. "The problem with the just 'adequate' sales representative is that he can never figure out who's making the decisions (in the buying center); he really doesn't know who to see or when to see them," reported the vice-president of marketing. In contrast, the vice-president of marketing reported that the "distinguished" sales representative knew all the persons involved in buying plates in the paper mill, when each was involved, and could predict accurately the next event based on the outcome of the last event in the buying process.

After a successful trial the mill manager and the purchasing agent usually met twice to discuss performance characteristics of the new plates, price quotes from the sales representative, and level of service history of the supplier. The machine foreman was often present for the first of these meetings and the sales representative was present for the second. The mill manager met face-to-face with the sales representative for negotiating delivery dates, quantities of plate orders, and price for the initial order of the new plate. The written order was placed by purchasing.

The machine foreman and the purchasing agent often inspected jointly the arrival of the first sets of new plates ordered. Box markings, order quantity, quality of plate surfaces, and date of likely use were discussed. Either the machine foreman or the purchasing agent would notify the quality control engineer that the new plates ordered had arrived. The engineer usually asked when the new plates would be installed but he was unlikely to be present for the removal of the old plates and installation of the new plates. The engineer and machine foreman would inspect the fiber quality produced using the new plates and usually met to confirm their observations with each other. The purchasing agent requested verbal comments on performance of using the ordered new plates from both the foreman and engineer.

At the end of phase four and during phase five in the decision process, the sales representative attempted to have the purchasing agent and mill foreman (assistant mill manager) informally agree on an order split favorable to the supplier (80-20, 70-30, or 60-40). The mill foreman and purchasing agent determined the size and direction (favorable or unfavorable) of the order split by (1) the relative advantage in performance and cost of the new versus old plates, (2) amount of prior experience with the competing suppliers, and (3) local policy of the mill managers. For most paper mills, the purchasing agent would not discuss a specific order split with the sales representative but would verbally guarantee future orders for the new plate.

THE PURCHASING AGENT AS COORDINATOR

The purchasing agent may be singled out from Table 1 and found to be the only individual in the paper mill likely to be actively involved in all phases of the buying decision process. The purchasing agent's major role appears to be coordinator of the buying process and gatekeeper for entry to other persons in the buying centers and information transfer within the firm. To the extent that the purchasing agent did not act as the coordinator of the phases in the decision process, the amount of delays, confusion, and conflicts among persons involved in buying new disc refinery plates increased. Purchasing agents who did not assume the role of coordinator of the phases in the decision process preferred not to agree to trials of new plates. Sales representatives reported a preference of "working with" purchasing agents who were involved in all phases of the decision process. The less able or willing the purchasing agent was in coordinating the decision process, the greater the involvement of the mill manager in all decision phases. In such cases, the decision to conduct a trial, choose a supplier, or place an order would often be made with reference to authority in place of problem-solving.

This research showed that buying is a process very diffused throughout the organization.

> That is, much information, many activities, and many people are crucial parts of the buying process, and yet are not parts of the "purchasing department." The more diffuse a process is, in this sense, the less appropriate it may be to think of the "buyer" only as a decision maker in a narrow sense.

> From an organizational theory point of view, it is increasingly evident that the more diffused the information-activities-persons process is, the more necessary it is to find a structural way to plan and coordinate such a process. The structural answer to the need for a planning and ongoing coordination is the creation of the "purchasing" department/manager (Nicosia and Wind 1977).

DISCUSSION

Management in vendor organizations may want to use the variables shown in Figure 1 as a starting point in developing their own method for content analyzing sales representatives' call reports. Some use of third party observations of meetings of the sales representatives and members of buying centers is recommended. The use of third parties from outside the vendor's organization (e.g., observers from an industrial research firm), is likely to provide more objective observations and descriptions of selling and buying activities. This procedure would need the understanding and support of both the customer organization and the sales representatives. Some sales representatives should be expected not to want to participate in such research. A voluntary research program is recommended initially.

REFERENCES

Hill, R.W., and T.J. Hiller. (1977). *Organizational Buying Behavior*. London: Macmillan.

Nicosia, F.M., and Y. Wind. (1977). "Behavioral Models of Organizational Buying Processes." Pp. 96-120 in *Behavioral Models for Market Analysis: Foundations for Marketing Action*, edited by F.M. Nicosia and Y. Wind. Hinsdale, IL: Dryden Press.

TUFTED CARPETS LIMITED:
THE PURCHASE OF A NEW MATERIAL—
NEEDLED WOVEN POLYPROPYLENE

Stephen Parkinson and Michael Baker

ABSTRACT

The following case study centers upon the purchasing process for a new material: needled woven polypropylene. Information for the case was drawn from a larger study on innovation in the carpet industry. The focus of this case study is one particular, and highly competitive, sector of the carpet industry—tufted carpets. In addition, it deals with the purchase of needled woven polypropylene (NWP) by one company, Tufted Carpets Limited, within the tufted carpet sector. The case study on Tufted Carpets Ltd. is introduced against background information on the tufted carpet market at the time of the introduction of NWP in 1972. This introduction is followed by an overview of the criteria applied to the decision to purchase NWP in the larger study that included twelve companies. This overview is based on Robinson, Faris, and Wind's (1967) methodology indicating the nature of management involvement at each stage.

Advances in Business Marketing and Purchasing, Volume 5, pages 79-95.
ISBN: 1-55938-364-X

Mintzberg, Raisinghani, and Theoret's (1976) theory of "the structure of unstructured decision processes" is also referred to throughout the paper. The case follows the emergence of three distinct stimuli which prove to have direct influence on Tufted Carpets Ltd.'s purchasing decisions in terms of the new NWP material. Additionally, the issue of the significance of timing in purchasing strategy is presented through its relevance to the issues of the case.

THE TUFTED CARPET INDUSTRY: AN INTRODUCTION

Tufted carpets were first introduced in the British carpet market in 1956. From 1957 well into the 1960s the market for tufted carpets grew rapidly. This growth occurred at the expense of other floor coverings, such as linoleum and matting. It did not interfere with the purchase of woven carpets.

The success of tufted carpets in those early years can be attributed to several factors. First, tufted carpets could be produced at up to twenty times the speed of the traditional woven product, without requiring additional labor. Second, the original manufacturers of tufted carpets adopted a policy of aggressive promotion of their products to both the public and to the trade. Third, consumer ignorance played a role in the market's development. When tufted carpets were first introduced, the public did not know that they were different from woven carpets; they only knew tufted carpets were cheaper.

The Economic Intelligence Unit estimated that the retail value of the total floor coverings market in 1961 was about £165 million. The same source estimated that British manufacturers' sales of woven carpets to the home market in that year totalled £69.4 million. Manufacturers' sales of tufted carpets were estimated at £19 million, including £6 million from Northern Ireland.

During the 1960s, differences between the structures of the woven and tufted sectors of the carpet industry emerged. On the woven side were a number of small manufacturers. The largest of these included: John Crossley—Carpet Trade Holdings, Blackwood-Mortons (BMK), The Carpet Manufacturing Company Limited, Firths, A. F. Stoddart, Templetons, Brintons and Bond Worth. Between them, they controlled 50-60% of the market for woven products. In this sector, no single manufacturer controlled more than 13% of the market.

Table 1. Estimated Market Shares,
Tufted Products 1968
(In percent)

Lancater	25
Shaw	20
Cyril Lord	20
Kosset	15
Others	20
Total	100

In the tufted industry, the number of manufacturers was much smaller, and therefore, the market share of each leading manufacturer was much larger. In 1968, the Economic Intelligence Unit estimate of market shares in tufted carpets are shown in Table 1.

By 1968, the market had become increasingly fashion-conscious and open to textural and pattern changes. In addition, carpet printing technology had advanced to the point where it was feasible to begin copying Axminster style patterns on tufted products.

Table 2 illustrates that in 1967, 1968, and 1969 the rate of expansion of the overall market for tufted carpets slowed down. Tufting manufacturers began to compete with each other for market share, rather than for a share of a growing market. Product innovation became a key competitive strategy as manufacturers fought to secure the favor of their customers.

Table 3 provides some background information on the carpet industry at the time of the innovation by providing the estimated sales potential of different types of tufted products for 1972.

INNOVATION IN THE TUFTED CARPET INDUSTRY (1972)

In 1972, changes in both demand and the channels of distribution affected the growth of the tufted carpet industry. In the area of demand, consumers became more aware of value for money, durability, and attractiveness in the carpets they bought; this forced manufacturers to be more consumer-oriented in their approach. At the same time, it seemed that the public was becoming more knowledgable about certain carpet fibers and blends of fibers; they were also better able to discuss their advantages and disadvantages at the retail level.

In the area of distribution, no one manufacturer exercised complete control over any sector of the retail trade. As a result, tufted carpet

Table 2.   Relative Importance of Different Carpet Types (1964-1970)
(Percent of Carpet Sales By Volume)

	1964	1965	1966	1967	1968	1969	1970
Woven Carpets	54.1	51.7	49.6	45.4	44.7	41.1	37.7
Tufted	31.8	34.7	39.1	43.8	43.8	43.5	46.6
Rugs	2.9	2.8	2.4	2.2	2.0	1.5	1.3
Other	11.2	10.8	9.9	8.6	9.5	13.9	14.4
Total	100.0	100.0	100.0	100.0	100.0	100.0	100.0
Overall Market for Carpets (000 square yards)	104.69	107.73	107.73	115.31	125.74	129.19	128.33

Table 3.   Sales of All Types of Tufted Products
(Projections for 1972)

Tufted Carpets Containing 50% or More by Weight	Number of Companies	000s Square Yds.		Value (£000) MSP	
Acrylic fibers	22	8,611	(8)	15,494	(13)
Polymide fibers	23	40,354	(37)	48,707	(39)
Viscose of Modified					
Viscose	23	42,701	(40)	33,438	(27)
Wool	14	4,853	(4)	11,470	(9)
Other	13	11,514	(11)	14,185	(11)
Total		108,034	(100)	123,295	(100)

manufacturers wanted to establish good relationships with their distributors in order to maintain or even expand sales. The majority of companies dealt directly with the retailer as well as through the wholesale market. A tufted carpet company seeking to increase its market share needed not only attractive carpet ranges, but also an efficient distribution strategy. Therefore, selection and servicing of the most appropriate marketing channels was of prime importance.

The six largest tufted carpet manufacturers were Associated Weaver, Lancaster Carpets, Rivington Carpets, Donaghadee Carpets, Shaw Carpets, and Kosset Carpets.

Although the tufting process was basically simple, considerable capital resources were required for large-scale operations. Also, tight margins were fairly common, particularly during the three or four years in which growth of the tufted market did not meet manufacturers' expectations. Thus, many manufacturers had excess capacity at this time. In response, manufacturers continued to produce at capacity, but reduced the price of the product. They did this by introducing new and cheaper fibers, and using less fiber per square yard.

Tufted carpets are made in a process which involves the stitching of tufts of pile yarn into a pre-woven backing material. The basic technology involved in tufting is simpler than that of manufacturing woven carpets. The primary backing material for tufted carpets was traditionally woven from jute yarns. However, uncertainties concerning the supply of raw materials developed and, consequently, prices increased. Jute became an unpopular material for backing fabric. Manufacturers began to examine polypropylene fibers and considered using non-woven fabrics.

Polypropylene was a comparatively cheap fiber with low specific gravity, negligible moisture absorbency, and good resistance to chemicals. It also offered manufacturers a savings of up to 40 percent on backing costs. However, the initial polypropylene product had several flaws. Polypropylene backings, when subjected to the twisting pressures of the tufting process, distorted the warp and weft of the material. This made accurate printing of carpets based on simple polypropylene backings difficult. Thus, there was a need to improve the mechanical properties of polypropylene-based backing materials in order to meet the needs of a rapidly expanding sector of the tufted carpet industry (i.e., printed carpets).

One of the innovative solutions to this problem, pioneered by Synthetic Fabrics Ltd., was the development of a new carpet backing manufacturing process. In it, the woven polypropylene backing and a loose synthetic fiber were passed under a spiked roller. The spikes on the roller had barbs which took some of the viscose material through the backing material. This effectively "locked up" the matrix of man-made fibers and reduced the tendency toward distortion in the finished carpets. In shag carpets, this reduced the number of necessary tufts per square unit; thus, substantial savings were realized.

The new product, needled woven polypropylene (NWP), had a further advantage. It was much easier to stick latex foam backing to NWP than to the conventional simple polypropylene. All tufted carpets must have some form of secondary backing; simple polypropylene backings were difficult to "back," as they were shiny and chemically inert. With an increased number of tussocks of fiber through the material, the latex foam vastly increased purchases of the backing material.

CRITERIA USED IN THE DECISION TO PURCHASE NWP—AN OVERVIEW

The initial decision to use NWP materials was dependent on a series of interrelated activities that led to the final buying decision. At each stage of the process, various factors interceded and influenced the direction of the decision.

Stage 1:   Recognition of need for low pile weight tufted carpets.

Stage 2:   Specification of required characteristics of low pile weight product.

Stages 1 and 2 are equivalent to the identification stage in the work of Mintzberg et al. (1976). Mintzberg et al. state that "the first step following recognition is the tapping of existing information channels and the opening of new ones to clarify and define the issues."

By early 1972, most firms in the sample had recognized the need to produce cheaper tufted carpets. In varying degrees of sophistication, management in these companies had analyzed the tufted carpet market and realized that the overall trend was toward downgrading the quality of the product. This trend emphasized the importance of reducing the cost of the carpet without sacrificing appearance. One way of downgrading quality involved using less pile yarn per square yard.

It appears that this trend in the market acted as a stimulus to initiate a decision process which would mobilize resources to meet this demand. In other words, the stimulus was sufficient to push the appropriate manager over his threshold decision level; he authorized resources to be channelled into dealing with the problem.

Stage 3:   Identification of technical problems associated with low pile weight products.

Stages 3 through 6 represent the development phase of Mintzberg et al.'s model. At this stage, the greatest number of decision-making resources are used. Mintzberg et al. defines development in terms of two basic routines—search and design. Search is used to find ready-made solutions and design is used to develop custom-made or modified ready-made solutions.

In the sample, the production of a low pile weight product was delegated to the manager responsible for technical functions. Some organizations employed a manager specifically for this function. In other companies, the manager of technical development had additional responsibilities.

Typically, when the manager was given a brief for a low pile weight product, he tested several methods of reducing pile weight. When conventional carpet backing was used, it was found to show through or "grin." The technical manager then had to find a new way to achieve a low pile weight. This search for a new method may be labelled a "memory search," as managers searched through the organizations' existing memory—on paper and in the minds of personnel.

Stage 4:   Awareness of NWP materials.

In June/July 1972, Synthetic Fabrics Limited met with the technical manager in each company, bringing samples of the NWP material. In several companies, this material filled a pressing need. It provided a backing material which would allow lower pile weights, particularly on piece-dyed carpets.

Evident in this stage were two principal types of search routines, and possibly a third. The first is a "trap search," in which search generators are used. These generators inform suppliers about what the searcher is looking for. The second is an "active search;" this involves a direct search for alternatives. The final one is a "passive search" in which the company awaits unsolicited alternatives. Not only do organizations seek alternatives, alternatives also seek organizations. In the case of NWP, searches by both supplier and buyer led to the proposed solution of using NWP.

Stage 5:   Decision to test NWP materials as a solution to problems defined in Stage 3 above.

Stage 6:   Technical evaluation of the performance of NWP backing materials compared with conventional backing materials.

The technical manager was responsible for testing the NWP material and subsequent technical evaluation of its performance. In most companies, the technical manager performed a trial production run using NWP materials with a given pile weight. He compared the results of this run with a second trial, in which simple polypropylene backing materials were used along a higher pile weight. Next, he examined various alternative carpet constructions; some of these included NWP material and others did not. He presented these alternatives to the managers responsible for product policy for evaluation. At this stage, "search" had narrowed down alternatives including NWP, and "design" was to modify the alternatives for internal application.

Stage 7:   Business evaluation of new products developed which incorporated NWP products.

This stage is an overlapping phase between development and selection based on Mintzberg et al.'s model. The development phase frequently involves factoring one decision into a series of subdecisions, each requiring at least one selection step. Thus, one decision process may involve a number of selection steps; many of these may be intricately bound up with the development phase. Therefore, the selection stage is an iterative process, involving a progressively deepening investigation of alternatives. As such, it cannot be separated from the preceding steps.

In the survey, the decision to use NWP materials in a particular carpet was typically made by the manager or group of managers responsible for product planning. If the product was suitable and met the required specification, the new tufted carpet product would be launched using NWP materials. The evaluation process varied between companies. Some formed sophisticated product planning committees; others judged the product according to whether it "looked right."

Two key interrelated decision criteria are apparent in the analysis. First, would the base fibers take up the same dye stuffs as the pile? This would eliminate "grinning." Second, did lack of "grinning" mean that pile weight could be reduced? NWP fulfilled both criteria, taking up the same dye stuffs and allowing for reduction in pile weight.

THE HOLDING COMPANY

Textiles International Limited is the parent company of a group of subsidiaries; these subsidiaries are engaged primarily in the manufacture and marketing of household textiles, floor rugs and carpets, and fabrics. They are divided into three main operating divisions—the retail division, the overseas division, and the manufacturing division. This case study focuses on the carpets subdivision of manufacturing. The carpet subdivision is represented by Tufted Carpets Ltd. Table 4 illustrates that this subdivision has been consistently the least profitable of Textiles' subsidiary companies.

Table 4. Contribution of Operating Devisions to Sales/Profitability

	1970 Sales £000	1970 Profit as a % of sales	1971 Sales £000	1971 Profit as a % of sales	1972 Sales £000	1972 Profit as a % of sales	1973 Sales £000	1973 Profit as a % of sales	1974 Sales £000	1974 Profit as a % of sales
Retail Division	3,200	16	3,692	16	3,628	16	3,759	17	4,393	16
Manufacturing										
Textiles	9,416	9	9,538	6	10,793	8	12,910	9	13,946	8
Yarns	2,019	5	2,184	8	2,362	9	3,197	10	4,341	8
Others	2,124	9	2,722	9	3,343	11	3,078	13	4,040	12
Carpets*	6,405	4	7,759	5	8,502	7	11,185	5	13,790	5
Overseas Division	3,338	23	4,062	21	4,927	17	5,423	19	6,604	19
Totals	26,502	10	29,957	9	33,555	10	39,552	11	47,114	10

Source: Annual Reports and Accounts.

A COMPANY BACKGROUND

Tufted Carpets Ltd. is a wholly-owned subsidiary of J. Tuft and Sons Limited. J. Tuft and Sons was first registered in 1936 as a holding company for a group which manufactured carpets, rugs, mats, furnishings, and textiles. Tufted Carpets Ltd. was registered in March 1966 as a private company to manufacture rugs and carpets within the group.

Until 1967, Tufted Carpets Ltd. had produced primarily the traditional woven carpet; however, the board of the company realized that tufted carpets were gaining an increasing proportion of the total carpet market. A decision was made in 1967 to acquire tufting machinery and enter the tufted carpet market. This would allow the company to defend its position in the woven carpets market; it would also enable them to gain a share of the new markets which tufted products had developed. In 1968, Textiles International and the Garde Corporation battled for the ownership of Tufted Carpets Ltd. In December of that year, Textiles International acquired Tufted Carpets Ltd. (TCL).

Tufted Carpets Ltd.'s policy has been to produce tufted products aimed at medium to high price sectors of the tufted carpet market and at heavy duty/contract applications. There were two reasons for this. First, the company had a large established contract sales force, which included strong contacts with major contract buyers. Architects and other major buyers, such as the Department of the Environment were among these. Therefore, the company was in a position to benefit from products which could utilize the same channels of distribution as the traditional woven carpet. The new product, however, would be aimed at installation areas for which the woven product was unsuitable. Second, TCL valued its reputation as a producer of medium to high price/quality products; they wanted to produce tufted products that would enhance this image. In 1972, the company invested in the Crawford Multi-Color Yarn Patterning Machine with tufting and backing machines.

The range of "standard" tufted products TCL produces is relatively small. In November of 1972, there were only eight products in the tufted product range. Four of these were designed for contract applications, and the other four were indicated as suitable for heavy domestic use.

The company does considerable business with the Department of the Environment, mail order companies and their multiples, each of whom commission individually designed products. This has recently led to a problem. Because most customers buy well before delivery, it is difficult to adjust prices in order to keep pace with the increasing costs of raw materials. This results in a pattern of falling margins. This is particularly true with the medium to high quality product TCL has traditionally produced. The firm's management is seriously considering the possibility of trading down the quality of its products by substituting synthetic materials for wool.

Tufted Carpets Ltd. has an active product development program through which new products are brought into the market. The primary objective of this program is to develop new products suitable for certain price sectors of the market. All new product ideas, for both tufted and woven carpets, are evaluated by a marketing development committee. Representatives of production, new product development, design and marketing are involved in this committee. Its goal is to ensure that woven and tufted products are developed in a complimentary, rather than competitive, way.

The technical manager and chief designer work together in the development of new products. The technical manager supplies technical input on such factors as wear resistance qualities, developments of the fiber suppliers, and the physical construction of the product, including backing material. The chief designer is responsible for the design and coloration of new products.

When product development decides to produce a particular type of product, the technical manager and the chief designer are given their respective specifications. The technical manager described the process as follows (December 1974):

> We might begin with a spec for a low weight, piece-dyed item. The first thing to do is to look at whose face fiber you will use, and do your own comparisons between the available fibers across the companies you deal with, checking on discounts available and hopefully ending up with the best product at the most economical price. You will then talk to the supplier, obtain samples of the yarn, and begin construction trials on a narrow width machine.

At the construction trial stage, physical samples of the most attractive product ideas are produced. Costs of alternative products are developed, and given to the tufting sales manager. He then tests the probable market reaction. If this is favorable, the products will be dyed (if piece-dyed), in a range of colors. From these, the final twelve or so colors will be selected. Finally, when the construction and design work is finished, and the final three or four products have evolved, these are formally presented to the board of directors. They are presented as a finalized group of alternative "packages." The board will then select an alternative to market.

The role of the company's buyer throughout this process is as a specialist. He is not involved in decisions concerning the technical or aesthetic merits of raw materials used in the production of new products. His role is to negotiate terms of transactions between TCL and the company's suppliers; he negotiates price, quantity discount and delivery once suppliers for certain products have been chosen. He does not influence the choice of source of supply.

THE PURCHASE PROCESS FOR
A NEW MATERIAL (NWP)

In June 1970, Mr. White, TCL's technical manager at the time, visited the United States. He examined patterns of development within the American tufting industry. While in the United States, he discovered a new primary backing material—fiber lock weave. This was the American equivalent of needle weave polypropylene. The first product he observed which used this new material was a very light "shag" carpet; it weighed about ten ounces per square yard. At that time, he felt that there was no use for the material in TCL's range of tufted carpets. This was because TCL manufactured only high to medium quality tufted products. TCL's tufting machinery was set up to produce only these high quality products. Mr. White stated:

> we used to develop what we thought was the right cloth—but because we had certain looms (of a particular gauge), we thought we would develop the cloths for those looms, which wasn't necessarily what the market wanted.

This attitude has changed since 1970; by 1972, a change of product policy enabled TCL's management to consider using the needled polypropylene backing material.

In early 1972, TCL's management was concerned that the company was not represented in one of the most rapidly developing sectors of the tufted market. This sector included loop pile products wholesaling at just under £2 per square yard. This type of product was just below the price of TCL's lowest acceptable price product; consequently, TCL was losing sales to this sector. Therefore, in April of 1972, the marketing development committee decided to begin trials on the development of a low weight piece-dyed, loop-pile product, to meet this particular market demand.

In order to produce a product which would wholesale at the target market price level, Mr. White reduced the carpet's weight of pile per square yard. However, at the target level of 14 to 15 ounces of pile per square yard, the carpet's appearance was unsatisfactory. When the product was used on stairs, the "nosings" of the stair tended to open up the pile; this caused "grinning," and in very bright lighting, the backing glared.

Then, in June 1972, Synthetic Fabrics contacted TCL and presented their version of needleweave. This new material met TCL's need. Mr. White commented:

> We were looking at the development of the product and became aware of the development of the backing and we put the two together because there were decided advantages in using the fleeced fabric, in that we could get down to a lower face weight in the carpet without the carpet backing showing through, because during the piece dying process, the fleece takes up the dyestuff and prevents the grinning.

He continued, pointing out that the economic justification for using needleweave depended on the weight of pile saved:

> We did development work at about 14 to 15 ounces, with an ordinary tape fabric (normal woven polypropylene). At the time, we were having problems until Synthetic Fabrics sent us a sample roll of needleweave down, which we tufted. In doing so, we managed to get the pile weight down to 12½ ounces, and still produce an acceptable product. So we sat down and worked out what the price of needleweave was and what we would have to pay for the extra yarn (to achieve the same cover), if we didn't use it. On that product you needed to save at least 2 ounces—it depends really on the construction of the carpet, with a 'shag' carpet you could save far more.

In the case of this particular product, the company was able to save 2 ounces of pile yarn. This paid for the incremental cost of this backing material over ordinary woven polypropylene. At the same time, the product produced at 12½ ounces per square yard using needleweave was more acceptable aesthetically than the same product produced at 14½ ounces per square yard, using ordinary woven polypropylene. In September of 1972, TCL launched "Majestic," their first product with needleweave, at the Harrogate Textiles Exhibition. By September 21, they were ordering needleweave in quantity. Figure 1 illustrates the purchasing process of Tufted Carpets Limited.

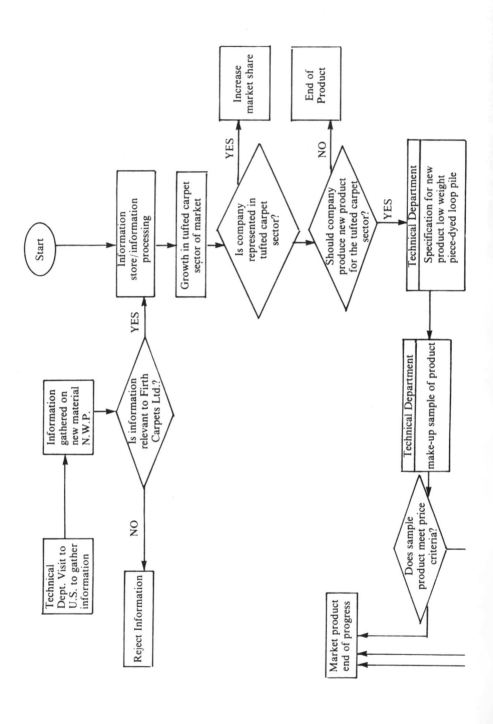

92

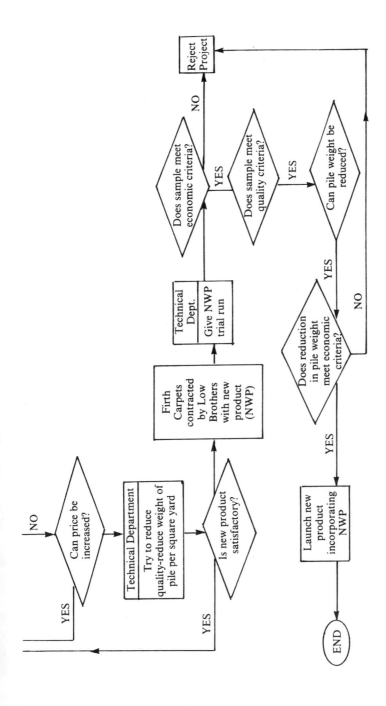

Figure 1. Tufted Carpet Ltd.

93

CONCLUSION

Because of the competitive nature of the tufted carpet market, Mr. White, the technical manager, collected information on new products and processes worldwide. While visiting the United States, he became aware of NWP materials. Although unsuitable for his company's product range at the time, he thought that NWP was a good idea. Information on NWP was stored for later use, in case a situation would arise where its use would be appropriate.

Two years later, such a situation did arise, and the threshold level for action on NWP materials was reached. Mintzberg et al. (1976) states that the moment of action (in this case, the decision to examine NWP for use) is dependent on the "force of the stimulus over time and the action threshold." They continue, "quick reinforcement of one stimulus by another magnifies their perceived combined amplitudes." The reinforcement of one stimulus by another is evident in the case study; three interrelated stimuli influenced the decision to utilize the NWP material.

The first recognized stimulus was the change in product policy. This was caused by movement in market demand which led to TLC's need for a new or modified product. The second stimulus occurred in the form of "grinning" problems associated with the initial proposed solution. The pressure to accept external innovation was greater because the potential internal solution had failed. The final stimulus was when Synthetic Fabrics contacted Tufted Ltd. offering a potential solution. At this point, management was receptive to the idea of using NWP to solve their problem. The stimuli acted not only as individual influences on the decision to initiate action, but also cumulatively.

The selection of the new material NWP was based on an "analysis" type of routine. Mintzberg et al. define this as "a factual evaluation generally carried out by technocrats, followed by managerial choice by judgement or bargaining." In Tufted Carpets Ltd., the evaluation of NWP was carried out by the technical and design managers; the final decision to launch a product using NWP material was left with the board of directors.

Related to this is the example of "satisficing" which the case study provides. That is, the problem is reduced to a series of simplified steps. These begin with a study of potential internal solutions to the problem of developing a less expensive carpet; only when none of these proved feasible did the company search for external solutions.

The decision to purchase NWP was not complicated. The advantages of cost, aesthetic appearance and non-fraying qualities easily outweighed any disadvantages of the material. Nevertheless, the initial decision to purchase NWP from Synthetic Fabrics might have benefited from increased purchasing involvement. In particular, the technical orientation would have been balanced by the commercial orientation of the purchasing staff.

Finally, the purchase of NWP material by Tufted Carpets Ltd. is significant from a "timing" perspective. Mintzberg et al. state that "managers may purposely speed up or delay a decision process to take advantage of special circumstances or to synchronize action with another activity." The Harrogate Textiles Exhibition is an important event for carpet manufacturers; therefore, the pressure to launch any proposed new product at the exhibition would be intense. Thus, the decision to purchase NWP may have been "sped up." This might help to explain why Tufted Carpets Ltd. was one of the first companies to purchase NWP materials.

REFERENCES

Robinson, P.J., C. Faris, and Y. Wind. (1967). *Industrial Buying and Creative Marketing*. Boston, MA: Allyn & Bacon.

Mintzberg, H., D. Raisinghani, and A. Theoret. (1976). "The Structure of Unstructured Decision Processes." *Administrative Science Quarterly* 21(June): 246-275.

A STUDY OF THE PURCHASING PROCESS FOR A JCB 110B CRAWLER-LOADER MACHINE

Stephen Parkinson and Michael Baker

ABSTRACT

This three-company case study is drawn from a larger piece of research that analyzed the decision to purchase a JCB ll0 Crawler-Loader Machine in nine different companies. These purchasing-related decisions were made over a period of two years, beginning with the initial launch of the JCB 110 in 1971. In the larger study, this period was divided into three purchase phases. The first phase includes those companies which purchased a 110B prior to January 1, 1973; these companies were classified as "early." The second phase includes companies which purchased a ll0B during 1973, hence they were classified as the "majority." Finally, the third phase includes companies which purchased a 110B after January 31, 1974, and thus were classified as "late." This methodology was applied in order to analyze the individual purchasing processes within each company and also to compare the three companies within a specified

Advances in Business Marketing and Purchasing, Volume 5, pages 97-126.
ISBN: 1-55938-364-X

time period to those in other time periods. Of particular interest are variances present in the structure and strategy of the purchasing processes between individual companies and also between companies grouped in different phases. The market analysis is followed by an overview of the main findings on the purchasing processes in the larger research study. This overview utilizes Mintzberg, Raisinghani, and Theoret's (1976) theory on "the structure of unstructured decision processes." This theory also provides the basis for the analysis of the three exemplary follow-up case studies: J.R. Equipment Limited, Engineering Hire Limited, and Builders Contracting Company Limited. To provide a complete range of examples, one case is taken from each of the three phases described above. Robinson, Faris, and Wind's (1967) methodology describing the nature of management involvement at each stage is also applied throughout the case.

THE MARKET FOR EARTH MOVING AND CONSTRUCTION EQUIPMENT

The market for earth moving and construction equipment consists of two main sectors. These include the building and construction industry sector, and the plant hire subdivision within the building and construction industry. The following case focuses on the former area and, in particular, earth moving equipment.

THE BUILDING AND CONSTRUCTION INDUSTRY (1974)

The building and construction industry, although one of the oldest established industries in the United Kingdom, was paradoxically one of the least developed. It was characterized by a few large, publicly quoted companies and many comparatively small firms. Entering the industry was relatively easy, and the managerial skills required to set up a building company were limited. Success, however, was difficult to achieve; the building and construction industry had one of the highest bankruptcy rates of all industrial sectors.

The industry itself encompassed a wide range of activities classified under the general heading of construction. These activities included building new structures such as houses, shops, roads, bridges, factories, and so forth. Repair and maintenance of these structures was involved.

The industry also provided services such as gas mains and drains and sewers. Firms in the industry varied in size, from the large publicly quoted company, to the individual craftsman working in house repairs.

In the years previous to the time of the study (1974), the number of firms in the construction industry was decreasing. In 1948, there were approximately 130,000 firms in the industry. By 1960, this number had fallen to 90,508; by 1970, the total had fallen to 73,420. Fluctuations in the level of demand for the industry's products and services were related to this decrease. Successive governments had influenced the volume of trade either by direct intervention in the public sector or by introducing fiscal policies which influenced demand in the private sector. Clearly, these fluctuations in the level of domestic demand for the output of the building and construction industry affected the industry's development. In an environment of "stop-go" economic policies, long-range planning was difficult. In periods of "stop," materials producers shut down capacity which might never be used again; firms shed employees, fewer trainees were employed. All of this undermined the industry's potential development. When demand did increase, it was difficult to keep pace with demand; as a consequence, "over-heating" took place.

THE CONSTRUCTION AND EARTH MOVING EQUIPMENT SUPPLY INDUSTRY

The construction and earth moving equipment industry existed to provide the plant and equipment required in the building and construction industry. This broad classification (construction) included companies manufacturing excavating and earth moving equipment such as excavators, crawler tractors, dozers, graders, scrapers, shovel loaders, and dumpers. It also included companies manufacturing road-making and maintenance equipment, such as asphalt mixing and laying machines, road rollers, concrete mixers, and pile drivers. The section of the market of particular relevance to the case study is that of "off the road" vehicles (earth moving machines).

In 1972, the total volume of sales in the earth moving machinery field worldwide was estimated to be U.S. $5,500 million. In global terms, the U.K. market was relatively small. It accounted for approximately 4 percent of sales, but was still one of the most important markets for earth moving and construction equipment (see Table 1).

Table 1.   Relative Importance of Major Markets
for Earth Moving Equipment

World Wide Sales (1972) (in percent)	
North American Markets	37
Japan	20
Germany	6
France	5
United Kingdom	4
Italy	3
Subtotal	75
Other	25
Total	100

Source: Chief Executive Officer, *Fiat-Allis Limited Contractors Plant Review*, July/August (1974).

The U.K. market was supplied by one major domestic producer and several large international companies; several of the international companies had set up manufacturing facilities in the United Kingdom. In terms of overall sales volume worldwide, the largest of these companies was Caterpillar. Caterpillar was followed by Komatsu, International Harvester, J.I. Case, John Deere, Clark Equipment, Ford Motor Company, and Massey Ferguson. From Table 2, it is evident that sales of the largest domestically owned supplier of earth moving equipment in 1972 (JCB Ltd.) amounted to £33 million, approximately $80 million.

The construction equipment industry can be divided into six major groups. These include:

- excavator loaders,
- wheeled loading shovels,
- crawler-loaders,
- bulldozers,
- crawler excavators, and
- others.

The "others" segment can be divided into two areas. The first market was for large, special purpose machines primarily used in civil engineering. Scrapers used to level highway sites are included in this group. The second was the market for a range of much smaller products,

Table 2.   Sales Turnover of Some Major
Equipment Suppliers (1972)

Sales Turnover ($ million)	
Caterpillar	2,500
Komatsu	300
International Harvester	400
John Deere	400
Massey Ferguson	150
JCB Ltd.	80

such as pumps, wheelbarrows, dump trucks, and so forth. This sector was typically a highly competitive, low-margin high-volume area.

With a few notable exceptions, manufacturers of "off the road" vehicles were reluctant to introduce new types of plant in a traditionally conservative market. The building and construction buyers were cautious about new ideas; they felt that technical innovations in new equipment should be proven reliable before the equipment was accepted. Reliability was more important to the buyer than potential cost savings gained by the introduction of new techniques/technology in new equipment.

THE JCB 110B CRAWLER-LOADER

At the time of the case study, JCB was a relatively small domestic manufacturer attempting to enter a highly competitive international market with an entirely new range of earth moving machinery. Fluctuating levels of demand in the domestic market had forced many U.K. manufacturers of construction equipment to turn to overseas markets to ensure stability and growth. JCB was no exception. An average of 40 to 50 percent of the company's output was exported per year. Future company growth was dependent on increasing the company's involvement in developing markets. Such markets included the Middle East, South America, and North Africa. JCB was represented in four of the five high-volume markets of the earth moving and construction equipment industry.

The 110 was a loading shovel designed to dig and load earth and similar materials on building sites or other construction areas. The design of the 110 was significantly different from other machines supplying the market at that time. Its engine was located in the back, behind the operator, and it was driven by hydro-static transmission.

THE MARKET FOR THE JCB 110 MACHINE

A clear decision had been made to sell the 110 to contractors rather than plant hirers. One important reason for this was that the plant hirer paid for machines on an hourly basis rather than on a performance basis. Therefore, he did not want machines which did the work twice as fast.

The market JCB had identified was supplied by several companies providing machines of the same basic configuration. All of these were crawler units with a bucket or a blade on the front. The Caterpillar Tractor Company had the largest market share. Their machines were not purpose-designed for a loading application, but for a dozing application. In a dozing operation, the machine performs most efficiently if its weight is in the front behind the blade. However, in a loading operation, having the engine in the front is a disadvantage; the operator cannot see what is happening in the bucket, and the machine requires a balance weight to counter balance the weight of the load in the shovel.

The 110 was designed for both loading and dozing applications. Hopefully, it would be difficult for competitors to imitate such a product. They were committed to plant and equipment used to produce front engined dozing and loading machines, and could not easily change to a new configuration of machine. In the 110, the operator sat between the engine and the bucket, and the engine did not obscure the operator's view of the bucket.

The machine was originally designed to sell to the market for crawler-loaders with a bucket capacity of one-and-one-quarter cubic yards. This meant that the 110 would fall between the Caterpillar 951 (a well-proven, reliable loading shovel more expensive than the 110 with a comparable output), and the International Series B125 (commonly called a Drot). The International machine was also a proven design for a loading shovel.

ISOLATION OF CRITERIA APPLIED IN REACHING DECISION TO PURCHASE: AN OVERVIEW

Reviewing the stages of the purchase decision process outlined above, the decision to buy the new crawler-loader machine was not the outcome of a "once and for all" decision made at one particular moment. Rather,

Table 3.   Summary of Management Involvement in the Decision Process

State in Decision Process	Manager Responsible	Nature of Involvement
a) Realization of need to buy a new crawler-loader machine	Plant Manger	"Discovers" need through review of cost-demand data, or through contact with supplier's salesmen. Specifies "crawler-loader" as a solution because of experience in industry. Obtains provision in forward budget for machine purchase. Gets managerial approval in principle for machine purchase.
b) Search for a short list of alternative machines	Plant Manager	Reviews existing files with information on available plant—if these exist. Contact potential suppliers to determine provisional terms of supply (e.g., delivery and price). Evaluates credibility of dealer service associated with each supplier. Evaluates past experience with similar machines.
	Director	Once it is generally known that the firm is in the market for a new machine, other members of the organization along with the plant manager will be contacted by potential suppliers. Such members may tell the plant manager to investigate a particular machine. Directors frequently belong to and use the same trade association as dealers and other plant operators who may already be operating new types of plant, and so are influential.
c) Evaluation of machines on short list	Plant Manager	Evaluates technical features—machines' ability to do the job (basically output and reliability). Evaluates cost features—cost of the machines, all aspects, fixed and variable. Evaluates associated dealer networks and machine back-up services.
	Technical Manager (technician in large companies—likely to be a workshop foreman)	Evaluates technical features of machine from a maintenance/servicing perspective.
	Site Engineer	Evaluates ability of machine to do specific job.
Choice	Plant Manager	Frequently in consultation with technical manager and/or site engineer if employed.
d) Authorization of a purchasing decision	Plant Manager	Recommendation to board of a specification.
	Director(s)	Evaluates financial implications of proposal presented by plant manager. *Less frequently:* Evaluates specific choice of machine. Authorization or nonauthorization of purchasing decision.

it was the result of a series of smaller decisions. These gradually led the organization to purchase a particular crawler-loader machine, the JCB 110 machine. In effect, the prospective purchasing organization gradually screened out alternative choices in favor of the 110 machine. Some organizations began this process with favoring certain machines, but all of them gradually became committed to purchasing the JCB 110. This accords with Mintzberg et al.'s (1976) research, which states that the "decision maker deals with unstructured situations by factoring them into familiar structurable elements." This research also showed that the individual decision maker used "satisficing" routines, reducing a complex environment to a series of simplified conceptual models. Therefore, "decision processes are programmable even if they are not programmed."

Realization of Need to Purchase a Crawler-Loader

This phase is equivalent to Mintzberg et al.'s "identification" stage in the decision process. Identification or recognition of the need to buy a 110 was prompted by as many as three stimuli.

The first and most frequent situation occurred when management within the buying organization realized that the new plant was required to solve a particular operating problem. The operating problem usually became apparent through a review of cost data and/or anticipated demand for the company's plant.

The plant manager was responsible for ensuring that the costs of operating the existing plant were kept at a minimum. In order to do this, plant managers in different organizations operated under a variety of cost systems, with varying levels of sophistication. Generalizing, the larger the organization, the more sophisticated the cost system. The decision to purchase a new plant was frequently precipitated by costs rising above an acceptable level. Thus, the more sophisticated the cost control system, the more quickly management would realize that a new machine was needed. These findings support the proposal that "once a cumulation of stimuli reaches a threshold level, a decision process is initiated and resources are mobilized to deal with it" (Mintzberg et al. 1976). In some cases, low amplitude stimuli are collected, cumulated and stored over a period of years before a more intensive signal finally evokes action. Mintzberg et al. conclude that "the force of the stimulus over time and the action threshold" determine the moment of action.

The plant manager was typically responsible for ensuring that the company's fleet was suitable for the mixture of work the company was engaged in. From the cases, it appears that companies that made a conscious attempt to forecast or monitor trends in demand for the types of plant they were operating, realized more quickly that new machines were required, and initiated a machine purchasing process.

The second, less frequent, situation which caused management to actively consider purchasing a new machine was contact with a potential supplier's salesman. The dealer's salesman, because of his knowledge of the potential customer's work or problems with existing machinery, may trigger a search process. He seeks to "sell" his own product as a solution for particular problems which the potential buyer may not have even noticed.

Mintzberg et al. hypothesize that "the perceived amplitude of an unattended stimulus decays over time; that quick reinforcement of one stimulus by another magnifies their perceived combined amplitude." A summary of the cases revealed that certain combined stimuli were required to initiate the decision to purchase. These stimuli included the following. The necessary financing had to be available. The new work had to be sufficiently extensive and rewarding to justify the purchase, if new work was a precipitating factor. Also, for those companies which did not have the technical expertise to service or maintain such plant material themselves, the potential purchase (of the 110) must be relatively simple, and the machine must be reliable. The first step following recognition/realization of the need to buy involved tapping existing information channels and opening new channels to clarify and define the issues.

Search for a Short List of Alternative Machines

This phase and the following evaluative phase come under Mintzberg et al.'s heading of "development" where "the greatest amount of decision making resources are consumed." The "development" phase is described in terms of two basic routines, search and design. Search is evoked to find ready-made solutions; design develops custom-made solutions, or modifies ready-made solutions.

From an analysis of the case study data, the decision to include a machine on the short list was crucial. Thus, the criteria used in determining the short list were of primary importance in the decision process.

Having identified the need for a new crawler-loader, most managers in the sample drew up a short list of suitable machines. They made this list either from memory, or using files on plant and equipment maintained on a continuing basis. For some managers, the decision to purchase a machine precipitated a search for information; for others, the relevant information was already available.

Mintzberg et al. identify four types of search routines. First, there is a "memory search" of the existing memory banks—both human and/or recorded. Second, a "passive search" involves waiting for unsolicited alternatives. Not only do organizations search for alternatives; alternatives search for organizations. Third, a "trap search" is when a company informs suppliers as to what they need. Finally, an "active search" directly seeks alternatives.

In drawing up the short list, managers applied two distinct sets of criteria. The first of these were machine-related criteria. For example, to what extent was the machine under consideration suitable for the task(s) to be done? The second factor, which was more important than the first at this stage, was the potential buyer's past experience with the prospective supplier. Even though it was important that the machine fit certain general requirements in terms of price and performance, it was also very important that the machine's supplier was perceived as credible.

Two factors were involved in the prospective buyer's perception of the credibility of the supplier. The first was his perception of the ability of the supplier's dealer network to provide effective servicing in a variety of dealer activities, such as providing spares, servicing, and finance. Second was his perception of the supplier's ability to produce reliable products. This reflected past experience with particular machines from the supplier.

Evaluation and Choice from Short List

This phase is equivalent to Mintzberg et al.'s "selection" phase which he describes as "typically a multistage, iterative process involving progressively deepening investigation of alternatives." The description fits this stage in the purchase process for a crawler-loader. In the sample, when a short list of suitable machines had been established, each machine on it was subjected to a more sophisticated analysis. In most cases, suppliers were asked to provide a detailed quotation, conditions of sale, and so forth, along with complete technical data on the machine.

Comparison of machines on the short list was done in varying degrees of sophistication in different companies. Two basic sets of criteria were identified:

1. Technical: Could the machine do the work efficiently and reliably?
2. Cost: Was the choice of this particular machine the best economic proposition?

The most important factor overall was the potential buyer's perception of the "reliability" of the machine. Reliability in an earth moving machine, however, is difficult to assess, until the machine has been on the market long enough for operating experience to accumulate. Estimates of a satisfactory testing period range from twelve months to four years. The second-most important group of factors included maneuverability, speed, all around vision and ease of servicing, followed by bucket capacity and life of the tracks. Purely "economic" factors such as price and running costs played a minor role in determining choice of machine.

Comments of managers in several case studies suggest that financial criteria played a secondary (though important) role in the evaluation process. Management was primarily concerned with reliable and consistent performance, even if a very high price had to be paid. This was largely because unplanned downtime could be very expensive.

Evidence indicated that a greater proportion of early purchasers than majority or late purchasers felt that the new 110 machine was a good "match" to their requirements in bucket capacity, cost performance ratio, and availability of after sales service. A significantly smaller proportion of early buyers than majority or late buyers felt that the 110 machine was a good deal in price and ease of servicing.

Finally, it is evident that many buyers perceived themselves as solely responsible for the choice of a specific machine, even while admitting that other members of the organization were influential in this process. This was because they bore the responsibility for machine failure, and felt that they had the authority to choose the machine they believed would best meet their needs. This point was further emphasized by the finding that the performance of the plant manager was primarily reviewed in strictly financial terms, rather than in terms of performance of specific machines. In the final stages, the buying decision became one man's responsibility, regardless of the nature of his organization. This individual decision-making responsibility is referred to as a judgmental routine by Mintzberg et al. who states, "one individual makes a choice in his own mind with procedures he does not or cannot explain."

Authorization of the Purchasing Decision

The final stage in the purchasing decision process can be identified as the authorization of the purchasing decision made by the plant manager or his equivalent. Mintzberg et al. define authorization as follows: "Decisions are authorized when the individual making the choice does not have the authority to commit the organization to a course of action." The relevant criteria at this stage were predominantly financial. It was difficult to identify specifically the nature of this authorization process, as most managers interviewed were not themselves privy to this stage of the decision process. A general impression was that the manager's recommendation was usually endorsed by the board as a matter of policy.

In order to break down the above-summarized version of the decision to purchase a JCB 110 crawler-loader, three individual cases will be described as examples of the individual company's decision-making process. These three companies were chosen to represent the three classes of buyer—early, majority, and late. The companies are J.R. Equipment Ltd., Engineering Hire Ltd., and Builders Contracting Company Ltd. The actual names of the companies have been changed; each company's decision process is presented in a buy chart (figure) within the case.

J.R. EQUIPMENT LTD.

Company Background

J.R. Equipment Ltd. was one of the largest civil engineering and general contracting firms in the building and construction industry. The Scottish Civil Engineering Division (the focus of the study) spent more than £200,000 on new plant and machinery in 1974. Mr. Green (name has been changed), the regional director, administrated the purchasing function. He was also responsible for monitoring the various types of plants the company operated and altering this mixture of plants when appropriate.

Information was continuously collected, as site engineers provided Mr. Green with reports on the types of plant the division was operating at each site, the operating costs of each item of the plant, as well as the utilization of that plant. Several plant inspectors also reported to

Mr. Green. They were responsible for ensuring that the plant was being used properly. In this way, the division's plant and equipment were continuously evaluated to ensure that they were suitable for the types of work the company was involved in.

Each year, all of the site engineers were required to submit to Mr. Green a detailed list of the types of plant required on site in the next twelve months. Combining these, Mr. Green was able to determine the division's requirements for the next financial year. His estimates formed the basis of a machine replacement budget, which was approved by the regional board.

As plant director, Mr. Green had complete responsibility for the plant purchasing decision—identifying the need to purchase new items of plant, determining specifications, and making final recommendations to the board. Within the limitations of his budget, he had autonomy in the choice of a particular machine.

Realization of the Need to Purchase a Crawler-Loader

In December of 1971, the division was awarded a contract for the development of a new sewage works. Examining the division's current supply of machines, Mr. Green felt that several new items were required for the new project. In particular, it was evident that two crawler-loading machines would be needed to grade the site and to move displaced earth to lorries for tipping.

The division already had several crawler-loading machines in its fleet which could have done the job. However, these machines were relatively old, and Mr. Green decided that it was time to buy replacement machines that would operate more efficiently. Specifically, he wanted machines that worked more quickly than the ones the division was currently using, and had greater maneuverability.

Before finally deciding to buy, however, Mr. Green considered the possibility of hiring equipment to do the work required. Two factors influenced his decision. First, would the cost of purchasing the machine and operating it over the life of the contract be greater or less than the cost of hiring such equipment over the same period? Second, would the machine have other applications when the contract was completed?

Mr. Green felt that it would be cheaper to buy and operate the machine over the life of the contract than to hire such a machine. He also felt that there would be plenty of work for such a machine when the contract was finished. Therefore, he decided that the division should buy a new crawler-loading machine and included a provision in the machine replacement budget for 1971 for the purchase of such a machine.

Search for a Short List of Alternative Machines

The need for the new machine was relatively urgent, and Mr. Green immediately began to search for information on the various types of crawler-loading machines available. He collected information on new types of plant and equipment on a continuing basis in an office file, and updated this when he received new information from suppliers. Initially, he reviewed this information file, searching for suitable machines. He rejected some machines in his file with little consideration, as he lacked personal experience with them, or because he felt that the dealer could not offer the necessary spares or servicing back-up.

As a result of this initial screening process, Mr. Green identified three machines which were potentially suitable. These were the JCB 110, the Komatsu D30s machine, and the Caterpillar machine. He had operating experience with both the Komatsu and the Caterpillar machines, and felt that both provided reliable and efficient performance. He decided to consider the 110 because he had been operating other types of JCB machines without problems.

Evaluation and Choice

Mr. Green felt that he knew enough about the Komatsu and Caterpillar machines to make a decision on the relative merits of each. However, he was less certain about the JCB 110 machine. It had only been introduced recently, and Mr. Green had not had the opportunity to test the machine as a hirer.

Mr. Green had first became aware of the JCB 110 machine when he visited the JCB factory in 1971. There, he saw the machine put through its trials as a prototype. At that time, he felt that the JCB 110 machine was a complete break from the conventional crawler-loader machine. It seemed that the 110 would be able to perform more quickly than existing, more conventional machines.

After visiting the factory, Mr. Green had received technical information on the JCB 110 machine from the local dealer. When he examined the machine's specifications, he determined that the JCB 110 machine was one of the best currently available. He commented that "one of the main advantages was the handling of the machine from an operator's point of view. You could slew this machine around with none of the traction problems of the conventional type of gear change."

Having drawn up a short list of three machines, Mr. Green compared these on a point-by-point basis, evaluating them on purely technical factors. In this technical evaluation, he compared each machine's ability to do the work required. This was recorded and formed part of the formal justification he presented to the board for choosing a particular machine.

When a technical evaluation of each machine had been completed, Mr. Green compared the relative economics of operating each machine. This was done on the basis of the estimated cost per hour of operating the machines. Costs including purchase price, overheads, and return required on investment were calculated; these were divided by the number of hours it was estimated that each machine would operate. This resulted in a machine hour rate, to which Mr. Green added the variable costs of operator's wage, running costs, and maintenance. This gave Mr. Green the information necessary to compare each machine's financial performance.

On purely technical grounds, he concluded that the Caterpillar was by far the best machine, both in terms of proven reliability and performance. However, he felt that both the JCB 110 and the Caterpillar machines could perform adequately and meet his requirements. Technical performance was not the only factor in his choice.

The Caterpillar was significantly more expensive than the other two machines. Its better technical performance did not, in Mr. Green's opinion, justify its higher cost. Mr. Green decided to buy two different machines—a Komatsu and a JCB 110. Working both of these on the same contract would provide the opportunity to compare the relative advantages of each machine. Having done this, he would be able to decide which machine would best standardize his fleet in the future.

At the time, he was not sure that the JCB 110 machine would be able to withstand the required pace. However, he determined that he should at least test the machine because of its potential advantages. This was not a particularly risky decision, as he had negotiated a "buy-back" arrangement with the dealer. According to this agreement, the dealer was obligated to buy the machine back at a guaranteed price, should it prove unsatisfactory.

J.R. Equipment Ltd. bought their first JCB 110 machine on February 14, 1972 (see Figure 1 for the buying process of J.R. Equipment Ltd).

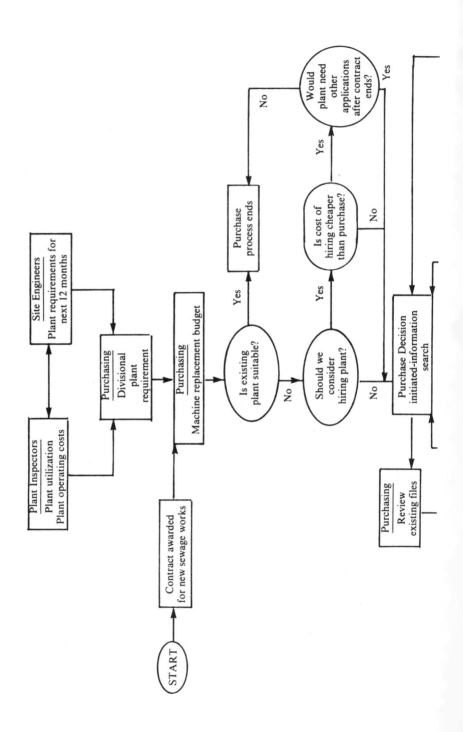

START

Contract awarded for new sewage works

Plant Inspectors
Plant utilization
Plant operating costs

Site Engineers
Plant requirements for next 12 months

Purchasing
Divisional plant requirement

Purchasing
Machine replacement budget

Is existing plant suitable? — Yes → Purchase process ends

No

Should we consider hiring plant? — Yes → Is cost of hiring cheaper than purchase? — Yes → Would plant need other applications after contract ends?

No

No → Purchase Decision initiated-information search

Would plant need other applications after contract ends? No

Would plant need other applications after contract ends? Yes

Purchasing
Review existing files

112

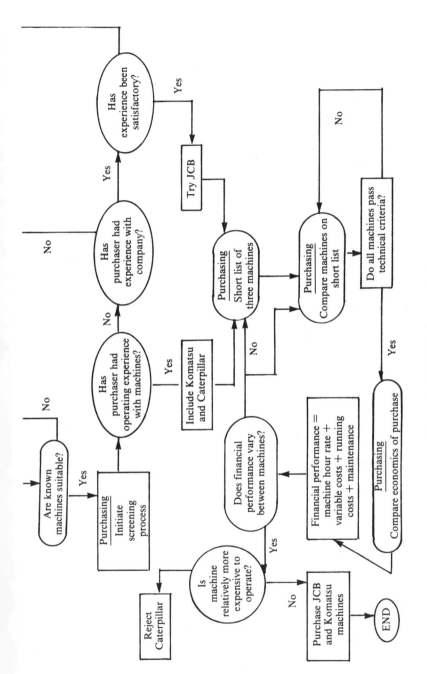

Figure 1. J.R. Equipment Ltd.

113

ENGINEERING HIRE LIMITED

Company Background

Engineering Hire Ltd. is a subsidiary of a group of firms in the building and construction industry. Other subsidiaries have interests in civil engineering, joinery, and electrical contracting. As its name suggests, Engineering Hire's primary business is plant hire, although the company does a certain amount of earth shifting and levelling work from time to time. Most of the company's business involves the hiring of construction industry equipment, ranging from a 2½ inch bore pump to a 1½ cubic yard excavator.

Mr. Black (name has been changed) is the plant director at Engineering Hire Ltd; he is primarily concerned with decisions to purchase or sell plant material. He reports to the group chairman, who is also involved in plant purchasing decisions. He described the way he and the chairman share the responsibility for plant purchasing. "Basically I am the one who is involved in fleet expansion—I usually discuss it with our group chairman, because he is also the managing director of this company, but the final decision is mine. Technically, he doesn't know much about the different machines available—he is a civil engineer not a technician—he knows the applications however, and obviously he knows the plant hire business. If I am considering expanding into a new range of machines, he is mainly concerned that the work for those machines will be available and that the machines could be kept busy—if it came to a choice between 2 or 3 different crawler tractors, then the actual choice of the make of machine would be mine."

Mr. Black, therefore, is primarily responsible for initiating the decision to buy new plant material. This decision is usually made on the basis of information available on existing demand for the company's equipment. Such information is compiled weekly for Mr. Black by the company's hire manager. Mr. Black commented, "We are keeping our eye on the market all the time as to what the demand for different types of equipment will be. One of the ways of checking this is by maintaining a record of all the enquiries for plant hire we have had. A sheet is produced for me each week which enables me to see what we have had to turn away or find—is it a request for a machine which we don't posses or is it a request for a machine which we do have on our books which is already working elsewhere?"

This sheet is compiled weekly, but there is no specific procedure followed for acting ón the information it provides. This is left to Mr. Black's discretion. A major factor governing his decision is the volume of future demand predicted for each category of equipment. In assessing such demand, it was necessary for him to discriminate between short-term fluctuations in demand and the long-term trend.

"You need to be careful though—sometimes there may be a sudden increase in demand for a particular type of tractor—you need to find out where this demand is coming from because it may well be that there is a particular contract in the area which is draining the area of plant but only on a short term basis—therefore, there is no point in buying such plant—you need to decide where the stop line is for you, and look around the market to find out why demand has been created."

Realization of the Need to Purchase a Crawler-Loader

In the early months of 1973, Mr. Black decided that the potential hire demand for crawler-loading machines was large enough to justify the purchase of additional machines. This was in line with general company policy at the time, which was to expand the company's activities "on all fronts." He commented, "At that time there was a very big demand for crawler-loading machines, which seemed to be quite a good long-term demand—we have a development plan in a way, but it has to be very flexible—at that time, we wanted general expansion on all fronts, and as part of this, we increased the crawler-loader section."

Evaluation and Choice

Having decided to buy additional loading machines, Mr. Black began to look for the most suitable machine. He had a general idea of the types of machine which would be suitable, because of his experience in the industry. In addition, he examined a file of information on manufacturer's plant and equipment which he maintained continually. This file was divided into different categories of plant, and contained data on prices and specifications. Most of this information had been provided by the representatives of local dealers.

Reviewing the information at hand, Mr. Black decided that only three machines were potentially suitable for the work he planned to do. These were the Caterpillar 951, the Massey Ferguson machine, and the new

JCB 110 crawler-loading machine. He had extensive operating experience with the Caterpillar and Massey Ferguson machines, but knew very little about the JCB 110 machine. He did feel that it met his requirements, in terms of price and ability to do the work.

He rejected the Caterpillar machine without serious consideration, because he had recently had bad experience with two new Caterpillar machines. Engineering Hire maintained detailed records on the reliability of each machine operated. These records were maintained by the service manager, who reported to Mr. Black.

These records provide information on the earnings of each item of plant the company operates; they also indicate the costs of repairs for each item. These records are analyzed annually, to compare earnings with running costs. Mr. Black and his managing director decide accordingly whether it is worthwhile to continue to run certain items in the plant. Examining these records, Mr. Black concluded that the Caterpillar machines had been unsatisfactory, and excluded them. He noted that, "These machines weren't up to Caterpillar performance, and the Caterpillar service had gone to rock bottom, both in spares supply and in servicing."

Thus, the final choice was between the JCB 110 and the Massey Ferguson machines. Mr. Black had seen the first version of the JCB 110 machine when it was launched in the early months of 1972; he had rejected it then because of several faults. In particular, the machine's running gear appeared suspect. In his initial examination of the JCB 110, Mr. Black was advised by his service manager. He described his relationship with the service manager as follows. "If I am looking at a new model of a machine, then I will involve my service manager, and we will go and examine it, to see if we think it is all right. Usually, we will see how different it is to the models we are already running and try to work out whether this is to our advantage or not. We usually express opinions to each other. Basically, I suppose we are looking for a machine with good performance, reliability and a good standard of operator comfort."

However, Mr. Black felt that the improved version of the 110 machine, introduced in 1973, was a significant improvement over the original machine. It was therefore worthy of consideration. Some of its original faults had been corrected, and he now felt that the risk of buying the machine was justified. He believed that this machine would prove to be far superior to the Massey Ferguson machine if it was reliable; therefore, he was prepared to take the risk of buying it.

He commented that, "We liked the concept of the 110 engine at the rear, bucket at the front to give it balance—the operator could see his bucket for the first time in his life—we liked the idea of the hydrostatic transmission and so on—I suppose to some extent we decided to stick our necks out. There was very little operating experience with them so we took a calculated risk."

JCB's reputation for manufacturing good machinery and providing good spares and after sales service was an important factor in the final decision. Mr. Black said, "Put it this way—we had JCB equipment before and had good results. Going by JCB's reputation and what we knew from our past records, we hoped that this machine would be suitable for the required workload it would get."

He was still hesitant about buying the JCB 110 machine, because there were very few of these machines in operation at the time. He had to rely upon leaflets and brochures and contact with the local dealer for information on the JCB 110. There were few dealers who could provide him with advice or an opinion.

The price of the machine was not a determining factor in his opinion. He was more concerned with reliability. He stated that, "What we are after is a machine we can buy, put out to work, and have no problems with—if it's a couple of thousand pounds more, you're better paying that and having no problems than buying a cheaper machine, which is persistently in the yard for repairs. Customer goodwill and loss of earnings are all important."

As the result of his evaluation, Mr. Black decided to take a risk and buy three JCB 110 machines. He had involved his managing director in the buying decision at all stages, and the decision to buy was approved by him. Mr. Black discussed their relationship as follows. "I think I know him (the managing director) well enough to know where he would gamble and where he wouldn't. I have to use my own judgment and stand by that. He was in on the discussions when we bought them and knew the story behind buying them. He knows the full history of it so any failure is not really held against one person. In this event it was a calculated risk that didn't come off—(you have to take risks though). In this instance, the machine didn't live up to its initial promise." (See Figure 2 for the buying process of Engineering Hire Ltd.)

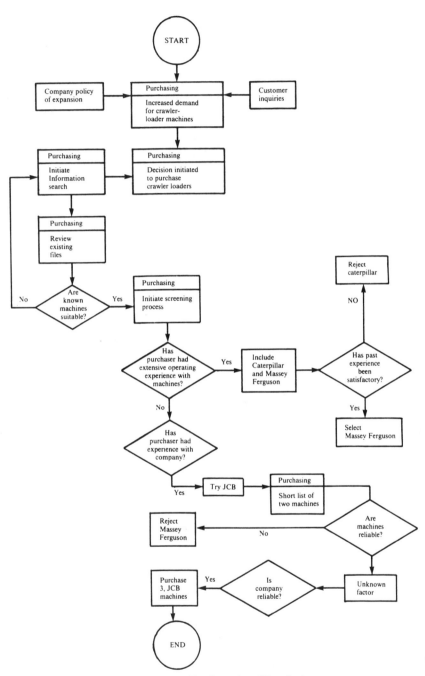

Figure 2. Engineering Hire Ltd.

BUILDERS CONTRACTING CO. LTD

Company Background

The Builders Contracting Co. is a general contracting firm with an extensive plant hire division. This division operates as a separate entity within the company under the direction of Mr. Hughes (name has been changed), the plant director. The philosophy of the plant hire division is to supply as wide a range of plant as is necessary to satisfy each customer's need for variety of equipment. This, they believe, is necessary to satisfy the contractor who does not want to deal with different sources for plant hire.

Mr. Hughes commented, "We are in the plant hire set up on an operated basis—you have to supply a total service—not completely restricted to high demand machines because you wouldn't give a complete service—most contractors tend to go to hirers because they are giving a total range of machines rather than go to one hirer for one item of plant and another for another item...we ourselves run wide range of JCB plant to give a total service . . . not always chosen on the basis of what's going to be a profitable machine to buy."

Mr. Hughes' responsibilities as plant director included maintaining a mixture of plant which would continue to be in demand by building contractors. He described his division's function as follows. "As plant hirers we are engaged in investing capital in machinery to put out on hire—we do not consciously evaluate plant and equipment to make sure it is suitable for the types of work currently being done—we just try and keep on top of it."

As his comments suggest, Mr. Hughes did not formally evaluate his mixture of plant; he did point out that he continuously considered changes which might be made. "You monitor demand, obviously—but it's more a 'seat of the pants' operation—nothing formal—mainly by conversation and general feelings—a plant hirer operates by feeling the pulse of the trade—there is no conscious attempt to evaluate different types of machines—it's more just something you feel you would make money out of. You have plant you are trying to keep on work for, and if work runs out for that type of plant that's the time to sell it-but that has never happened yet—you always come to the end of its useful life before the trend has gone for that type of machine."

Realization of Need to Purchase A Crawler-Loader

Over a period of months in early 1974, it became increasingly apparent to Mr. Hughes that there was a demand for a crawler-loading machine not currently part of his company's fleet. Builders Contracting Co. had covered this demand by "cross-hiring" such a machine from other plant hirers. This involved hiring the machine at a fixed charge, and then re-hiring it to customers. He commented that, "We weren't represented in that particular market but we had already tapped it— we were cross-hiring to satisfy the demand we had, and had metered the demand over a considerable period."

By the middle of 1974, Mr. Hughes was convinced that it was time to buy this type of machine. He explained the decision as follows. "This was a decision to buy into another range which we felt we had to cover— we hadn't covered it before—it was a thing which I felt I wanted to go into to give this type of service so I went in for this machine."

The range of plant which the Builders Contracting Co. provided had evolved in this way for as long as Mr. Hughes could remember. In effect, the current mixture of plant available was the result of a series of ad hoc decisions made by the company over a period of time. The critical criterion on which decisions were based was profitability. Mr. Hughes said, "As plant hirers, we are engaged in investing capital to put out on hire to make money—our stock of machines has evolved over time to suit the demand we are supplying—at the time (of purchase of the 110), I was aware of the need for a machine to fill a gap in our current range of plant."

He had an idea as to which machines would be most suitable. This was the result of a continuing process of mental evaluation of the various plant available. Again, he commented, "I did not sit down and say, 'Here is a problem I have to get information for'—I keep it going all the time— you collect information in your head really, as you go to shows and listen to various salesmen as they come in—I prefer trade shows myself, especially if it's a demonstration type show—it gives you a look at current machines."

Evaluation and Choice

Mr. Hughes, as plant director, has sole responsibility for the purchase of all new items of plant within Builders Contracting Co. He quickly decided which machine to buy. His comments indicate the way he evaluated the machines to determine which would be most suitable.

I did not draw up a short list because I had already chosen in my own mind over a period of time, through going to trade shows, talking to salesmen, that sort of thing, where I could obtain the best deal from— I could go straight to a source and know exactly what the deal was going to be at any one moment, and what machine I would have—even before I wanted the machine, I would know which machine I would go for straight away.

I do not formally sit down and write out all the pros and cons of the machine, because I trust my own judgment more than that—I don't need to have to sit down and work out all the statistics of it really—if I make a decision, it's made because of the information which I have gathered over a period of time and is my own personal thing. I certainly don't have to justify my decision to anyone or give a formal explanation of why.

The overwhelming factor, in Mr. Hughes' opinion, was the relative cheapness of the JCB 110 machine when compared with the Caterpillar 951. He felt that these machines were the two he must choose between.

The two machines available were the Caterpillar 951 and the JCB 110 machine . . . in that size bracket the Cat 951 costs a lot more money than the JCB 110 machine, I felt we could put the 110 out to hire and get the same rate as the Cat 951—less money out and the same return— basic economics really.

He did not feel that a comprehensive point-by-point comparison of all of the machines available was necessary. Mr. Hughes said:

There is a specification on all machines, isn't there—but it comes down to this "seat of the pants" stuff again. You know what the machine can do—you have seen it working in the field—you have stopped and looked at it, and have talked to contractors who have used it, and you have formed the opinion that "Yes, they will go out as 951s"—contractors will be happy to accept them on site at the same sort of rates as the 951. This was basically it—right down the line.

Mr. Hughes did not buy the JCB 110 immediately after it was put on the market. At that time, there was little concrete evidence to show that the machine would work satisfactorily. Therefore, he chose to wait until others had proven that the machine was mechanically sound. He described his reluctance in this way.

> I was very anti-110 to start off with because of the track wear on them—
> when they slowed the tracks down and developed the machine into the
> "B" series I thought it was time to try it. My reaction with a thing like
> hydrostatic drive was not to buy it until it was proven. You have got
> to have something to form your own opinion on—it's no good jumping
> into the cab of one, driving it and saying yes, we will have two . . . when
> the buck ends here, you have got to take your time.

Despite his initial hesitation, Mr. Hughes was impressed by the
technical features of the 110 machine.

> These features weren't new in an earth moving machine, but in the 110
> they were all together for the first time—this was the thing—basically
> it's a great tool; anyone could have built it had they wanted to go into
> hydrostatic transmission, but the parcel as a whole—the 110 was very
> good.

These features, however, were of secondary importance to the price
of the machine. He repeated his initial comments, "Price-wise the
machine met our requirements very well—this was the major factor.
On October 10, 1974, Builders Contracting Co. bought its first JCB
110 machine. (See Figure 3 for the buying process of Builders
Contracting Company Ltd.)

CONCLUSION

The first notable difference in the cases is in methods of information
gathering and processing. Considering each case in turn, the difference
becomes clearer.

First, the plant manager at J.R. Equipment Ltd. collects and monitors
information on potential and actual plant and suppliers in a routine,
coordinated way. He reduces information problems into subdivisions
to which he applies "general purpose, interchangeable sets of procedures
or routines" (Mintzberg et al. 1976). That is, he attempts to deal with
the unstructured situation of monitoring information in a multitude of
areas by "factoring the situation into familiar, structurable elements."
According to Mintzberg et al.'s theory, the plant director should be more
receptive to stimuli, as he has eliminated key problem areas by
routinizing procedures. From this, it is evident that the plant director
at J.R. Equipment Ltd. has reduced his total number of problems. He

is therefore more likely to be in a position to search actively for opportunities.

In the second example (Engineering Hire Ltd.), the information gathering process is less routine. Because of this and the fact that procedures for appropriating information are unclear, the stimuli are more widely dispersed across a greater number of decision makers. Thus, the build-up of stimuli necessary to activate a decision to take action (i.e., on the new 110 machine) is less likely to occur.

Builders Contracting Co. Ltd. is at the end of the continuum opposite J.R. Equipment Ltd. The information gathering system is completely ad hoc. The plant director "simply tried to keep on top of it." If the previous assumption is carried through, the plant director's problem threshold is probably higher than those of the previous cases. Therefore, he is likely to be less receptive to opportunistic stimuli than problem-solving stimuli. This may shed light on the fact that this company did not purchase the 110 during its "early" launch phase.

Throughout the cases, a build-up of stimuli toward the final purchase decision is apparent. In the first case, there was a gradual build-up of stimuli resulting from the use of out-dated machinery. The additional stimulus of the contract for a new sewage works was sufficient to reinforce existing stimuli, and trigger the realization of the need to purchase a new crawler-loader.

In the second case, corporate policy was the crucial stimulus. Finally, in the third case, the need to solve a problem (hiring was no longer suitable) led to action. The fact that a temporary solution had been implemented partially explains why this company purchased a 110 machine "later." The decision process had followed the cross-hire route for a certain period of time, until this became unsuitable. This led to a delay in the decision process, as decision makers returned to the beginning of the decision process to re-examine alternative solutions.

During the search phase, existing information provided the short list of potential machines for evaluation in all three cases. The search phase in each company was relatively short, because potential solutions were "ready-made." This helped to shorten the decision process by reducing the number of feedback loops and failure recycles often existent when a solution is "custom-made," or does not exist at all.

In each company, the selection process differed. The plant director in J.R. Equipment Ltd. was influenced by the fact that JCB was attractive from the operator's viewpoint. This perspective provided the background for the final decision. Other key points apparent during

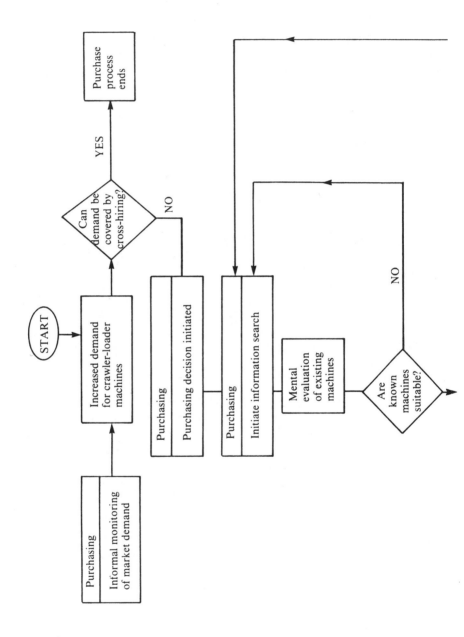

124

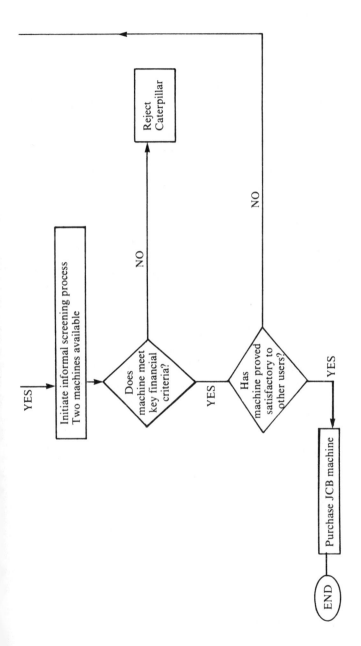

Figure 3. Builders Contracting Co. Ltd.

125

the evaluation of the machines were technical and financial considerations. The financial criteria were more important to the plant director, and the Caterpillar machine was screened out. This can be partially explained by the fact that the plant director did not need approval for purchasing. However, he did need approval for budgeting decisions. Therefore, in his mind, financial criteria were most important.

The decision process in the second case, describing Engineering Hire Ltd., was extended by negative influences. In particular, the time of decision was delayed because the key criterion was reliability. Neither of the final two machines had a satisfactory reliability rating. The Massey Ferguson had not proven reliable in its daily operation, and the 110 was new to the market, and its reliability was unknown. This led to a feedback loop in the decision process. The first set of criteria (reliability) did not provide sufficient data for a decision to be made; therefore, substitute criteria had to be examined. Theoretically, the greater the number of feedback loops, the longer the decision process.

In the final example, Builders Contracting Co. Ltd., the criterion for decision making is more clearly measurable. At the time of purchase, the 110 had been on the market for three years, and its reliability was proven.

REFERENCES

Mintzberg, H., D. Raisinghani, and A. Theoret. (1976). "The Structure of Unstructured Decision Processes." *The Administrative Science Quarterly* 21(June): 246-275.
Robinson, P.J., C. Fairs, and Y. Wind. (1967). *Industrial Buying and Creative Marketing*. Boston, MA: Allyn & Bacon.

THE CASE OF STEEL CASTINGS

Orla Nielsen

ABSTRACT

The Case of Steel Castings describes the highly complex purchasing
process utilized by A.B. Nielsen & Company (ABN), a Danish firm. The
type of purchasing situation described is a modified rebuy of a production
material component (steel casting) which is commonly used in turn-key
contracting, ABN's primary business. Because of the substantial level of
capital involved in subcontracting work, the efficiency of the purchasing
process plays a vital role in ABN's operational success. A main issue in
the case involves a recognition by management of the need for a more
aggressive purchasing policy in order for ABN to secure the most
advantageous blanket purchasing contracts. The need for purchasing
efficiency is so pressing as to require a complete reorganization of the
purchasing department. Another key issue of the case is a question of
the balance of authority between the ABN head office and the subsidiary
offices regarding the specification of requests for quotes (RFQs). Such
a conflict must be resolved in a timely manner before it leads to even
more serious autonomy-related problems within the firm. The buyflow
process for ABN routinely involves three basic stages. The case also

Advances in Business Marketing and Purchasing, Volume 5, pages 127-170.
ISBN: 1-55938-364-X

reflects use of the common industry-wide practice of allowing existing vendors preferential treatment in purchasing situations for new materials.

THE COMPANY

A.B. Nielsen & Company (ABN) is a Danish firm located in Copenhagen. The firm was founded about 100 years ago, and now has subsidiary offices in Europe, North and South America, and Japan. These subsidiaries employ about 1,000 people. The total company employs approximately 4,400. The company supplies extractive and processing equipment which is used to manufacture basic materials such as cement, lime, iron, and metals.

In 1980 the ABN-Group had sales of more than 6 billion d.crowns or $1 billion, a 30 percent increase over sales in 1979. Sales in 1979 were 30 percent higher than in 1978. Profit amounted to 200 million d.crowns or approximately $30 million in 1978; this figure fell by 10 percent in 1979 and remained at a similar level in 1980. In 1979 the company actively considered some degree of reorganization for two reasons. Profit was unsatisfactory and international competition was increasing. By the end of 1980, the initial investigation was complete. The inquiry led to planned changes in the organization of the purchasing department and buying procedures.

ORGANIZATION OF PURCHASING

The purchasing department at the head office is run by a commercially educated director. The purchasing director previously reported to the director of sales and supplies; he now reports to the director of production, purchasing, and shipping, who in turn reports to the general manager. The department employs about 75 people, including personnel located in the ABN offices abroad. The principal personnel have engineering degrees, and many have a supplementary commercial education or inspection background. The department is divided into seven sections: staff, project coordination, ABN machinery, foreign machinery, steel castings, electrical equipment, and service functions. Quality control also reports to the manager of production. Due to the complex nature of the turn-key contracting (where many subcontractors are involved), it is necessary to continually inspect the subcontractor's production process to control product quality. This department also plays an important role in identifying and accepting vendors as possible suppliers.

Establishing turn-key points is one of the most important activities of the firm. The first stage in choosing suppliers for a turn-key operation is evaluation of raw material. Bore samples are sent to ABN laboratories where they are analyzed using electron microscopes and advanced computer-controlled equipment. This analysis determines the initial specification of the extractive system. From this analysis individual machines can be designed to operate at optimum levels of production efficiency. The extractive machines themselves are either produced at the ABN factory or subcontracted. Subcontract work may go to a domestic manufacturer, a manufacturer in the country where the factory is to be built, or a manufacturer in another country.

Each plant requires several different types of steel castings in its manufacturing process. In this case study castings will be labelled A to H. The steel castings are all purchased from subcontractors. ABN drawings and specified materials using different norms (e.g., Deutsche Indurstrie Normen) provide the basis for steel castings patterns. These patterns remain the property of the ABN Group, but are normally held by the supplier. Therefore, additional costs are involved in choosing new suppliers. Due to the emphasis on quality, the purchasing department often finds itself in a position where it cannot place an order without first consulting the quality control and inspection department. The steel castings vary in size from type H, which is measured in grams or kilograms, to types A and B, which may weigh up to 180 tons each.

The ABN Group must inspect all the potential vendors' facilities as part of its quality control program. Three general criteria are considered important. These are the capability of the machinery to produce consistent standards of quality, the firm's capacity and ability to handle large steel castings, and finally, transportation available to the firm (i.e., railroads, shipping, and trucking).

The ABN Group sends inspectors and/or representatives with inspection experience from the purchasing department to visit existing and potential suppliers and to prepare detailed reports on their capacities and abilities. The inspection form is given in Exhibit 1 and is used to evaluate all potential vendors.

Each plant is designed according to the type of raw material used in production. Although this means that the steel castings may vary in composition, it does not put many constraints on the choice of suppliers,

Exhibit 1. The Case of Steel Castings

SUPPLIER DATA

Name:
Address:
Telephone:
Telex:
Other information:

Supplier No.
Line of business:

Type of business: ☐ Private ☐ Co. Ltd./Inc. ☐ Public-owned

Contacts:

Contact language:

Bank connections:

Condditions of tender and sale:

General terms of payment:

Incoterms:
Others:

Price index: ☐ Yes ☐ No

General credit/financing terms:

Which:

Year established:
Share capital:
Equity capital:
Total annual turnover:
Annual turnover, own manufacture:
Extension plans:
Total number employed:
Number of workers:
Workshop space, sa.m.:
Finished goods storage space, sa.m.:
Quality assurance:

Ownership/affiliation:

Is the firm service minded?

☐ Yes   ☐ No

Transport limits:	Max weight	Max height	Max width	Other data
Tracks				
Berth				
Roads				

Understanding of
ABN's technical basis:

☐ good   ☐ medium   ☐ little   ☐ none

Co-operation with ABN commenced on: _____ based on:

☐ Client requirement   ☐ Price conditions   ☐ Financing   ☐ Geographical location

Visited on   By   Up-dated on   By   Estimated available cap   Comments

Exhibit 1. (*Continued*)

INFORMATION ON ABN-RELATED PRODUCTS

product	quantity	mat.	dimensions	d.kr./ kg.	ex./ fob	client	Year	insp. date	qual. 1-4

Other production/agencies

Supplier recommended for:

General quality level

| | excellent | | good | | acceptable | | bad |

General observance of
delivery time

| | excellent | | good | | acceptable | | bad |

Price level

| | low | | medium | | high |

Exhibit 1. (Continued)

Boring mill:

Nos.	Max. dia.	Max. Height	Max. weight	Copy device	Latest Design (Year)

FACE LATHE:

Nos.	Max. Dia.	Max. Height	Max. Weight	Copy Device	Latest Design (Year)

Shafting Lathe:

Nos.	Max. dia.	Max. length	Max. weight	Latest design (year)

MACHINE SHOP

Crane capacity:

Nos.	Max. weight	Max. lifting height

Radial drilling machine:

Nos.	face plate dimension	max. height	max. length	Latest design (year)

Cylindrical grinding machine:

Nos.	Max. Dia.	max. length	Max. Weight	Latest Design (Year)

Milling machine:

Nos.	Horizontal	Vertical	Process l x w x h

134

Plane

Nos.	Max. length	Max. width	Max. Height	Max. Weight	Latest Design (Year)

Gear cutting:

Type	Nos.	Max. m	Max. Weight	Process

Horizontal boring machine:

Nos.	Max. Height	Max. length	face plate dimension	Latest design (year)

Supplier of cast iron:
Name:
Max. piece weight:
Supplier No.

Own design dept.: ☐
Own inspection dept.: ☐

Inspection equipment:
☐ Ultrasonic
☐ magnaflux
☐ capillary
Others:
Scope and standard of control equipment

Standards usually applied:
☐ ISO ☐ ASTM ☐ ASME ☐ DIN ☐ BS
Others:

Updated on:
Name:

Comments:

Exhibit 1. (*Continued*)

PLATE SHOP			
Rollers/Presses:			
Type	Nos.	Max width	Max. thickness	Latest design (year)

Welding equipment: powder welding

Electroslag: max.t

protection gas, kind:

Others:_____

Correction facilities:

Edge press:			
	Max width	Max. thickness	Latest design (year)

Weld prep.:

☐ Edge planer

☐ Flame cutting

☐ -----------

136

Crane capacity: | Nos | tonnes | lifting height

Heat treat furnaces: | l x w x h | temp. control | ☐ ☐ ☐

MACHINING

PROCESS

see

MACHINE SHOP

Material: mat. 120, time of delivery (local: _____ (import: _____

z-plate., time of delivery (local: _____ (import: _____

Own design dept: ☐

Own inspection dept: ☐

Standards usually applied:
☐ ISO ☐ ASTM ☐ ASME ☐ DIN ☐ BS

Others:

Inspection equipment:
☐ Ultrasonic
☐ X-ray, max. thickness
☐ Magnaflux
☐ Isotope
☐ Capillary
☐ Others

Comments:

Up-dated on:

Name:

137

Exhibit 1. (*Continued*)

Melting furnaces: Type Nos	Max. melt	Max. finished weight	FOUNDRY
			MOLDS:
			MAX. DIM.:

MAX. PIECE WEIGHT

Crane capacity: Nos	Tonnes	lifting height	MACHINING PROCESS
in workshop			see
fin. prod. stock			MACHINE SHOP

Heat treat. furnaces l x w x h	Max. temp.	temp. yes	Control No	Material testing
		☐☐☐	☐☐☐	☐ Spectograph ☐ Chemical ☐ Microlab. ☐ Mechanical

138

Work piece weight distribution in %

Material		Annual-production	10-100 kg	100-1000 kg	1-5 ton	5-15 ton	15-35 ton	15-35 ton	above 35 ton	max. piece weight
	Non-alloyed									
Steel	Heat resistant									
	high alloy									
	low alloy									
	Wear-resistant									
	Ducrodan									
	Manganese									
cast iron	Grey									
	White									
	Shell moulding									
	Meehanite									
	licence									
Bronze										

☐ Own pattern shop   ☐ Automatic moulding machine   max. piece weight _____

Own design dept. ☐

Own quality control dept. ☐

Quality control equipment:
☐ Isotope
☐ X-ray, max. thickness
☐ Ultrasonic
☐ Magnaflux
☐ Others: _____

Standards usually applied:
☐ ISO ☐ ASTM ☐ DIN ☐ BS

Others: _____

Comments: Updated-on:

139

and the specifications are usually so definite that responsibility lies clearly within the purchasing department. However, the fact that ABN is producing to order has meant that buying tends to be on an "on-off" basis, although some measures have been taken to decrease costs by combining orders to increase the volume of the purchase and therefore negotiating power.

The geographical location of a new plant influences the transportation costs of the steel castings. Location may also influence supplier choice due to individual government policies. These may include restrictions on the choice of subcontractors, willingness to grant import licenses, and credit facilities.

Recently, the organization has been attempting to increase the efficiency of purchasing operations through the development of blanket contracts covering 80 percent of the yearly demand for steel castings, and to leave ABN free to place the remaining 20 percent with the most suitable suppliers; that is, ABN has freedom to maneuver the 20 percent between suppliers when faced with variable market conditions. The 80:20 policy has been accepted by the board and was put into operation for the first time in 1981. This case study focuses on:

1. the development of RFQs (request for quotes) for blanket contracts for steel castings as a whole;
2. the decision process of granting blanket contracts for type H and type B steel castings; and
3. the decision process of placing specific orders within or outside the particular blanket contract.

THE DEVELOPMENT OF RFQs FOR BLANKET-CONTRACTS FOR STEEL CASTINGS

The flowchart showing the development of blanket-contracts for steel castings as a whole is shown in Figure 1. The buyflow process begins in the sales department. A list is carefully constructed based on existing knowledge of projects currently planned around the world. This list includes firms involved in the projects and characteristics of these projects. Only those projects which are likely to be ordered from either ABN or its competitors within a four-month period are considered.

Every two weeks the sales director meets with his sales managers to evaluate the company's current and potential sales performance. In some cases where a letter of intent (i.e., information from the buyer stating that he intends to grant the order to ABN) is at hand, sales probability amounts to nearly 100 percent. In other cases, evaluation depends on the sales manager's impression of negotiations to date. Expected orders are recorded on the list which is then forwarded to the purchasing department.

In the purchasing department the section head (steel castings) considers the list then consults with various project engineers to determine the demand for different items of steel castings within the overall project. This information is added to existing knowledge and forms a basis for calculating demand for castings. It may take a long time from the issue of letter of intent to construction of a plant. In one of the ABN brochures potential buyers are informed that "an ABN factory can be ready in . . . days, anywhere" (more than two years).

Because these calculations are tentative, the forecasts are compared to actual purchases of the various items in the last five years. Currently, a basic decision rule is used to determine the size of the base volume to be covered by the blanket contracts. The rule is as follows—choose whichever is the larger, either:

1.   75 percent of the expected demand, or
2.   75 percent of the lowest actual yearly buy in the last five years.

One of the respondents stressed that this rule is not always followed exactly. Expected demand will always form the basis of the calculation, even when it is smaller than lowest yearly buy, but a low expected buy figure will certainly call for careful recalculation.

Before the decision can be made, the time period for the blanket contract must be set. Several criteria are used in this process. These include expectations about price and/or currency rate fluctuations and risk regarding possible delivery or demand problems. These criteria would appear to suggest a short delivery time period, but this is counterbalanced by ABN's desire to give suppliers an order large enough to create certain interest and thereby negotiate for favorable prices. After careful consideration, ABN fixed this period at six months when the procedure for establishing blanket contracts was adopted and used for the first time.

The rules regarding size and time period may be altered in the future as the company gains experience. The 75 percent compared to the "circa 80" mentioned previously reflects the expectation that the rule will result in a smaller proportion of demand being awarded to blanket contractors

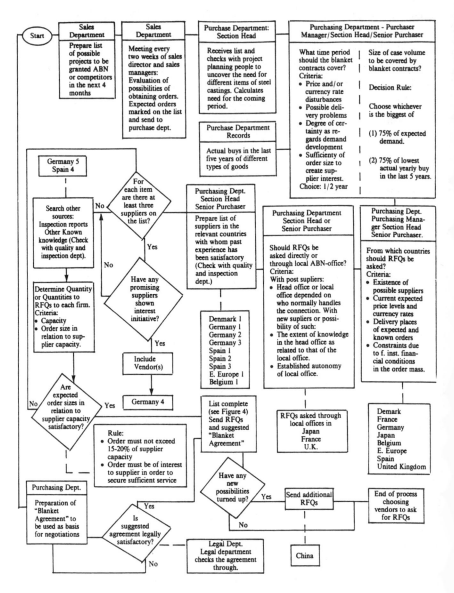

Figure 1.   Buyflow: Development of RFQs

due to growth greater than that shown by the calculations. This is a "hidden" source of freedom welcomed by the purchasers. Decisions concerning size and time periods are made within the purchasing department and involve the purchasing manager, section head (Steel Castings) and a senior purchasing engineer. These managers also determine the countries and potential vendors to which RFQs should be sent.

Throughout this decision process, four composite criteria seem to be applied. First, the expected price levels and currency rates of possible suppliers are considered. This resulted in the exclusion of suppliers in Italy and the United States. Past experience showed that quotes from Italian vendors were always too high, and that Italian vendors were too large to be sufficiently interested in ABN orders. In the United States, eight to ten vendors were investigated in 1980; this investigation resulted in RFQs being sent to five vendors for two standard types of type H. Three vendors responded, quoting prices higher than their European competitors. Because of the high value of the dollar at the time, ABN then excluded U.S. companies from the search. The high value of the English pound nearly excluded the United Kingdom. In 1979, the head of the quality and inspection department along with a buyer visited several vendors in South Korea. This visit resulted in favorable reports on technological skills and the capacity of South Korean vendors; further, actual business relations in connection with fulfilling a turn-key project in the country proved satisfactory. These factors may make South Korea a possible choice for RFQs regarding blanket contracts. However, the country was not included in this phase.

The second major constraint on country choice is consideration of expected geographical location of the new plants and relevant policies of the governments in question. The third influencing criterion is ABN's knowledge of potential suppliers. In many countries there are either no potential vendors, or their capacity is too small. A fourth criterion is ABN's impression of the level of technology in the country's steel castings supply industry. If the level of technology is too low, this may result in the exclusion of certain countries.

The choice possibilities are not identical for each type of steel casting. For example, one piece of machinery is manufactured in the ABN plant in Germany or in Copenhagen. Because of high transportation costs, the steel castings needed to manufacture the item (types D, E, and F) must come from vendors located near the plant. Types A, B, and C are delivered directly to the site on which the turn-key plant is to be built; this considerably increases the choice area for blanket contracts.

At the first stage in the buying process, the following countries were chosen: Denmark, Belgium, France, Germany, Japan, Eastern Europe (one country), Spain, and the United Kingdom. Denmark is on the list because ABN has a financial interest in a Danish firm. If ABN wishes to obtain export credits from the government, then an investigation into potential Danish suppliers has to be undertaken as well.

Because ABN had a satisfactory relationship with a country in Eastern Europe in the past this region was included. Usually vendors in Eastern Europe are considered only when there is no other option, frequently because of government stipulations in the country where the plant is to be built.

The next question to be addressed by the section head and the senior engineer concerns whether RFQs should be sent directly from the head office in Copenhagen or through the local ABN offices. This question reflects both efficiency and organizational problems.

When past suppliers are involved, the RFQs will be sent through the normal local channels. With new suppliers two factors must be considered. First, does the head office or local office have knowledge of the supplier, and second, to what extent is the local government autonomous? The blanket agreement policy argues in favor of the head office handling all the work itself. On the other hand, the section head argues that greater autonomy for local offices should be considered. For example, the local offices in the Far East may be more efficient simply because they have a better knowledge of the cultural background and the vendors themselves. Local offices are needed to coordinate delivery schedules, and in some countries the local office also has to sign the order to the local subcontractors. This is the case where a company must document its exports for the authorities in order to be recognized as an independent firm, thereby gaining access to credit facilities. In this case study RFQs were sent through the ABN local offices in France, Japan, and the United Kingdom.

The section head and the senior purchasing engineer then prepare a list of vendors who will receive RFQs directly from the head office. The first step involves searching through past suppliers in appropriate countries which have a satisfactory record. If there are fewer than three potential vendors for each type of steel casting, the search will be continued. This figure will be raised to seven whenever possible, a result of a policy decision to take all necessary steps to secure the lowest possible prices. ABN always considers any promising vendors who have shown initiative and an interest in doing business with the firm.

In this case study nine vendors were chosen: one from Denmark, three from Germany, three from Spain, one from Eastern Europe, and one from Belgium. A fourth vendor from Germany was included as "promising." This firm had made a sufficient impression on ABN (through its salesmen and sales calls) to be included in this low-risk operation.

ABN embarked on a further search for suppliers suitable for RFQs. This search resulted in the selection of another German firm. This firm had been recommended earlier by one of the German firms already short-listed, as it supplied items which the short-listed firms no longer manufactured. The senior buyer added a Spanish company to the short list. This company was selected from several vendors visited in 1980 during a routine inspection in Spain.

Vendors are requested to quote prices for quantities based on their production capacity. Very few vendors can supply the range of different types of steel castings required. Those suppliers which could satisfy all ABN's requirements operate on a large scale. ABN's orders would be too small as a percentage of the output of such firms for ABN to exert any significant leverage or control in price negotiations. Medium-sized companies are thus preferred according to ABN policy. ABN policy states that the size of an individual order must not exceed 15-20% of supplier capacity. This policy was introduced because ABN did not want one supplier to become too dependent on ABN purchases. Blanket contracts should be large enough to cut prices; but, they must not be so large that ABN grows too dependent on any one supplier. The final selection of suppliers is shown in Figure 2.

Meanwhile, the purchasing department has worked out a preliminary "blanket agreement" which has already been checked by the legal department. The preliminary blanket agreement is to be used as the basis for negotiations, and is therefore sent along with RFQs to the vendors chosen. Because this was the first time the procedure had been used, it took more time than it is expected to take in the future. On this occasion, the list of suppliers was checked again before the final decision was made on all the items.

During the final checking phase, vendors from the Far East appeared to be competitive. An RFQ was sent to China and a visit to specific South Korean vendors was arranged. The search was widened, possibly due to "pressure" from the sales' and quality and inspection departments.

VENDORS

Item	ABN Japan	ABN France	ABN U.K.	1 Den.	1 Ger.	2 Ger.	3 Ger.	4 Ger.	5 Ger.	1 Sp.	2 Sp.	3 Sp.	4 Sp.	E. Eur.	1 Bel.	Base Vol.
A	770	770			770			770				770				772
B	800	320		320	800		500					800		320		798
C	100	100			100	100				100			100			118
D		140		140	140	140			140							138
E		95			95	95										94
F		50			50	50										45
G		200	200	200						200	200				200	243
H	500		500	600						500	500				500	2018
Total Tons	2170	1675	700	1260	1955	385	500	770	140	800	700	1570	100	320	700	4266

Figure 2. List of Venders to be Asked for RFQs

Notes: Germany 5 and Spain 4 are new possible suppliers. Only type C was relevant for Spain 4. The base volume in the right column shows the calculated 75% of the expected demand covering the chosen time period.

146

THE DECISION PROCESS FOR AWARDING BLANKET CONTRACTS: THE CASE OF STEEL CASTINGS, TYPE H

This decision process is shown in Figure 3. Spain was the only vendor who did not bid. Spain 1 was a trusted and efficient supplier, and at the time had large orders from ABN. Late in 1980, Spain 1 demanded an 8% price increase and a shorter payment period, contrary to the conditions specified in the contract; Spain 1 remained on the short list in spite of this, but refused to bid. The section head believed that Spain 1 felt so secure in its current order position that it expected orders would continue to be given to them, without extra effort on their part. That is, Spain 1 did not feel inclined to risk getting involved in price cutting in order to win a blanket contract.

It was decided that Spain 1 should be "put on ice," that is, the vendor only received orders when it had a comparative advantage over competition on geographical location or already held the necessary patterns for castings. However, the section head still intended to include Spain 1 on the short list for the next period. At this point, Spain 1 has not received any orders from ABN, and it is suspected that the vendor now has trouble filling production capacity.

At this stage the bids are compared, based on criteria such as price per kilogram (including stipulated delivery conditions, e.g., ex works, fob), method of payment and packaging costs. Negotiations will be made with all the bidders, the comparison shows with which bidder to begin.

In this case study negotiations were facilitated between ABN and Belgium 1, Spain 2, and Denmark; U.K. 1 had not yet been contacted for two reasons. The purchasing department had capacity problems, and the United Kingdom's bid prices were not competitive. ABN's past experience with U.K. 1 was not satisfactory, and when an RFQ was sent out, ABN did not expect to receive a favorable bid. At this point, the vendor contacted the section head and convinced him that negotiations would be worthwhile. A meeting was arranged with U.K. 1 and the head of the quality and inspection department. As a result of this meeting, U.K. 1 was included in subsequent negotiation. U.K. 1 made an impression not only through its new management team, but also through its reorganized quality assurance department.

In face-to-face negotiations, ABN is represented by either the section head or the senior purchasing engineer and an assistant. The recommended procedure calls for no less than three to five rounds of negotiations, applying a squeezing policy; bidders are constantly pressed to cut prices or better their offers in other ways. However, no definite negotiation strategy is determined. The first meeting usually seems to be a tentative discussion on prices and the various paragraphs of the blanket contract. The ABN representatives focus on price, while the bidders try to avoid price discussions, and instead focus on other factors such as delivery and quality. In the second or subsequent negotiations each bidder is informed as to the competitive status of his bids, compared with those of other bidders, and he is asked to make concessions. It seems that the strategy of the section head is not to develop counter offers, but rather to encourage bidders to take the initiative to better their own offers. After the third round of negotiations, ABN projects the probable results, and at this point a decision is made whether any bidders should be rejected. At this stage, Denmark 1 was rejected because its prices were too high.

Negotiations are time-consuming, and ABN felt the need to finalize the blanket contract so that it could award specific orders to meet immediate demand. A blanket contract was signed with U.K. 1—the most promising bidder. By comparing immediate demand and the figure proposed in the original plan, ABN determined the final order quantity (450 tons $+/-$ 10% covering the period of May 1 to November 1, 1981). The financial department was consulted about the currency to be used for payment. As shown in Figure 2, the contract covers not only the ABN head office, but also ABN offices in various countries. The contract is distributed to them as well. To illustrate the time frame, in the course of eight days, U.K. 1 was awarded orders of more than 600 tons, including orders from the local office in the United Kingdom. The fact that this amount is an additional 33% in comparison with the $+/-$ 10 percent specified in the contract does not seem to have created difficulties.

Although up to five rounds of negotiations are recommended, it would appear that no more than four rounds are necessary. The decision to halt negotiations after the fourth round was influenced by the contract with U.K. 1. Belgium 1 and Spain 1 (with whom negotiations were almost ended before U.K. 1 came into the picture) were awarded contracts of 200 tons $(+/- 20\%)$ type H and 150 tons type G $(+/- 30\%)$ covering the period June 1981 to December 1981, and 500 tons $(+/- 20\%)$ type H covering the period August 1981 to January 1982.

Meanwhile, negotiations were initiated with bidders from Japan. Bids for different types of steel castings appeared to be competitive, and a decision was made to send the senior purchasing engineer to Japan.

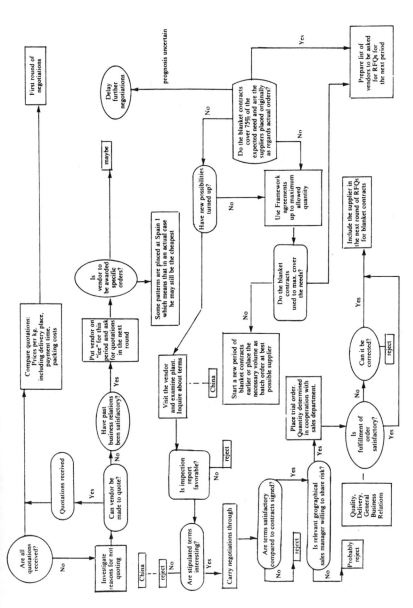

Figure 3a. The Decision Proces For Awarding Blanket Contracts: The Case of Steel Casting, Type H

149

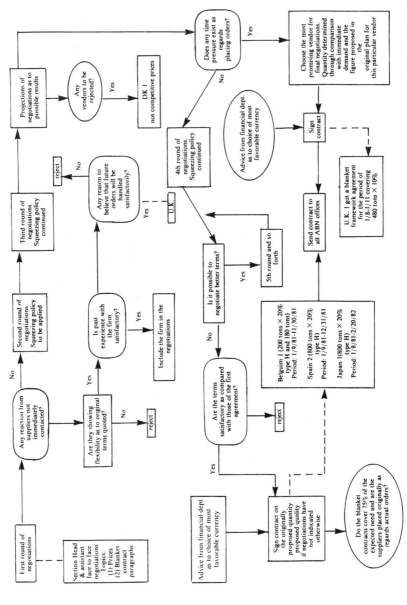

Figure 3b. The Decision Proces For Awarding Blanket Contracts: The Case of Steel Casting, Type H

150

An earlier report suggested that South Korean vendors might supply type B—but not type H castings—causing the senior purchasing engineer to include South Korea in his trip as well. During his stay in the Far East, the senior purchasing engineer was informed of developments in negotiations with the European bidders; he was able to use this information in negotiations with the Japanese bidders. One was awarded a contract and one was rejected because of too high prices. The most important features of the final contracts with suppliers U.K. 1, Belgium 1, and Spain 1 were as follows (see Exhibit 2):

Exhibit 2. Framework Agreement

between

A. B. Nielsen & Company A/S,

Denmark

hereinafter called ABN

and

Hereinafter called L.

Besides covering the ABN head office in Copenhagen, this agreement shall cover supplies to ABN subsidiaries in Europe, North and South America, and Japan. Orders placed at one or more of said ABN subsidiaries shall thus be regarded as part of the fulfillment of this agreement, and L shall accept orders from one or more of said subsidiaries in accordance with the conditions of agreement between L and ABN as laid down in the undermentioned.

1. *Period of validity*
   This agreement shall be valid for the placing of orders in the period from _____ 19_ to _____19_ with successive deliveries in the period from _____ 19_ to _____ 19_.
2. *Scope of supplies in terms of weight*
   With regard to the delivery periods stated in Clause 1, L shall be obliged to accept orders successively and to deliver _____ tons steel castings, the consignment weights being as required by ABN, though at a rate of approximately _____ tons per month. L accepts to plan his production in such a manner that deviations from the agreed quantities shall be kept within a limit of $+/-$ 20%, the observance of said limit being regarded as in quantitative compliance with this Agreement.

(*continued*)

Exhibit 2.   (Continued)

3. *Supply itemization*
Supplies shall comprise:

Type A	approx. _____ % of supplies
Type B	approx. _____ % of supplies
Type C	approx. _____ % of supplies
Type D	approx. _____ % of supplies
Type E	approx. _____ % of supplies
Type F	approx. _____ % of supplies

The above specifications are purely for guidance purposes and as such they shall not be regarded as binding upon ABN, though said specifications should be observed by ABN to the greatest possible extent.

The supplies are specified in more detail in Appendix 1 in connection with prices of individual products. Other (but similar) products than those stated in Appendix 1 can be ordered by ABN and shall be accepted by L.

4. *Price and supply clauses*
The enclosed price list, Appendix 1, shall apply for the whole period of validity of the Agreement.

With regard to products which are not included in the price list, the prices thereof shall be based on that of the product of closest similarity while adhering to price levels. This matter can be negotiated at a later stage. The prices are firm and _____ packing and understood to mean _____ in accordance with _____ terms 1980.

5. *Rust protection and packing*
Rust protection carried out in accordance with _____
Packing to be in accordance with Instructions _____ unless otherwise agreed.

6. *Terms of payment*
Current month plus _____ days.

7. *Times of delivery*
In order to ensure the supply of the relevant quantities in the periods concerned ABN 4(2) shall, wherever possible, place orders prior to product delivery times in accordance with the following schedule:

Type A	_____ months
Type B	_____ months
Type C	_____ months
Type D	_____ months
Type E	_____ months
Type F	_____ months

(continued)

Exhibit 2. (*Continued*)

The provisions of the present Framework Agreement also imply that L shall place the necessary production capacity at the disposal of ABN in order to observe the delivery times concerned.

L shall likewise ensure the necessary production capacity for any recasting work which shall be carried out promptly when notification of defects are received from ABN or when L ascertains defective castings prior to their dispatch, thereby avoiding undue delay.

L agrees to comply with any reasonable request by ABN to expedite an order. In the event L is not in a position to observe delivery times, written notification to this effect shall be sent forthwith to ABN stating the cause of the delay and revised times of delivery.

L shall pay a penalty of 1% of order purchase price for a delay of each whole week or part thereof, up to a maximum penalty of 10%.

8. *Dimensions and weights*

When supplies are based on weight, the consignment weight concerned shall be that as ascertained by L, in that the weight of a workpiece shall, subject to agreement, correspond to the weight calculated by ABN according to drawings or to specified manufacturing dimensions.

Workpieces exceeding ____% in excess weight may be rejected. The measurements shall be those as stated in ABN supply specifications and any deviations therefrom by L are subject to ABN consent.

9. *Quality*

Material qualities shall be those as stated in ABN material specifications and other technical documentation and instructions issued by ABN. Possible defects in castings shall not affect the applicability of said castings, and any repairs by welding or by the use of other materials shall not be undertaken by L without the prior written consent of ABN Quality Control and Inspection Department.

Any flaws on the surface of castings shall not be of a nature giving rise to doubts as to quality—irrespective of whether such doubts are justified or not.

ABN reserves the right to reject castings supplied by L.

10. *Guarantee*

L shall be obliged to rectify all defects occurring in manufacture, machining, or in materials, and in agreement with ABN to:

- supply replacements
- rectify defects by undertaking repair work at own foundry
- repair faulty castings at ABN or ABN client
- credit ABN with the amounts for castings returned

(continued)

Exhibit 2. (*Continued*)

All costs in connection with remedying faults shall be defrayed by L. Guarantee periods shall commence on the day castings are put into service, though not later than 24 (twenty-four) months after delivery date. The compensation rates to be paid by L are as follows:

One year	100% of purchase price
Two years	80% of purchase price
Three years	60% of purchase price
Four years	40% of purchase price
Five Years	20% of purchase price

11. *Checking*

L shall be obliged to follow suitable checking procedures as stated in the aforementioned Clauses 7 and 8, while ABN shall be entitled to carry out continuous checking of the steel castings supplied by L, both with regard to quality and delivery schedules.

The quality control undertaken by ABN shall not relieve L of the responsibility for manufacture, machining, and materials.

When placing orders, ABN reserves the right to have issued a certificate stating the analysis and physical properties of the castings concerned.

12. *Technical cooperation*

Either party to the present Agreements shall be entitled to acquire supplementary technical information from the other party with regard to current supplies to ABN, and both parties shall cooperate as required on pattern work, on the manufacture of castings, and on other matters contributing to efficient production and suitable prices.

13. *Patterns*

All patterns without exception shall remain the property of ABN regardless of their being manufactured by L or ABN.

L shall ensure that pattern material in use and in store is handled with care in a technically correct manner.

Minor maintenance jobs and pattern adjustments to facilitate production shall be undertaken by L for own account. Major repair work, adjustments or remaking work ordered by ABN shall be effected according to quotations sent to ABN.

L shall store the patterns for ABN without charge for a period of three years after use, at which time ABN shall be consulted with regard to further storing. ABN shall be responsible for insuring the patterns.

(*continued*)

Exhibit 2. (*Continued*)

Patterns shall at all times be at the disposal of ABN so that they can be sued at another foundry if so required.

L shall assist in despatching patterns according to ABN instructions and for ABN account and risk.

14. *Special circumstances*

All drawings, technical documents, and patterns which are forwarded to L in connection with supplies to ABN shall not be copied, reproduced or in any way whatsoever brought to the knowledge of a third party without the constent of ABN. L shall not offer or manufacture steel castings based on ABN drawings, material specifications, and patterns for a third party without the written consent of ABN.

15. *Default*

If supply orders are not executed in a satisfactory manner due to faults, defects, unsuitable quality or excessive delays in deliveries, ABN shall have the right to wholly or partially terminate the present Agreement with immediate effect.

If such a situation should arise, ABN shall be entitled to place outstanding orders or parts thereof elsewhere, the extra expense involved being borne by L.

16. *Arbitration*

In any case of any dispute arising from the contractural obligations of the present Agreement or default thereof, both parties shall meet and endeavor to reach an amicable settlement.

Failing agreement within a period of fifteen days from the date on which either party with reference to the present Clause requests in writing an amicable settlement, the matter will be settled by arbitration conducted in English and to be held in Copenhagen.

The Arbitration Tribunal shall consist of three members. Each party shall appoint one umpire to said Tribunal. Should either party fail to appoint an arbitrator within fifteen days from the date of the request in writing from the other party to do so, said other party shall be entitled to appoint a member of the Tribunal on behalf of the first party.

The two arbitrators so appointed shall jointly appoint an umpire. In case the two arbitrators fail to agree on such appointment within thirty days from the date on which the first arbitrator was appointed, said umpire shall be appointed by the President of the International Chamber of Commerce in Paris.

(*continued*)

Exhibit 2.   (Continued)

The arbitration shall be conducted in accordance with the Rules of the International Chamber of Commerce and it is agreed between the parties that there shall be no appeal to the Courts on the decision of the arbitrators.

It is furthermore agreed that the arbitrators shall not be bound by strict rules of law in reaching their decision but may pronounce judgment as "amiables compositeurs" (ex aequo et bono).

The Arbitration Tribunal shall determine which of the parties is to defray the expenses of such arbitration or the proper proportion thereof to be defrayed by each party. The arbitration expenses so allocated shall be paid direct to the party or parties by which such expenses are directed to be paid.

The provisions of this Agreement shall be governed by Danish law.

17.   *Stamp duty, taxes, and so forth*

Any Danish stamp duty shall be shared equally by both parties while each party shall pay their own taxes, duties, and other expenses.

In foreign countries, each party shall be responsible for their own costs incurred.

---

1.   ABN negotiators must be certain that a vendor is able to produce steel castings which meet ABN quality standards and specifications before serious negotiations can take place. Past experience with the vendor will influence the degree to which the following clauses will be negotiated—dimension and weight (paragraph 8), quality (paragraph 9), guarantee (paragraph 10) and inspection (paragraph 11) (Exhibit 2). In this case study these clauses were more detailed in the blanket contract with U.K. 1.

2.   Price is reflected in paragraphs 1, 4, 6 and of course on the price list. Prices are firm during the contract period, and as inflation results in a steady rise in production costs, the longer the period, the more advantageous the contract is for ABN. In this case study, the half-year period suggested by ABN was accepted by all suppliers. Paragraph 4 deals with price and supply clauses specifying the terms of packing costs and place of delivery, and paragraph 6 with terms of payment, which included the question of credit and possible means of financing. The possibility of utilizing export credits from the Spanish Government created a potential payment time of three years, which compensated somewhat for higher prices from Spain 2; but this meant that the contract was not valid for steel castings used in Spain itself. This clause

may also specify case-by-case negotiation when credit possibilities are dependent on where the steel castings are to be used. The choice of currency for payment was also important. This can be illustrated by the case of the Japanese supplier. The problem was one of choosing between yen and d.crowns to be used as payment currency. The senior purchasing engineers succeeded in neutralizing the problem by introducing the question of currency risk insurance, which in Denmark cost 8 percent and in Japan only 4 percent. If the contract specifies yen as the preferred currency, ABN has to cover the currency risk insurance, but as this insurance costs 4 percent, the prices quoted are correspondingly lower. If d.crowns are preferred, the Japanese supplier covers the insurance fee, but prices are correspondingly higher.

3. Paragraphs 2, 3, and 7 (scope of supplies in terms of weight, supply detail, and time of delivery) reflect the agreed terms relating to ABN's degrees of freedom ($+/- x\%$), the possibilities of ordering non-standard items, rush orders and the suppliers' wishes for production planning. Paragraph 7 also specified penalties for delays in delivery (ABN normally has to agree to such penalty clauses for turn-key projects). It should be mentioned that all of the suppliers introduced a "force majeure" clause in the contract, which probably was simply forgotten in the ABN original version.

At this stage, blanket contracts for 1,650 tons of type H (80% of the predicted figure) have been signed. It is now necessary to decide whether additional contracts are needed. This decision is based on current information of requirements determined by the sales department. The decision will also reflect the geographical position of the chosen suppliers in relation to the turn-key projects.

If demand is met (including the possibility of using the maximum allowed quantity), then the process of awarding blanket contracts ceases, and preparation for the next period begins. If ABN is uncertain about whether demand is being met, negotiations may be drawn out, and final decisions postponed. The buyflow chart indicates what would happen if demand is not met.

It is interesting to note that general management will be (unofficially) involved in the decision to place orders for ABN in a new country, and that preliminary business contacts will never lead to anything more than a trial order. The risk involved in establishing new relationships is estimated to be so high that it is shared with the sales department. The sales manager is involved through his role in determining the quantities to be ordered. Even if the supplier does not fill the trial order satisfactorily, he will not be rejected without an investigation into the possibility of correcting his faults.

THE DECISION PROCESS FOR AWARDING BLANKET-CONTRACTS: THE CASE OF STEEL CASTINGS, TYPE B

Type B castings are much heavier than type H castings; their weight per piece is measured in tons. The heavier weight results in a need for the suppliers to have a much greater melting capacity. Demand for type B castings is more directly related to turn-key projects and can therefore be more easily predicted over longer time periods. Consequently, the time factor is less important than it was for type H castings, and more suppliers will be sent requests for quotations.

Type B products can be divided into two groups: small (measuring less than 1,800 mm.) and large (measuring more than 1,800 mm.). Demand was calculated at 320 tons of small and 500 tons of large type B. Requests for quotations for the supply of 320 and 800 tons were sent out because of the different melting capacities of different suppliers.

At this stage the buyflow charts for type B and type H items are very similar. The main differences are caused by situation specific factors; for example, the senior purchasing engineer has full responsibility for the purchase of type B items. Throughout the decision-making process, individual influences are moderated as important problems are discussed among the members of the purchasing department—purchasing manager, section head, senior purchasing engineer, and assistants. Individual influence is further moderated during negotiations with vendors. The individual chosen to negotiate will vary according to situation; for example, in negotiations with the Japanese vendor (for type H) the senior purchasing engineer was involved. The buy flowchart for type B castings is shown in Figure 4. The RFQs which were sent out followed the same format as Figure 2, with bids being received from all vendors. Bids were compared using the relevant criteria, as for type H castings. Due to the considerable weight of each piece of type B, special consideration was given to alternative shipping methods. Type B's weight was considered a major cause of price variance, with the highest price 160 percent above the lowest. To facilitate comparison, bids are ranked according to price variance. This information is used along with comparative data, and vendors are chosen to participate in negotiations.

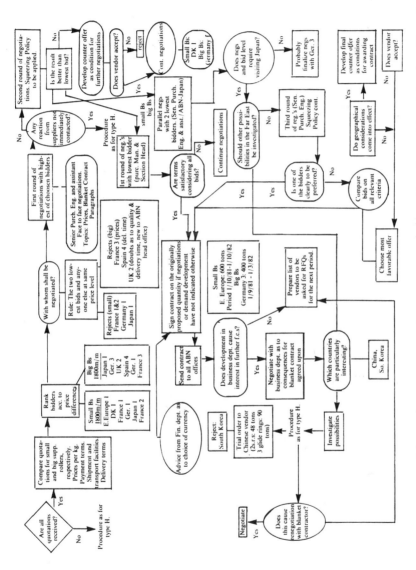

159

Figure 4. The Decision Proces For Awarding Blanket Contracts: The Case of Steel Casting, Type B

Four bidders were rejected from the "small B" group, leaving only Denmark 1 and Eastern Europe 1. In the "large B" group three bidders were rejected. One bid, from Spain 4, was rejected as too high because of long delivery times and U.K. 2, due to doubts about the vendor's ability to produce products which met ABN quality standards and delivery times. Additionally U.K. 2 would be a new supplier for the head office, and therefore could only be given a limited trial order.

Company policy dictated that negotiations take place with the two lowest bidders. This did not occur in this case study. Negotiations were initiated with the highest bidders for both the small and large groups. After two rounds of negotiations, the projected result is compared to the lowest bid, and the vendor is presented with a counter-offer which he must accept if negotiations are to continue. In this case, Denmark 1 (small group) and Germany 1 (large group) did not accept, and were therefore excluded.

In the small group only Eastern Europe 1 remained. Negotiations began with the section head visiting the vendor. The deal was closed, except for details, during that first visit, in spite of the established company policy of conducting several rounds of negotiations. Eastern Europe 1 was awarded the contract largely because it offered to extend the period of the blanket contract to one year. Eastern Europe 1 was awarded a contract for 600 tons covering the period October 1, 1981 to September 30, 1982. This was an improvement over the original requirement of 320 tons over six months.

Meanwhile, the sales department was under pressure from the Chinese market for barter trading. This pressure was so great that the sales manager with responsibility for the area recommended renegotiating with Eastern Europe 1 to make room for Chinese suppliers. The sales manager and the head of the quality and inspection department knew that the Chinese suppliers were potentially attractive through earlier visits to China. These managers also had favorable reports on South Korean suppliers. In the final appropriation of business, a trial order went to China, and the contract with Eastern Europe 1 was unchanged.

In negotiations for large group contracts, ABN-Japan suggested that the senior purchasing engineer visit Japan before he concluded his negotiations with Germany 3. The first few rounds of negotiations showed a fierce competition between these two suppliers; therefore, ABN felt justified in giving a trial contract only to the Chinese vendor. The South Korean vendor was rejected when the senior purchasing engineer visited the plant. He found that the majority of the vendor's melting capacity was reserved for his own rolling mill; this left insufficient capacity for external orders. It was further determined that the South Korean vendor lacked manufacturing expertise.

The choice of supplier for the large B contract was now between Japan 1 and German 3. A more detailed comparison of the suppliers was needed, for example, a calculation based on a division of the different weight classes and their respective part of the base volume, patterns, and the price of the protection of materials during transport. At this stage it was decided that although the Japanese offer was favorable even when costs of insurance for currency fluctuations were taken into account, Germany 3 held a stronger position when the construction locations of the relevant turn-key projects were considered. A final counter-offer to Germany 3 stating the conditions for awarding the blanket contract of 400 tons (100 tons lower than the original quantity) met with acceptance, and the process was completed.

THE DECISION PROCESS FOR PLACING SPECIFIC ORDERS

In Figure 5, the buyflow illustrates that the decision process for placing specific orders is relatively simple. The technical departments develop detailed specifications for the steel castings needed for each individual turn-key project following ABN standards as closely as possible. Product and machine specifications are drawn up very early in the process so that the turn-key price can be calculated. This involves buyers from the coordination department, who supply information principally on prices. The final specifications are negotiated between the sales department and the buyer of the turn-key project. These negotiations often take a considerable amount of time, leaving ABN buyers with little time to carry out other duties. This problem highlights the need for a blanket contract procedure to save time.

All the "requisitions" are written up by the sales department, then passed on to an assistant buyer. The assistant buyer must decide whether the items are specified in the blanket contracts. If they are not, a separate agreement will be made with the supplier. If they are, then the assistant buyer will determine which blanket contractors can deliver on time. He must then calculate the total costs involved, including prices, packaging costs, transport and patterns, and rank potential vendors in order. Some of the blanket contracts may offer the possibility of renegotiating vendor

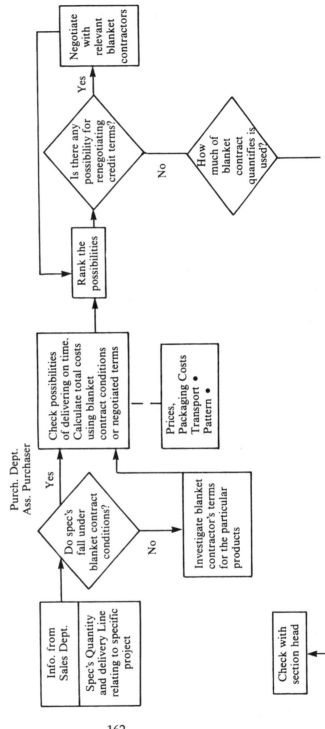

Purch. Dept.
Ass. Purchaser

Info. from Sales Dept.

Spec's Quantity and delivery Line relating to specific project

Do spec's fall under blanket contract conditions?

No

Investigate blanket contractor's terms for the particular products

Yes

Check possibilities of delivering on time. Calculate total costs using blanket contract conditions or negotiated terms

Prices, Packaging Costs
• Transport
• Pattern

Rank the possibilities

Is there any possibility for renegotiating credit terms?

Yes

Negotiate with relevant blanket contractors

No

How much of blanket contract quantifies is used?

Check with section head

162

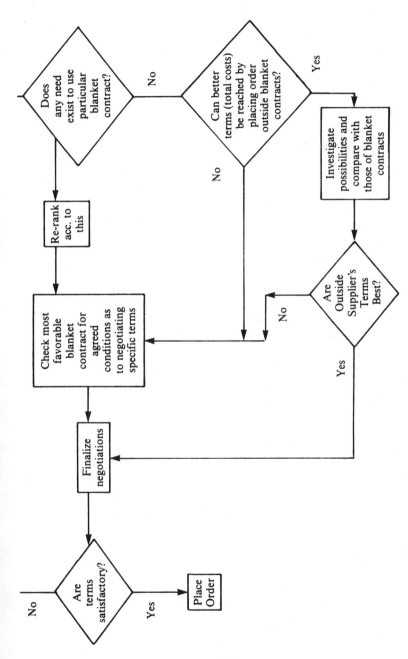

Figure 5. Buyflow: The Decision Process for Placing Specific Orders

163

credit terms for specific orders. Such new negotiations may result in a re-ranking of the suppliers.

The blanket contracts dictate a minimum quantity which must be ordered within a specified time period. Because of this, ABN may be forced to choose one particular blanket contractor, or re-rank the suppliers if there is uncertainty about ABN's ability to order the minimum quantity required as stated in the blanket contract. However, the "25% degrees of freedom" normally provides ABN with the flexibility to investigate other potential vendors for more favorable terms. The need to use this "reserve" (i.e., buy outside the blanket contractors) is most likely to occur when the turn-key project involves relatively high transportation costs because of geographical location. However, the purchaser has to be careful, because this "25% degrees of freedom" also covers the situation in which the customer for the turn-key project (and his government) demand reciprocal purchases in the customer's own country.

STRATEGIC IMPLICATIONS

ABN called in a professional consultancy firm to investigate the possibility of reorganization primarily because of unsatisfactory trends in net earnings. The consultancy firm also investigated ABN's purchasing processes. This investigation resulted in the recommendation that ABN introduce aggressive purchasing behavior in addition to establishing blanket contracts. The need to reorganize in order to increase profit is probably felt in many companies, and as the areas of production and administration probably have already been objects of reorganization efforts, it would not be surprising if reorganization of the purchasing function spreads to other companies. Analyses have shown that general managements are often satisfied with "passive buying." If this is correct, aggressive purchasing will be more widely used, and the ABN purchasing strategy may be implemented by other companies with similar purchasing problems.

This case study deals with subcontracting and involves large amounts of capital. The purchasing department has been shown to play an important role in this process. A turn-key operation is technically very complex, but the machinery, parts and components, and so forth are standardized, because ABN drawings and patterns are used. Detailed specifications for steel castings to be used in a particular turn-key project are developed through cooperation between the sales department, construction department, and representatives of the customer, sometimes also with the help of the quality and inspection department. Thus, all technical decisions are made before the purchasing department makes the commercial decision of selecting the subcontractors. The fact that this division of the two types of decisions is possible may be viewed as necessary for leaving the choice of subcontractors solely to the purchasing department. However, throughout this process, many influencers are evident. The sales managers and, to a lesser degree, the quality and inspection department, are influential during reciprocal purchases. General management finalizes decisions in purchasing when politically sensitive areas are involved. The quality and inspection department, and occasionally the business engineers (who cater to ABN's worldwide interests) play the role of gatekeepers.

The composition of the buying center varies from situation to situation, depending on the type of decision to be made; technical, commercial and calculation of demand—and any situation-specific factors. The purchasing department is always involved in the critical choice decision. The buyflow itself is clearly divided into three stages: (1) The development and choice of who receives RFQs; (2) the choice of suppliers for blanket contracts; and (3) the choice of suppliers for specific orders. Two principal decisions are made early in the process. These are the time period for blanket contracts and the minimum volume for different types of steel castings.

The consultancy firm appointed to look at ABN's purchasing behavior suggested that it should attempt to allocate 75 percent of its requirements to blanket contracts. The recommended purchasing strategy was accepted by the board and became a rule. Whether 75 percent or any other figure was optimal was not discussed within the purchasing department. In order to implement the new strategy, the purchasing department was reorganized. All employees except for the purchasing manager were discharged. They were then asked to reapply, in competition with possible applicants from outside the firm. This put pressure on employees to comply with new procedures.

The time period for blanket contracts was fixed at six months. The source of the "six months" choice is not clear, but it is evident that two factors played an important role in the decision. These were the quality of the demand forecast and the expected degree of cost inflation. Still, the choice of six months seems somewhat arbitrary.

The choice of countries as the first step in the process of selecting vendors for RFQs seems to be guided by past experience and knowledge/impressions about the technological level of the steel castings industry, the currency rate level, and the possibility of gaining financial advantages. As the choice is a low-risk decision, nearly any country will be included that is suggested by internal or external parties.

The employees did not comply with the procedural rule set by the consultants, which recommended a minimum of seven vendors for quotations at this time. This was especially apparent in the purchase of type H. The reasons for failure to comply included insufficient suitable suppliers. The difficulties associated with forecasting precise demand for type H were also influential in rejection of the procedural rule. Type H is also required for other plants, and demand may arise suddenly.

Work has begun on a "supplier matrix" which would contain information on potential suppliers worldwide. It would include information on supplier capacities, price levels, and so forth. The information for the matrix would be electronically processed, thereby creating the potential for making current information on potential suppliers immediately available for any product type, in any given area, should a purchasing problem arise.

The particular problem of deciding whether RFQs should be sent by the ABN head office or through ABN local offices reflects an area of conflict, which is also evident in the later negotiation phase. The process does not exhibit exactly the characteristics of a game for power, but it does indicate that distinct rules are probably needed to avoid future conflicts.

The initial search process is dependent on past experience. Only a few "new" vendors are asked to quote prices. In spite of this, it is fairly easy for internal influencers, such as the sales department, and vendors who show initiative and interest in ABN orders to expand the number of vendors under consideration, even if past experience is not satisfactory (see, for example, the U.K. vendor for type H). Unsatisfactory performance does not automatically lead to rejection. More often than not, ABN investigates the possibility of correcting the problem. The vendor's action in this instance often influences ABN's final decision.

Seven bids followed by seven rounds of negotiations using a price-squeezing policy as recommended by the consultancy firm can be seen as "aggressive" when compared to previous purchasing strategies. The "two times seven" figure is relatively high, suggesting that management is striving to achieve more effective buying, not simply introducing a rule-of-thumb approach. The case presented for type B is closest to this recommendation. The only difference was that the forecast of time required for negotiations resulted in the rejection of some bidders early in the process. The price variances supported the decision to reject the highest bidders at an early stage. This decision was not made until a compensatory decision model had been applied. A compensatory decision model includes assigning positive and negative scores (e.g., $+/-3$) for each attribute for each vendor, and summing the scores for each vendor across attributes. The vendor having the highest positive score is selected.

Compensatory judgmental rules are used throughout the decision process, except during the early, less critical stages, where a satisficing/conjunctive model is applied in order to dichotomize the vendors into acceptable and unacceptable groups. A conjunctive model includes setting minimum acceptance levels for each attribute (e.g., delivery must be in 20 days or less), and rejecting vendors who fail to meet the minimum standards on any one attribute.

When the buyflows for type H and type B are compared, structures are similar, but buying styles are different. In the type H process, the initiative to improve the bids is left primarily with the competing vendors; in the case of type B, counter-offers are developed, especially during the last phase. This may reflect differences in the situation as it develops, but the individual characteristics of the buyers with major responsibility for the purchase are important factors. Face-to-face negotiations were considered both necessary and preferable in both cases.

The buying is done for each type of steel casting, not for the total volume or for any group of castings. Figure 2 shows that negotiations regarding groups of different castings should be possible, at least with some of the vendors. The reasons for this separate buying are difficult to assess. They may include differences in the characteristics of various types of steel castings and customs in the industry. But it may also be that a possible method of aggressive buying is not being used.

ABN's new buying strategy cannot be fully evaluated yet. ABN appears to have an aggressive and professional buying process. This has resulted in better contract agreements, according to the purchasing department. The question concerning an efficient tool for measuring the effectiveness of the department's work is still unresolved. The consultancy firm has recently recommended the construction of a price index which could be used as a basis for comparison; prices would be obtained by ABN. This recommendation is being considered, but this would present many difficulties, particularly in keeping the price index up-to-date.

One short-term disadvantage of the blanket contract is the discrepancy between the challenge being put to the purchasing assistants, and their capabilities. There is also an advantage. Benefits may be accrued from the existence of blanket contracts because the opportunity exists for increasing the level of relevant information available. This information is required for a more accurate calculation of the costs involved in contracting for turn-key projects.

Appendix 1

****
TELEXTELEX***TELEX***TELEX***TELEX***TELEX***TELEX***TELEX***
****

(Dette telex behover ikke hulstrimmel, nar det afsendes fra xx-7)
(TX-H81-1530)

Date: 09.30.81
Telex til: Germany 2.
Telex nr.:   732513/1 xyz-a

price inquiry/framework contract

in connection with possible future negotiations concerning framework contracts for steel castings, kindly quote us the following parts by telex by 1/4/81:

item 3:

Type C: 100 tons

expected distribution:

quantity:	weight:	
55%	25%	4-10 tons
10%	15%	10-20 tons
35%	60%	more than 20 tons

(*continued*)

Appendix 1. (*Continued*)

A, type C:

mat. 332/295
min. 255/310 hb

B, type C:

mat. 322/332 or 212

item 4:

Type D: 140 tons.

expected distribution:

quantity:	weight:	
75%	65%	11 tons or smaller
25%	35%	more than 11 tons

item 5:

Type E: 95 tons

expected distribution:

quantity:	weight:	
40%	20%	2-6 tons
60%	80%	6-8.5 tons

item 6:

Type F: 50 tons

total: 385 tons.

(*continued*)

Appendix 1.(Continued)

We kindly ask you to quote the total volume of the 385 tons. Please also specify itemized prices of the 4 items. Your prices are to be firm and valid for delivery ex your works, according to terms 1980, and for placing of order between May 1, 1981 and October 31, 1981, with successive normal delivery time. The percentages stated are only for your guidance and are as such not binding for A.B. Nielsen and Co. A/S Proposed terms of payment current month plus 30 days. Regards, Purchase/xx/xxx tx-h81-2530

ABNEL COMPANY:
SEARCH FOR AND CHOICE OF A
SUPPLIER IN THE PRODUCT DEVELOPMENT
AND TEST PRODUCTION PHASE IN A
DANISH ELECTRONICS COMPANY

Orla Nielsen

ABSTRACT

This paper follows the case of the A.B. Nielsen Electronics Company
Limited (ABNEL), which is a part of the ABN Group discussed in the
previous paper. At ABNEL, "passive buying" prevailed, as purchasing
was widely viewed as a service to the Production Department. This notion
evolved primarily in response to the company's struggles for survival in
recent years. As competitive pressures grew more intense, research and
development, marketing, and financial problems subsequently became
the forefront of managerial concern, with purchasing being downgraded
to a secondary problem. Greater interest in purchasing was prompted

Advances in Business Marketing and Purchasing, Volume 5, pages 171-193.
Copyright © 1992 by JAI Press Inc.
All rights of reproduction in any form reserved.
ISBN: 1-55938-364-X

by the company's decision to invest in developing the "P-System," a new product with exceptional market potential. To develop the system, ABNEL needed to secure a supplier for the "c-component," a critical system part. The purchasing situation for the c-component will likely progress from a new buy to a straight, or occasionally a modified, rebuy situation as sales of the P-System develop. Specifications of the research and development department are anticipated to play an ongoing and instrumental role in purchasing activity, due to the frequency of technological devlopment in the industry.

THE COMPANY

In the case study "The Case of Steel Castings," a descriptive model of the decision process is presented for a firm producing to order, a description of one of A.B. Nielsen & Company's purchasing processes was given. The purchasing process examined was related to steel castings for turn-key operations, for example, the construction of cement factories. The steel castings' case study provides background information relating to this study, as A.B. Nielsen Electronics Company Limited (ABNEL) is part of the ABN Group.

ABNEL became part of the ABN Group in 1973. Before 1973, ABNEL, which was amalgamated from two of ABN's key suppliers, supplied the ABN Group with automatic process control systems; these systems were utilized, for example, in cement factories. Today ABNEL supplies complete automatically controlled monitoring and warning systems, tailored to individual requirements. The company also has production facilities for the manufacturing of highly developed power electronics. This equipment can be used for hospital emergency systems, vital industries, EDP Centers—in short, wherever power cuts must be avoided. This equipment is purchased to ensure continuity in power supplies. These products are marketed worldwide. ABNEL has subsidiaries in Norway, the United Kingdom, and Germany, as well as a number of agency and licensing agreements in other areas.

In 1981, the company employed about 500 people, and had sales of 160 million d.crowns, about $18 million. When the 1980 and 1981 figures are compared, a growth of almost 50% is evident. A total of 90% of sales went to export markets, and the gross profit margin was 20 million d.crowns, or approximately $2 million in 1981. This result was clearly better compared to the unsatisfactory year, 1980.

THE "P-SYSTEM"

The "P-System" is a recent innovation, the result of a 5-year cooperative effort between the ABN Group laboratories, ABNEL, and the Technical University of Denmark. The P-System cannot be described in detail because the company wishes to remain anonymous; therefore, only a brief description will be given.

The P-System is aimed at a new and expanding market in areas where ABN and ABNEL have already gained considerable experience with earlier, more conventional products. The P-System is a major breakthrough for three reasons. First, possible savings of 25-30% in initial installation costs may be achieved; second, power consumption can be reduced by 60-65%; and finally, if a company should decide to use the system no modifications are necessary. Installation can be done during routine, planned maintenance downtime.

In 1978, the project was so far advanced that the first half-size pilot plant was built and installed in a Danish company. The system was monitored for two years, and the results met expectations. ABN has now built six large P-Systems for demonstration purposes. Three of these were built in the United States, and the remaining three were built by ABNEL.

In order to manufacture the P-System, several components must be purchased from external sources of supply. This case study examines the purchasing process for the key c-component. In particular, the study investigates the problems encountered during the pilot project, the subsequent product development work relating to the demonstration units, and the preparation for first series production.

Having provided background information on the P-System, some background information on the organization of the company, and the purchasing department is presented in the next section.

THE ABNEL ORGANIZATION

There are four main divisions within the ABNEL organization. The first division is the Main Program Division (MPD), which supplies process control equipment and high-power electronics. The second division is the Special Program Division (SPD), which supplies special electronic equipment to consumers who operate under extreme environmental conditions and therefore have exceptional needs. The third division is the Uninterruptable Power Supply Division (UPS), which deals with continuous power supply. The final division is the newly established P-System Division (PSD). Each division (except PSD) has its own staff departments for engineering, documentation, purchasing, stock, quality control, assembly, planning, and dispatch.

The P-System Division is responsible for the new product and its assumed large market potential. This division is not as fully developed as the older divisions, and has neither production nor purchasing departments. Production and purchasing activities are handled by the MPD. The general manager is responsible for the individual divisions, as well as the departments of purchasing, R&D, sales and marketing, personnel, and the special tasks department. In the MPD, the purchasing manager reports to the plant manager, who reports to the divisional head.

When the research began, the purchasing department was staffed by a purchasing manager, three buyers (all engineers), and four secretaries. As well as supervising, the purchasing manager is responsible for important contracts, purchasing research, and department budgeting. The three buyers are responsible for buying mechanics (e.g., aluminum platers), electro mechanics (e.g., connectors and high-power components), and electronics (e.g., semi-conductors, diodes and resistors), respectively.

General Purchasing in the MPD

The field of process control advanced rapidly in the 1970s/1980s due to the appearance of microprocessors. This has resulted in the development of increasingly specialized equipment which relies heavily on software, especially programming. Consequently, production tends to be "tailor-made" for individual customers. Series production does occur, but only in very small amounts. However, considerable energy has been put into developing standard modules for software, with some success.

As a result, the company has a highly differentiated purchasing program. In July of 1982, 17,000 different articles were held in inventory; 10,000 of these were "active" purchasing problems. The average order size was 2-3,000 d.crown or about $333, and only a few suppliers received annual orders of over 1 million d.crown, about $100,000. From a total of 850 EDP-registered suppliers, 59 received orders valuing between 200,000 and 1 million d.crown ($20,000-

$100,000), and the remainder received orders totalling less than 100,000 d.crown per year ($10,000).

Facing this type of purchasing program, where most of the items represent only a very small share of the total purchase, it is not surprising that the purchasing task is routinized as much as possible. The principal task of the purchasing department is to have the quantities of the respective articles ready when needed for production and assembly, in the qualities specified.

The purchasing department has to have in-depth knowledge of all possible suppliers because customer requirements tend to be unique, and many suppliers have only limited assortments of such "niche" products. These assortments tend to be minimal because of the high rate of product development and change. From the purchasing department's point of view, the ability to deliver according to specification is more important than price. The department, however, would not accept prices assessed as higher than "reasonable."

The purchasing department receives very detailed specifications. Thirty percent of the purchases made stem from customer orders through the ABN sales department. The purchasing department also receives a quarterly demand forecast based on information from sales and production, broken down into demand for components at the lowest possible level—for example, the exact dimensions of a resistor. The date the article is needed is also given, along with weekly lists of required components, written up by production planning. Components listed are those not carried in stock.

In this case, the concept "purchasing research" describes the work done primarily during the product development phase. A company management decision some time ago stated that the purchasing department should be involved at this early stage, but the normal procedure is that the work is done primarily by the product development engineers. However, the purchasing manager has been able to get involved to some extent. For example, he may supply the product development people with information on possible suppliers gathered during visits to expositions in different European countries. For the first time, the purchasing manager has truly cooperated with the R&D engineers, and one in particular, who is now heading the new division. This cooperation took place during the development of the P-System.

THE PURCHASING PROCESS

Development of the Prototype and Demonstration Units

In 1976 the idea for the P-System was presented to ABN management. A committee to develop the idea was formed with members from ABN, the Technical University, and ABNEL. It was soon decided to produce a half-size prototype. Based on the work of the committee, the R&D department of ABNEL decided on summary specifications. Concerning the c-component, specifications were sent to ten companies perceived as capable of supplying it. Choice of suppliers was based on previous knowledge of the R&D department. Six of these were later sent detailed specifications, and finally an Irish supplier was chosen to deliver the c-component for the prototype. The choice criteria appeared to be ability to satisfy demand, a competent and flexible product development department, quick delivery and reasonable price. The decision process is summarized in the flow chart shown in Figure 1.

The responsibility for searching for suppliers as well as the final choice lay with the R&D department; this search was motivated exclusively by the wish to implement the decision to build and test the prototype P-System as quickly as possible. While the R&D department was deciding how to best carry this out, the technical patent rights were secured.

The half-size prototype was built and installed in a Danish plant during the summer of 1978. The primary objective was to test the efficiency of the P-System, including the reliability of different components. A second objective was to gain experience in order to develop the system further. The results were satisfactory, and the committee decided to have six full-size mobile units built for demonstration purposes. Three would be manufactured by a U.S. company, an ABN license contractor, and three by ABNEL. Each company was given the option to choose the supplier they preferred. No information is available on the U.S. company, except that the company found a supplier who delivered three c-components; one of these was imperfect and later replaced by the same supplier.

ABNEL inspected the Irish supplier's plant and decided to give the order for the three c-components to the supplier. The order involved new specifications because of changes in the size of the c-component, but the basic technology was the same. ABNEL did no research for other suppliers. When the components were delivered, it was discovered that during operations, the components' temperature got too high, threatening other components.

Negotiations followed which raised doubts about the supplier's technical knowledge and competence. When the supplier refused to recognize his failure and supply new components free of charge, the relationship was terminated. At the same time, the purchasing manager, who had been employed for about twelve months, and the product development engineer began preliminary work to select a supplier for the production of the first series. This work was interrupted by the problem of finding a replacement for the Irish supplier.

Neither the purchasing manager nor the product development engineer presented a possible U.S. supplier for discussion. The potential U.S. supplier chosen for investigation was recommended by a firm that supplies medicines. The U.S. supplier provides the medical supplier with c-components used in heart attack machines, through an agency in Germany.

Research into the U.S. supplier revealed that the company had previously been considered as a supplier for the prototype, and ABNEL had copies of its production program and brochures on file. Research also produced an advertisement for the U.S. supplier in "Electronic Design." At this point, the product development engineer had planned to visit San Francisco, and it was decided that a visit to the U.S. supplier should be included in the schedule.

The American company's production facilities were inspected and the technological expertise of the staff was evaluated during the visit. ABNEL's representative evaluated the supplier on technical criteria. Besides impressions of technological competence gained through discussions with the company, the following "objective criteria" were used:

1. the ability to handle pure plastics, which required advanced technology;
2. the amount of care taken in conditioning the raw materials; and
3. the amount of care taken to ensure that the production area is dust-free and has a continuous supply of filtered air.

The results of the evaluation along with a satisfactory list of references led ABNEL to believe that the U.S. supplier had sufficient expertise. The final consideration in the evaluation was price. This was also considered satisfactory. Despite some minor skepticism apparent in the following statements, it was decided to place the order for the three c-components with the U.S. supplier (see Figure 2).

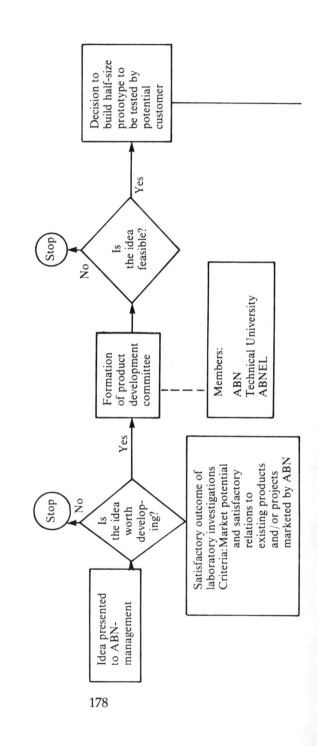

178

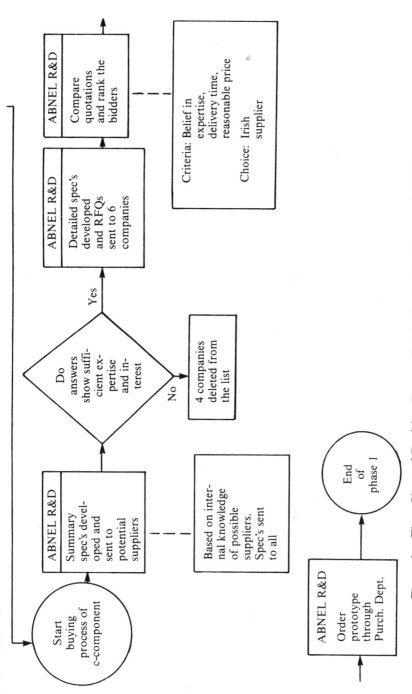

Figure 1. Flow Chart of Decision Process Related to the Development of the Prototype

179

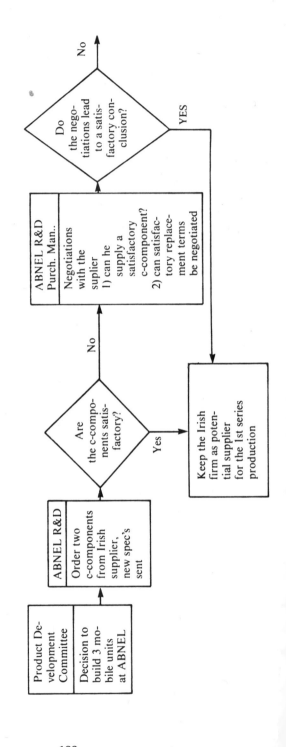

180

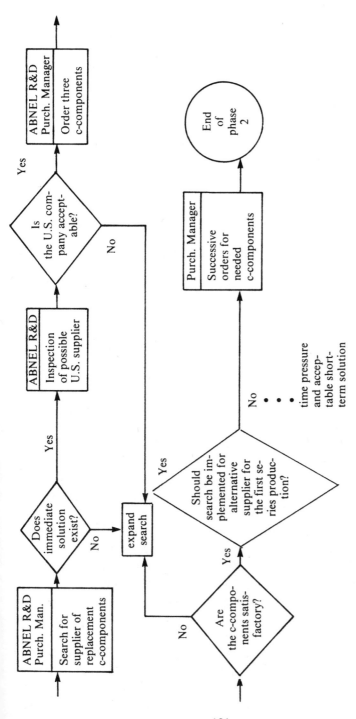

181

Figure 2. Flow Chart of Decision Process Related to the Production of Mobile Units for Demonstration Purposes and the 1st Series Production

> When we visit a firm they can solve any problem, but trouble always turns up.
> American suppliers do not have the German precision, and they are not famous for keeping promises on delivery dates.

The question of visiting the supplier of c-components to the U.S. company never arose. When questioned, the product development engineer stated his belief that unconsciously three factors may have played a role in this:

1. one of the three c-components was not satisfactory and had to be replaced;
2. the supplier to the U.S. company was not known to be "export minded," whereas the other did already export to European countries; and
3. the U.S. company being an ABN-licensed contractor might later be a competitor in the world market.

Preparation of the First and Second Series Production

Having solved the immediate problem of securing replacement c-components, the company continued to plan the first series production of twenty units to be manufactured during 1981. The U.S. supplier delivered satisfactory c-components and because of time pressure, no further search was conducted regarding this first series (see Figure 2).

However, the problem had not been fully solved. There were three reasons for this. The price of the component increased due to changes in the exchange rate of the U.S. dollar. In addition, the distance between buyer and supplier resulted in heavy transport costs. The need for maintaining security of supply through dual sourcing was apparent. Finally, communication problems due to the time difference were disturbing. As a result of these factors, the product development engineer and the purchasing manager renewed the search for an alternative supplier. The purchasing manager had already gathered relevant information while visiting exhibitions, and discussing the problem with sales representatives.

Suppliers from various countries were considered. A discussion with a German representative, who thought his company could meet the demand, resulted in a mutual agreement that the firm did not have the necessary technology to become a supplier for the P-System. A Danish company was also considered. After visits to Copenhagen, it was decided that the costs relating to financing a joint test were too high, and there was also a risk of the company closing down. The third company considered at this time was Swiss. The proposed solution would have resulted in larger, more expensive c-components than those supplied by the United States; therefore, the Swiss company also dropped out of contention.

In the spring of 1982, the purchasing manager visited a French exhibition, in spite of rumors that French companies operating in the field of electronics were not particularly export-minded. Contrary to expectations, the purchasing manager found, in his words, "a truly exciting industry" with five possible suppliers of c-components.

The product development engineer and the purchasing manager compiled a list of 24 possible suppliers, based on available information. Careful scrutinization revealed one definite supplier possibility (the U.S. company) and several possible suppliers. Some companies were excluded because standard answers to earlier inquiries revealed no understanding of technical problems and no willingness to investigate and understand the problems of ABNEL. Others did not seem competent enough to manufacture satisfactory c-components, based on inspection of available background information on the companies concerned.

Because both the product development engineer and the purchasing manager were convinced that mutual advantages would be gained by close cooperation, it was decided that they would jointly visit three possible suppliers, one in Switzerland and two in France. These visits were not only to solve the problem of finding a source for the c-component, but also to establish the soundness of product development and purchasing working together, developing lateral relationships between departments. This cooperation was consistent with new management policy, but not with the traditional perception of the way things had been done in the company in the past.

The two ABNEL representatives visited the Swiss supplier first to evaluate its potential as a supplier of two different c-components. The usual evaluative criteria were applied (technological and objective factors), and it was found that the company could supply one type of component, but not the particular type desired for the P-System.

The other visits were to two French companies. At the first company, the two representatives talked with a "very competent" sales engineer, and informed him about the c-components and another product which was needed. He immediately decided that his company could not supply one of the c-components, but could supply the other. During the meeting he was shown the specifications and responded, "This is amazing! These look just like the specifications we have from another firm." As a result, the documents were withdrawn. The risk involved in establishing a business relationship with this supplier was perceived as too great. A contributory factor which militated against establishing a commercial relationship was that it was not possible for the ABNEL representatives to inspect production facilities.

The visit to the second French company proved to be more satisfactory. Expectations were now at a rather low level, but because the company was known to have considerable sales and it heavily advertised its ability to manufacture c-components, the visit was made as planned. The representatives had a positive impression of this company after inspecting the production facilities.

There was a good atmosphere among the workers and personnel seemed satisfied. The production facilities were not as highly automated as those of the other suppliers, but the representatives felt that the positive working atmosphere more than compensated for this shortcoming. The usual evaluative indicators were deemed satisfactory, and the supplier had the additional advantages of a sales engineer who seemed highly competent, and a product development engineer who was very intelligent. The final factor beneficial to the supplier was that the company was a private independent company. After a good deal of discussion, the supplier received the order to supply a prototype c-component.

The subsequent relationship between the two companies revealed that the French supplier was pleasant to work with. At the beginning of August the prototype was delivered. Because the c-component was half the size of its American equivalent, it was cheaper. However, during testing it did not meet expectations. At this point the French sales engineer met with the purchasing manager and two ABNEL development engineers to investigate the unsatisfactory performance of the prototype. The parties presented various possibilities, and finally agreed to perform a new test on the component based on the supplier's own criteria.

This suggestion has been made to the production development engineer, who is now head of the PCD. The purchasing manager expects the engineer to accept the new testing procedure, and he also expects the French supplier to realize that the dimensions of the c-component are too small, and that a satisfactory component will have to be developed.

Currently, there are various options open to ABNEL. The purchasing manager plans to visit an exhibition in Germany shortly, and will continue his search for a c-component supplier. He has also maintained discussions with the U.S. supplier; as a result, this supplier has made an offer matching the lower French price. Consequently, the purchasing manager is considering purchasing the U.S. prototype and hopes that its new test will be satisfactory. If this occurs, he will have both a well-defined product and the possibility of double sourcing. Figure 3 briefly summarizes the decision process and related activities.

PRACTICAL IMPLICATIONS AND RECOMMENDATIONS

This description indicates that the company has become increasingly reliant on its ability to design advanced technical solutions using existing or newly developed components produced elsewhere. If such a policy is approved as future strategy, then it is clear that purchasing becomes a key function in the firm.

As the situation unfolds, a serious question to be asked is whether or not the purchasing departments are working at an optimum level. The MPD purchasing activities can best be described as "passive," that is, the R&D and production departments define material codes; this leaves the problem of finding appropriate sources to required specifications to purchasing. Because of the enormous quantity of components that are "active purchasing problems" and the small purchasing staff, there is no time for strategic purchasing. The relative unimportance of the cost of each component to the finished solution indicates that the costs of purchasing research may be too heavy. As a consequence, management has not developed a long-term purchasing strategy nor specific purchasing policies. Also, no distinctive goals for purchasing have been formulated (except budget control), leaving the purchasing manager to set his own goals for measuring the efficiency of the department.

If the purchasing manager is ambitious, then the lack of a corporate purchasing policy may lead him to try to increase the influence of the purchasing function in relation to other functions. An example of this in this case study occurred when cooperation took place between R&D

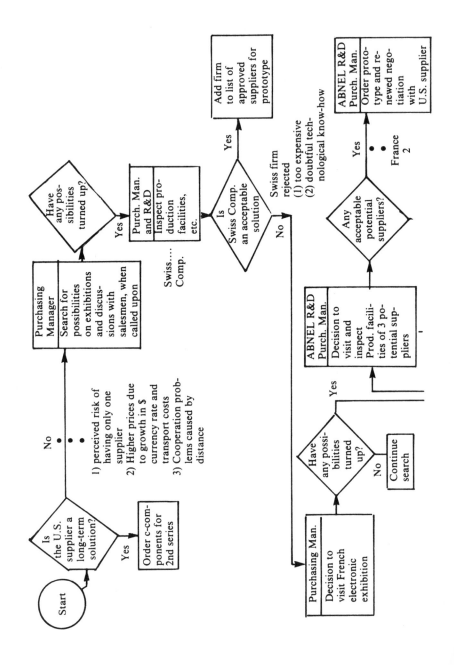

186

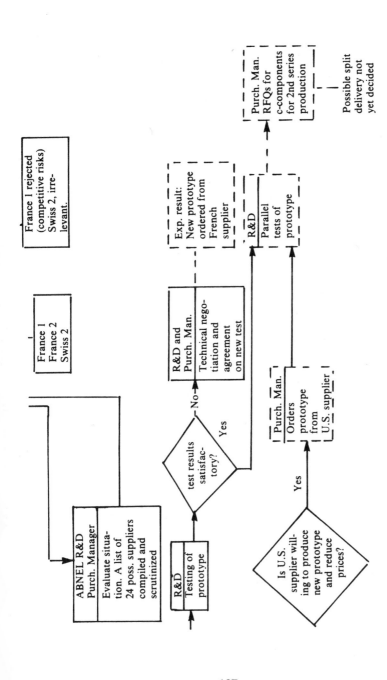

187

Figure 3. Flow Chart of Actual and Expected Decision Process Related to the 2nd Series Production

Note: Stipled boxes refer to expected decisions and activities.

and purchasing, with the "quiet" support of the MPD general manager. This type of "informal" activity between departments can lead to internal conflicts, particularly with the production department, considering that purchasing reports to production on a hierarchical basis.

A final point is that the production department is responsible for stocks, and a special department within the production function is responsible for component control. The research did not identify any cooperation problems between component control and purchasing. On the other hand, there were no guidelines for cooperation in routine work situations. In conclusion, it would be advisable for ABNEL's general management to discuss the purchasing function seriously, and decide on its future level of importance within the organization.

Changes in the organizational structure seem to be necessary. A materials administration department could be created and given responsibility for purchasing, logistics, stock and component control. This department would take the form of a staff section reporting directly to the general manager of ABNEL. He would work for all relevant divisions—MPD, SPD, and PSD.

From an external viewpoint, there is no advantage in having a separate purchasing department for each division; on the contrary, there is the possibility of utilizing past experience and combined learning, through a centralized policy of materials administration. Security problems related to the SPD may also be solved under this type of organizational framework.

A further recommendation is that the management decides on a set of strategic items which are important in one or several dimensions (e.g., relative price, criticality in production, delivery security); these would then receive special attention by the materials administration department. These strategically important items should be the subject of specific purchasing policies. Examples of such items include purchasing research, market assessments, and rules relating to the number of bidders and choice of suppliers. The following policies should be developed.

1. Goals and efficiency measures to control the work of the department and simultaneously guide and inspire the personnel should be set.
2. Cooperation between the materials administration department and R&D should follow loose rules to allow for interdepartmental creativity.

3. Ad hoc relationships would be preferable between purchasers and product development groups when different types of components are being discussed. This rule may not be particularly creative at first, but would be considered a necessary contribution to the purchasers' learning process, ensuring profitable cooperation in the latter stages.

The above recommendations are those adopted by a Finnish Electronic Company (Möller and Allos 1983).

There appears to be no formal connection between the ABN purchasing department and ABNEL. When implementing the recommendations, it seems desirable that ABN buyers help in the design of the new system, and help train future buyers. In this case study, purchasing behavior for the c-component is characterized by finding satisfactory solutions to problems as they arise. This search is carried on exclusively by the two representatives, and is expanded only if no solution is found. Note, for example, that potential supply from Japan is not discussed, and the supplier of c-components to the U.S. company was not considered. Concerning marketing c-components to ABNEL, purchasing behavior has certain implications; therefore, the following suggestions have been made.

First, the suppliers are immediately divided into two categories— possibles and nonpossibles. This division is based on the impression given by existing information on the potential suppliers' technological knowledge (written material in the archives and memories of the persons involved) and highlights the need to secure current information on the marketers' product development ability. Second, the marketer should be made aware of the importance of ABNEL's first visit and the "objective indicators" applied in the evaluation. The marketers should also be aware of ABNEL's sensitivity to competitive risks.

Taking into consideration the organizational structure of the purchasing function at the moment, marketing efforts should be concentrated on the R&D personnel. These efforts should reflect the marketer's interest and ability to find solutions to ABNEL's problems. If the marketer is not accepted during the first stage, then a strategy of aggressive pricing is probably the only way to gain acceptance.

In the case of a supplier who has been accepted at the main production phase, the focus of activity must be on evaluating the demand for his product relative to the total product of ABNEL. If the supplier's product is relatively important, ABNEL will continuously try to secure multiple sources. If it is not important, then the supplier will be able to remain the sole source of supply, provided he does not deviate too much from the agreed specifications.

THEORETICAL COMMENTS

Despite the fact that this case study is based on a quite large company (500 employees) with purchasing departments employing up to four buyers and secretaries, purchasing is still viewed as a service function serving the production department. Purchasing tasks involve mainly routine response behavior (straight rebuy), information input, prespecified and predictable content and output, and finally, specified alternatives (Howard, Hulbert, and Farley, 1975). The above tasks are completed only to a "satisfactory" level; therefore, the end result is "passive buying."

The general manager believes that the "passive buying" situation is caused not by a failure to recognize the advantages which could be gained by more active purchasing, but rather by the fact that the company has been struggling for a long time to survive. The company strategy for survival focused on efficient R&D and marketing and solving financial problems. The managers have been busy solving problems related to the rapid rate of development of electronics and the competitive situation, and have not had time to work on "secondary" problems (i.e., purchasing).

The author has come across this secondary/service function view of purchasing in earlier research. It is theorized that this is most common among small- to medium-sized industrial companies, particularly those producing to order, and working in fields where technology is developing rapidly.

Situations like the one described demand a technological competence not usually evident in buyers. Consequently, the primary work is done by R&D people. Only when content is precisely specified may purchasing take over. This gives rise to "traditional" conflicts between R&D, production and production planning, and purchasing; thus it invariably creates frustrations for the ambitious purchasing manager. The purchasing manager is likely to develop strategies to enhance the influence of the department and to convince general management of the need to improve the department's lateral position to make purchasing more efficient. The R&D engineer's interest in helping the purchasing manager and his belief in the mutual benefits of such a cooperation were therefore met with eagerness by the purchasing manager.

The purchasing process for the c-component can be viewed as an example of content development during the product development phase. This process will probably result in routinized response behavior at a later stage, when the P-System becomes standardized. In other words, it is predicted that purchasing behavior will move from exhibiting new buy characteristics to those of straight rebuy, and then possibly back to exhibiting modified rebuy characteristics whenever relevant external changes are perceived.

However, "new buy characteristics" (or extensive problem-solving) is rather loosely defined. There is no doubt that actual behavior may vary considerably from company to company and product to product. This case gives only one example, and the applicability of the comments to a general model must be considered limited at most, as a few pieces in a complex jigsaw puzzle.

In this case study, buying behavior was initiated by the decision to develop the new P-System. The evaluative criteria are formed gradually during the development of the system, from the prototype to the production of the demonstration units, and the first and second series production. At first, such criteria were defined by the R&D department, and appeared to be exclusively concerned with the product. Subsequent criteria involved the supplier's ability to provide a satisfactory component. Evaluative criteria relating to the question of supplier stability were not implemented until the project reached the stage of first series production planning. The supplier may have the opportunity to influence the choice and importance of criteria used, as this case illustrates, by proposing and carrying out an "in-house" test on the critical components. The only evaluative criteria used previous to the prototype production stage, which refers to potential supplier choice, is that of sufficient technological competence.

At the specification stage, suppliers are evaluated using a new criterion, that is, the perceived interest of the suppliers in cooperating to solve ABNEL's problems. In the final choice, delivery time and price (5-7% of total buys for the P-System) are examined. Subsequent criteria seem to be influenced by perceived problems, such as product specified, price development, and cooperation problems; they are also affected by experience gained during the process, for example, indicators for evaluating a company's technological competence may be developed.

The risk of future competition is also relevant. In the final stages, the criteria are formed by R&D and the purchasing manager.

The search for suppliers is connected with the formation of evaluative criteria, and in this case is aimed at finding a satisfactory solution at each stage. This situation is comparable to the "classical" finding of Cyert and March (1963), as the purchasing process is motivated by an identified problem, and only expanded when no satisfactory solution has been found.

The decision heuristics belong to the satisficing models, but different models seem to be applied during the process. In the beginning, the judgmental rule is probably a conjunctive model, serving to dichotomize the suppliers into acceptable and unacceptable categories. Later, during the choice of supplier for prototype production, the rule becomes a disjunctive model. Perception of technological competence is believed to have top priority. Later, the conjunctive model is applied again; this develops into a compensatory model, which is used in the final choice without clear weighting.

The perceived risk seems to be closely associated with the problem identified at each step. At the beginning of the process, risk concerning "quality type" is dominant; later, risk regarding "buying tasks" which are perceived and acted upon is dominant. Throughout the process, the two representatives seem to be aware of the risks involved in competition. It can also be argued that there is a risk of the situation "slipping out of control," which influences problem identification and search throughout the various steps.

The buying process as a whole is somewhat obscure when one tries to ascertain whether clear independent steps exist. As one goes through the process, it is evident that the decision to develop the P-System is clearly an independent step taken, which initiates the purchasing process. The next independent step involves the choice of c-component and supplier for prototype production. Subsequent decisions are incremental, and the process involves several feedback loops. This is a characteristic of the new buy situation; or it could result from the fact that the organization has no prespecified policies to handle such a project.

The nucleus of the buying center changes only once throughout the process, from R&D to the divisional head and purchasing manager. The fact that the purchasing manager is involved at an early stage is probably due to the situational factor that the intention of the representatives was also to prove to the organization that cooperation with the purchasing department is beneficial during the product development phase. Another important situational characteristic influencing the process seems to be the repeated difficulties of finding a satisfactory c-component. These difficulties occurred both during the process of obtaining replacement components for the demonstration units as well as the parallel testing procedure in the final stage.

Finally, even if the buying process as such seems sensible as a whole, the absence of political guidelines from the general management results in a dependency to the extent that the two principal parties involved understand and follow the company's objectives, their enthusiasm, and other individual characteristics. Because of this, the problem-solving procedures will vary according to which individuals are involved.

REFERENCES

Cyert, R.M. and J.G. March. (1963). *A Behavioral Theory of the Firm*. Englewood Cliffs, NJ: Prentice-Hall.

Howard, J.A., Hulbert, J. and Farley, J.U. (1975). "Organizational Analysis and Information—Systems Design: A Decision-Process Perspective," *Journal of Business Research*, Vol. 3, pp. 133-148.

Möller, K., and J. Allos. (1983). *Buying of Production Materials: An Intensive Study in Three Finnish Corporations*. Helsinki: Helsinki School of Economics.

DELSOLA COSMETICS:
INDUSTRIAL BUYING BEHAVIOR—RESTYLING
THE BOTTLE OF A SHAMPOO RANGE

Jan B. Vollering

ABSTRACT

This case describes a modified rebuy purchasing situation for Delsola Cosmetics, a medium-sized Dutch cosmetics producer. Acknowledging the significance of packaging as a marketing tool for consumer products, Delsola management seeks a restyling of its present shampoo product packaging. Such a restyling involves a rather complex problem solving process, based on the substantial investments in capital and management time that it entails. The relationship between Delsola and existing shampoo bottle suppliers can be characterized as long term. As such, the relationship plays an influential role in all company buying decisions. The buying decision process can, in fact, be described as a linear, sequential process with limited feedback loops. The Delsola case effectively illustrates the challenge inherent to alternative suppliers seeking to influence the industrial buying process, when long-term supplier relationships are in existence.

Advances in Business Marketing and Purchasing, Volume 5, pages 195-205.
Copyright © 1992 by JAI Press Inc.
All rights of reproduction in any form reserved.
ISBN: 1-55938-364-X

DELSOLA COSMETICS

Delsola Cosmetics is a medium-sized Dutch producer of a range of cosmetics, including shampoos, setting lotions, bath oils, bath foams, and permanent wave solutions. It employs 135 people, and has annual sales of about Dfl. 30 million ($12 million). The company has a strong position in the Dutch cosmetics market. It is a leader in the shampoo market, holding more than 15 percent of the market, and ranks second in the market for setting lotions. The company has little overseas activity. Delsola has concentrated its efforts on the consumer market, having sold a sister company which produced basic raw materials for shampoos, to a large Dutch chemical firm some years ago.

The Market for Packaging Materials

The market for packaging materials in general, and plastic bottles in particular, has the following characteristics.

- The appearance and cost of packaging is important.
- Frequency and reliability of delivery and constant product quality is also important.
- When developing new packaging, or restyling existing packaging, large investments of management time and money are required to cover development costs.
- Technological development is steady, but involves heavy investment. Alternative production technologies (such as extrusion blowing and injection blow molding) result in differing restrictions on the measurement and appearance of bottles. It is a "gentlemen's agreement" in the industry that a supplier who has a two-year claim on the production of the mold. This provides compensation for the development work done on the mold.
- Because of differences in the various production processes, extensive development is necessary if the manufacturer wishes to use the bottle molds of other competitive suppliers.
- Complicated molding tasks are carried out by companies which specialize in molding. In the case study, the supplier of the bottles was in continuous contact with the mold producer.

ORGANIZATION OF BUYING IN DELSOLA COSMETICS

The company is administered by a marketing director and a technical director. Together, they are responsible for overall business strategy. Subsequently, they will be referred to as the "management team." The purchasing department consists of a head of purchasing and a purchasing officer; the purchasing officer reports to the financial director. Certain procedures have been developed for the procurement of materials. For example, technical items needed for repair and maintenance are bought by the maintenance and repair department. In this situation, purchasing will be informed as to the department's intention to buy, and the prices negotiated for specific items. When more important items are involved, close cooperation between various departments is instrumental in drawing up specifications and discussing potential suppliers. The atmosphere of the relatively small company encourages good formal contacts. A number of multi-disciplinary task groups meet on a regular basis to address long-term issues. The head of purchasing is a member of several task groups which include:

- *Search committee*: this committee monitors changes in competitive offerings, and advises management about strategic decisions which must be made; the search committee meets every three months.
- *Value analysis committee*: this committee has the task of monitoring the quality and appearance of products and packaging, and discussing possibilities for cost reduction.
- *Project development committee*: this committee monitors the progress of projects which have been approved by management.

In the event of important product developments, clear specific procedures are used. Each product development process is divided into three stages: pre-orientation, orientation, and realization. Management must give the formal "go ahead" at the end of each stage, before the next stage can begin. A "consolidation report," which integrates the contributions of various disciplines to the project, is required to gain the approval of management. The development of new packaging or the restyling of existing packaging for cosmetic products involved relatively large projects, which require a great deal of time and attention from various departments, because the appearance and quality of packaging are of paramount importance in selling cosmetics.

The Buying Decision Process for Restyling the Shampoo Range

The decision process for restyling is summarized in Figure 1. The flowchart indicates the sequence of stages, the persons and departments involved, the criteria used and decisions made. The numbers in the flowchart correspond to the numbers in the description given below.

The process of restyling the shampoo range was triggered by the EEC directive of 1979 on informative labelling (particularly of contents). Delsola shampoo bottles contained 185 and 285 ml., which did not meet the new standards set in this EEC directive. Delsola therefore decided to introduce bottles with 200 and 300 ml. contents [1] into the Dutch market. The numbers in brackets refer to the numbers in the flowchart of the decision process.

The EEC directive initiated the restyling process, but marketing also felt that the shampoo range needed a "face lift" to give the product range a new lease of life in the saturation phase of its lifecycle. The management team agreed with the proposal to restyle the bottle, and the pre-orientation stage was approved.

The marketing department formulated the following requirements for the new range of bottles:

- they should be recognizable as Delsola shampoo bottles;
- they should look bigger than the existing bottles;
- they should raise associations of modernity, as Delsola products were perceived as too old-fashioned;
- they should be more attractive to look at than existing bottles;
- they should allow the firm to distinguish the traditional range of shampoos from a new specialty range.

The production department and the purchasing department also formulated criteria for the new range of bottles [2]. An external designer was commissioned to develop new models for the shampoo bottles. Within the framework of the restrictions of marketing, production and purchasing, the designer had relative freedom in the design and execution of his work. Three alternative designs were developed and tested by a market research agency. All three models met the requirements [3]. The final choice of model was made by the marketing department, with consumer recognition as the primary criterion [4].

After additional market research, the marketing department estimated the type and size of response the market would make to this bottle restyling. The next decision to be made involved the type of granulate (plastic raw material) to be used for the model chosen. Four types of plastics, both in transparent and colored versions, were evaluated on 28 characteristics (see Table 1). Marketing, production and purchasing finally decided to use LD-Polyethyene. LD-Polyethyene was chosen for the following reasons.

1. It gave a "cosmetic feeling," smoothness, distinctiveness, light glossiness.
2. It had a low deformation.
3. It had good printability.

Decisions about Caps Were Made in a Similar Way to Those about Bottles

All of the decisions made were described in a "plant orientation report," which also included suggestions about potential suppliers [5] (August 1979). After the marketing, production and purchasing departments had made their final decisions regarding the model and material to be used, a preliminary mold was made by the designer. The financial department calculated the investment needed for restyling. After much consultation and discussion, the management team approved the proposal to begin the realization stage of the project [6](January 1980).

Selecting Suppliers for Quotation

Upon receiving approval to begin the realization of the project, a number of simultaneous and/or sequential actions were taken. The logistics department developed a "matrix realization plan," which scheduled the actions to be taken by various departments. The marketing department extended market research activities in order to estimate the size of market segments for various products within the shampoo range.

The head of the purchasing department and the head of production visited five potential shampoo bottle suppliers and requested quotations. Upon evaluating existing production facilities and potential new production equipment, both the head of production and the head of purchasing expressed a preference for the existing supplier, supplier B.

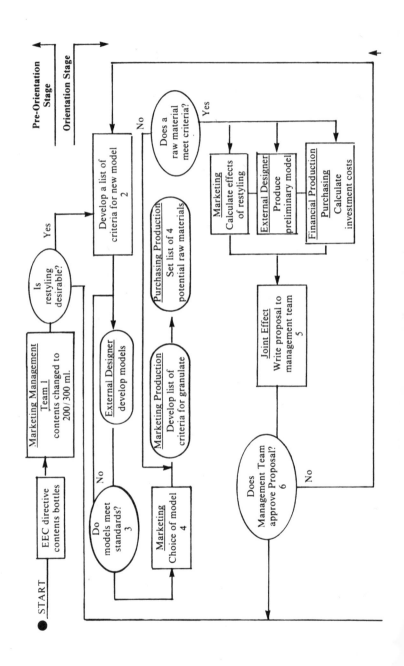

START

EEC directive contents bottles

Marketing Management Team 1 contents changed to 200/300 ml.

Is restyling desirable?

Yes

No

Develop a list of criteria for new model 2

Pre-Orientation Stage

Orientation Stage

External Designer develop models

Do models meet standards? 3

No

Marketing Choice of model 4

Marketing Production Develop list of criteria for granulate

Purchasing Production Set list of 4 potential raw materials

Does a raw material meet criteria?

No

Yes

Marketing Calculate effects of restyling

External Designer Produce preliminary model

Financial Production Purchasing Calculate investment costs

Joint Effect Write proposal to management team 5

Does Management Team approve Proposal? 6

No

200

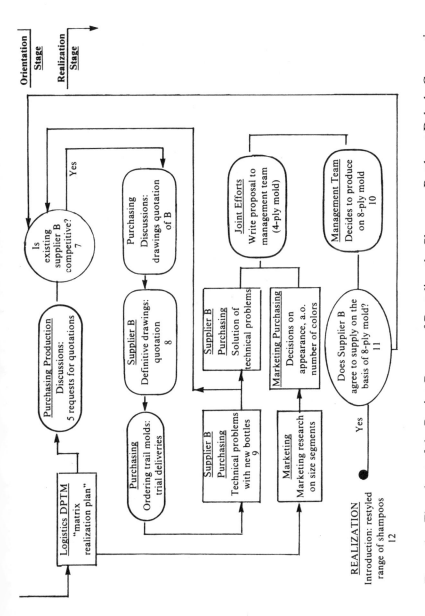

Figure 1. Flowchart of the Buying Process of Restyling the Shampoo Bottles at Delsola Cosemetics

Table 1.   List of Criteria for Evaluating Granulates
for the Shampoo Bottle

Suitable for both contents (200 and 300 ml.)
Deformation sensitivity
Deformation during use
Stress cracking
Tarra weight
Gloss
Scratch sensitivity
Extrusion stripes
Press at stocking
Cracking after fall
Supply of raw materials
Visibility of shampoo
Width of filling tolerances
Chance of filling disturbances
Width of tolerances on color stability of shampoo
Tolerances on stability of the emulsion
U.V. absorber necessary in shampoo or raw material
Printability
Number of colors for transparent shampoo
Printing possible on both sides
Shrinking during printing
Deformation during printing
Feasibility of a label on both sides
Feasibility of a label on one side
Shrinking during labelling
Restrictions due to environmental pollution

The head of purchasing stated that, "We have already had a good relationship with the supplier for 12 years. They maintain a reasonable price level, offer good delivery conditions; they deliver on time, and have established good quality control for the products they deliver to us." Preference, therefore, lay with the existing supplier because of the technical and commercial importance of the project. The four other suppliers visited were not able to supply the required quantities of bottles to Delsola Cosmetics [7].

Supplier Selection

A special visit was made by the head of the purchasing department to supplier B. Two weeks later, representatives of B visited Delsola and offered a preliminary quotation, which included drawings of the new bottles. Certain changes in bottle design were necessary, especially in the 300 ml. bottle; the angle of the neck had to be reshaped on the front and back, and the width of the base was too large. Four weeks later, definitive drawings and a quotation were offered [8] (March 4, 1980).

At this point, commercial, technical, and financial aspects were evaluated. The majority of potential suppliers evaluated could produce only on a 4-ply model; therefore, flexibility in supplier choice was an important variable for discussion. Other variables included:

- the number of colors to be printed on the front and back of the bottle, and
- the type of mold to be used for simultaneous production of 4 or 8 bottles.

The head of purchasing ordered trial molds, with the approval of production. Some minor modifications were made on the first trial mold.

The purchasing department ordered trial deliveries of 2 x 1000 bottles on June 9. A delay of three weeks was caused by technical problems with the thickness of the bottom of the bottle, and the presence of a thin place on the shoulder of the first "scale" bottle. The head of purchasing and a technical expert from Delsola visited B to discuss these problems on July 22, 1980 [9]. In the meantime, the purchasing department examined the possibility of contacting other suppliers.

After supplier B had solved its technical problems, the purchasing department recommended that management proceed with the 4-ply mold, as only a few potential suppliers were able to produce an 8-ply mold; if they chose to produce only an 8-ply mold, Delsola's flexibility in supplier selection would be limited. Management decided to produce the range with an 8-ply mold in light of price differences between the bottles produced in 4-ply and 8-ply molds [10].

Supplier B began production on September 8, 1980, using a 4-ply mold. Trials with the 8-ply mold began after production runs with the 4-ply mold were successfully completed. The head of purchasing discussed price options on 4-ply and 8-ply molds with supplier B, and it was agreed that supplier B would calculate bottle price on the 8-ply mold basis, even when they were produced on a 4-ply mold. Supplier B preferred to produce initially on the 4-ply mold, as the risk of breakdowns and problems with delivery times were decreased when the 4-ply mold was used. There were 11 breakdowns during the first quarter of 1981. Introduction of the restyled range of shampoo took place in May 1981 [12].

EVALUATIVE COMMENTS:
IMPLICATIONS FOR MANAGEMENT

The development process for restyling a shampoo bottle is complicated and time-consuming. The small company carrying out this process must usually work in close cooperation with one supplier, as is evident in this case study. In this study, supplier relations were good. Visits made by the heads of purchasing and production to the five suppliers cannot be viewed as part of the supplier selection process; in reality, it was a search for information. The search for alternative suppliers occurred only when technical problems with the new bottles arose.

Once started, the buying decision process contains many elements of sequential planning, and limited elements of choice. It is important for the head of purchasing, as well as the present supplier, to be present at the outset of the process, where decisions which determine final outcome are frequently made. The next stages can be characterized as a more or less linear planning process. Again, it would seem important for the purchasing head and present supplier to participate in decision subprocesses, as each process partly determines the outcome of the subsequent stage. The management team incorporates certain go/no go decision points, as it is important that they review the development process continually, and to discuss alternatives and consider feedback loops back to the starting point. On the other hand, it is doubtful that the management team can really influence the process once started, because the development process seems to be linear in nature, and each step is partially determined by the former step.

Two explanations can be given for the four alternative suppliers who stated that they "had no capacity to supply the required quantities of bottles." First, the market has the character of a "domesticated market" (Arndt 1979), where existing positions have been essentially frozen, leading to vested interests and a certain amount of inertia. Second, Delsola perceives the statement of the alternative supplier in this particular way because Delsola has no intention of considering these alternative suppliers seriously.

STRATEGIC COMMENTS

The interaction that takes place between existing suppliers of shampoo bottles is characterized by a long-lasting relationship (Hakansson 1982).

This relationship influences the buying decision process a great deal. Because restyling involves a complex problem-solving process, complexity and certainty are reduced when Delsola remains with the existing supplier. In a small company, such as Delsola, it is especially important to reduce "transaction costs" (Williamson 1979) because human resources are limited. The organization thus strives for satisfactory solutions to problems that arise.

In the buying decision process, a limited number of feedback loops can be distinguished. The process may also be characterized as a linear, sequential process. Several types of decision heuristics may be analyzed; two of these include the disjunctive ("choice" of the existing supplier) heuristic and the compensatory (choice of the type of granulate, using 28 criteria) heuristic.

The inductive, analytical description of the buying decision process, a description made by the IBB Group of researchers, seems to be a useful approach, as it clarifies the complex reality in industrial buying decision making. One striking element in this particular case is that a number of important choices usually mentioned in the literature (e.g., supplier selection) do not really exist. Another interesting aspect is that alternative suppliers have limited power, and limited will, to influence this particular process.

REFERENCES

Arndt, J. (1979). "Towards a Concept of Domesticated Markets." *Journal of Marketing* 43: 69-75.

Hakansson, H. (1982). *International Marketing and Purchasing of Industrial Goods.* Chicester: John Wiley.

Williamson, O.E. (1979). "Transaction Cost Economics: The Governance of Contractual Relations." *The Journal of Law and Economics* 22: 233-261.

GUM ROSIN:
RAW MATERIAL BUYING IN A
CHEMICAL INTERMEDIATES INDUSTRY

Jan B. Vollering

ABSTRACT

This case study examines a modified rebuy purchasing situation involving a material used in a process of production. The product is gum rosin, the application of which in this case is as a gelling agent in the production of printing ink for a subsidiary of a Dutch multinational firm. Distinctive features of the buying process for gum rosin at the Dutch subsidiary are the influence of long-term company and client research and development activity, as well as constraints on the procurement of gum rosin from natural resources. As a result, Mintzberg, Raisinghani, and Theoret's (1976) model of "unstructured" strategic decision processes is most applicable, based on its many feedback loops. The gum rosin case reflects a situation involving a series of complex operational decisions. As a result, it illustrates the need for a sound strategic plan to serve as a framework in guiding business decision making.

Advances in Business Marketing and Purchasing, Volume 5, pages 207-216.
Copyright © 1992 by JAI Press Inc.
All rights of reproduction in any form reserved.
ISBN: 1-55938-364-X

A DESCRIPTIVE MODEL OF STRATEGY
FORMULATION AND IMPLEMENTATION DURING
GUM ROSIN PURCHASING

The present study analyzes a buying process in a subsidiary of a Dutch multinational firm. It examines the procurement of gum rosin, which is applied as a gelling agent in the production of printing ink. The product range of the company consists primarily of gelling agents for paint, printing ink, polyester, and adhesives. Its production of rosin based agents for printing ink amounts to 20,000 tons. The number of employees is about 350.

The buying process for gum rosins has the following characteristics. First, it is influenced by long-term research and development by the paint company, as well as that of clients and the clients of clients. Second, procurement of gum rosins from natural resources has become considerably more complicated during the last few years because of the increased number of petrochemical and "tall" based substitutes. The final influence on buying is political instability in the countries of suppliers and changes in the markets for end-products.

Buying Process

The decision process itself is represented in Figure 1. There are three basic stages in this process:

1. preparing the preliminary guidelines for a new three-year plan, labelled the "3-year operational plan";
2. incorporating relevant dimensions of internal corporate and company policy of the markets served into the plan; assessing trends and developments in the raw materials markets and their impact on procurement in the "3-year operational plan";
3. finalizing the 3-year procurement plan.

Events and decisions are exhibited in boxes, and questions to be answered are in diamonds in the figure. Evaluation criteria are shown as dotted lines.

Preparing Preliminary Guidelines for the
New 3-Year Operational Plan

In this decision process, departments and groups take action and make decisions, rather than individuals. This is because of the complex nature of the product task. Solutions are derived through extended discussions within and between groups. Attaining maximum commitment and consensus is an important goal.

The 3-year operational plan is initiated by top management. The accountant supplies the necessary data to begin the discussion. The first exercise is to discuss the results for the next 3 years if no changes are made in present policy. Decision criteria include: corporate guidelines for the next planning period; the mission of the company; the strategy for becoming renowned as a specialist supplier; and developments, trends and conditions in the markets served. Alternative strategies are identified. The accountant calculates the consequences of various alternatives. When top management reaches agreement about the chosen alternatives, rough guidelines are developed, which provide limits useful in preliminary planning in the marketing department. The four product group leaders in marketing discuss the guidelines on the basis of their knowledge of the markets and initiate a discussion with top management to revise guidelines where necessary. When agreement with top management has been reached, or when top management does not want to revise its guidelines, the product group leaders make a preliminary estimate of quantities and prices for the following 3 years. Based on this information, the accountant calculates profits, production usage, and bottlenecks. Based on this analysis, the product group leaders make necessary revisions to their plans.

Preparing a Statement of Procurement's Role in the Operational Plan

On the basis of the preliminary marketing plan for the next 3 years, the controller calculates the required total amount of gum rosins, based on predicted quantities of end-products. Using this information, the head of the purchasing department calculates the required quantities of different types of gum rosins—natural gum rosins, gum rosins from petrochemical sources and "tall" gum rosins.

The sourcing decision for gum rosins is complex, and there are many different decisions to be made; each decision operates on a different time schedule. A procurement strategy is drawn up by the head of purchasing and of the gum rosin section of the R&D department, in close cooperation. The R&D department has the majority of the expertise on internal production and processing requirements, as well as external requirements, and problems of clients.

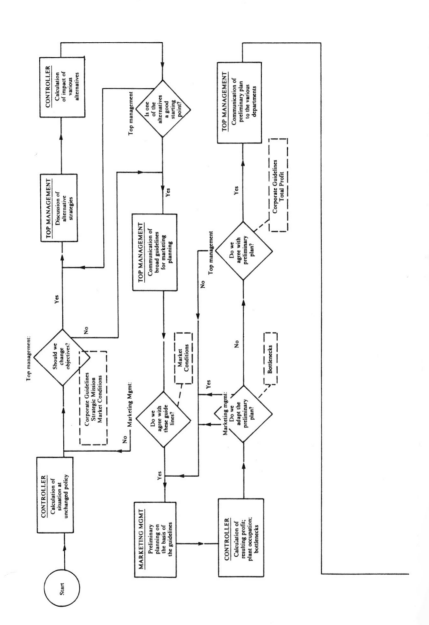

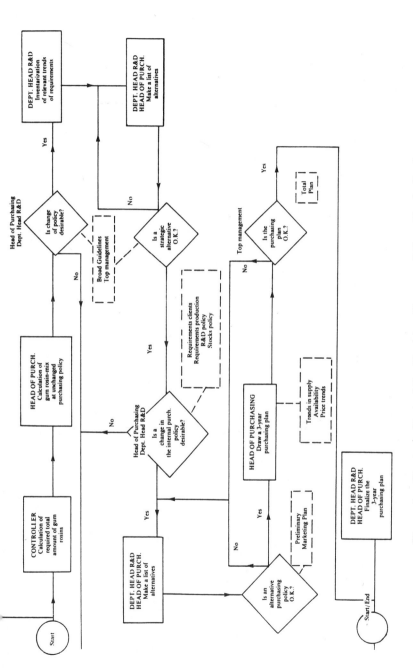

Figure 1. Strategic Part of the Decision Process of Gum Rosin Buying

211

The department head of R&D plays a coordinative role in the decision process on changes in printing inks throughout the drawing-up stage of the new procurement strategy. Factors influencing the development of a procurement strategy, which are studied carefully by the head of purchasing and the department head of R&D, include:

- availability of materials both from established and new suppliers,
- political environment,
- quality,
- price, and
- value.

When a draft procurement strategy has been established, the head of purchasing puts it in writing, and submits it to the company's accountant for approval.

Finalizing the 3-Year Procurement Plan

When the preliminary marketing plan is set, and agreement has been reached between the product group leader and top management on quantities, market prices, and corresponding profits, the final qualities of the products to be sold are translated by the financial department into quantities of gum rosins. Using these figures, the draft procurement plan is updated and submitted to top management for agreement.

Recurrent Purchases of Gum Rosin

Figure 2 describes the routine purchase of gum rosin. Routine buying decisions are made within the parameters of the overall purchasing plan. If there are unexpected problems, the decision makers refer to their experience in drawing up the strategic plan, and it is relatively simple to repeat it quickly. Top management may be consulted relatively quickly about this decision. When repeat purchases are consistent with the strategic plan, the head of purchasing or one of his subordinates will take the actions necessary for implementation. In this situation, the decision process is different from the earlier process. Fewer departments are involved and more is left to the discretion of the individual.

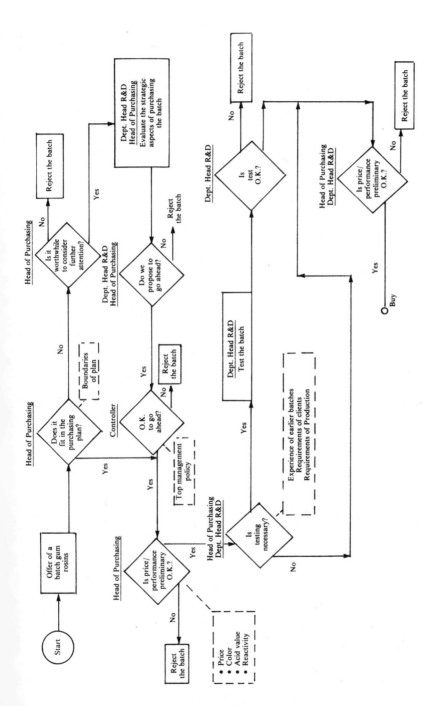

Figure 2. Operational Part of the Decision Process of Gum Rosin Buying

213

Implications for Purchasing and Marketing Management

The role of the head of the purchasing department is quite different in the strategic decision process than it is in the operational decision process. It is helpful to consider decision making as a 2-stage process. In the strategic decision process, the head of purchasing is to organize the decision-making process rather than to make the decision. In this sense, his task is fundamentally a "staff" function, and he relies upon its strength. Its strength must be derived from acquiring and processing data and managing the information-activities-persons process.

In the operational decision process, the head of purchasing is clearly a decision maker. Boundaries for making decisions, and the criteria to be used, have been formulated in the strategic plan.

Concerning communication strategy from suppliers, it is important for the firm to handle strategic information differently than operational information. Strategic information must be distributed as widely as possible. When a strategic plan is constructed and implemented, strategic input can be incorporated simultaneously with the drawing up of the strategic plan. It is important that the supplier employs a wide range of communication channels during the strategic part of the decision process. Apart from personal selling, public relations, advertising, seminars, and so forth may be used.

In the operational phase, the decision process involves less communication with fewer people. Personal visits and/or telephone calls are appropriate as a means to finalize the decision process.

COMMENTS

One characteristic element of the strategic decision process is the occurrence of frequent feedback loops, interferences, and dead ends. The extensive multi-stage descriptive model of Mintzberg, Raisinghani, and Theoret (1976) for "unstructured" strategic decision processes proved appropriate for the analysis of organizational buying decision processes of strategic importance with its many feedback loops, but also to analysis of the operational part of the decision process. The model provides the opportunity to add or omit feedback loops. It is also possible to investigate decision processes of groups as well as those of individuals. A shortcoming of the model is the absence of description and post-evaluation after the decision has been made. Conflict resolution is not considered explicitly in the model; it is restricted instead to political routines such as bargaining, persuasion, and cooperation.

How does the model of Mintzberg et al. compare with other models? In their descriptive research on decision processes, Farley, Hulbert, and Weinstein (1980) distinguish decision components as: input, communication, evaluation and recommendation, decision making, conflict resolution, decision implementation, and monitoring. In fact, they separate, more or less hierarchically ordered and loosely interrelated activities. For the operational part of a decision process, this is an appropriate method of analysis. But for a strategic decision process, with its dynamic character and feedback loops, the model of Mintzberg, Raisinghani, and Theoret (1976) seems more suitable, concentrating on decision substeps and how they are interrelated.

One specific characteristic of the type of markets examined in this research is the influence of the long-term activities of research and development of the company concerned, as well as the developments of the clients and the clients of their clients. The value of the "3-year operational plan" is that important inputs from previous years are taken into account. In the operational phase, one can concentrate on decision implementation. Because many of the long-term inputs are from persons other than the head of purchasing (especially from the R&D department), who has particular knowledge of the requirements of clients and production, concentrating the decision process on one process is relatively easy because decision processes have already been completed.

From the description of the decision processes, it is clear that the construction of the "3-year operational plan" is an exercise in double-loop learning (Argyris 1976) with characteristics of participation, power sharing, group discussions, and confronting alternative goals. It provides the basis for implementing decisions in a simple, single-loop learning process when no major changes in input occur. As the environment for making operational decisions becomes more complex, with greater uncertainties about availability, value, and so forth, a good strategic plan is increasingly important as input for daily decision making.

REFERENCES

Argyris, C. (1976). "Single-Loop and Double-Loop Models in Research on Decision Making." *Administrative Science Quarterly* 21(September): 363-377.

Farley, J.U., J.M. Hulbert, and D. Weinstein. (1980). "Price Setting and Volume
    Planning by Two European Industrial Companies: A Study and Comparison
    of Decision Processes." *Journal of Marketing* 44(Winter): 46-54.
Mintzberg, H., D. Raisinghani, and A. Theoret. (1976). "The Structure of 'Unstructured'
    Decision Processes." *Administrative Science Quarterly* 21(June): 266-275.

BUYING ABCD CHEMICAL:
ANALYZING PURCHASING DEVELOPMENT
IN A PHARMACEUTICAL FIRM FOR A
NEW PRODUCTION MATERIAL

Wouter Faes and Jacques de Rijcke

ABSTRACT

The ABCD case study reflects a situation of "Purchasing Development," the most creative and complex of all industrial buying decisions. In the case, Company Z, a highly innovative pharmaceutical firm, faces a new buy situation for raw material ABCD, a primary component needed in the production of a new drug. Anticipating favorable consumer acceptance of the drug (and pending FDA approval), Company Z plans an extensive marketing campaign to maximize awareness levels for the product. A key promotional component of the campaign is free sampling, thus raw materials are immediately necessary to fulfill the sampling requirements.

The most formidable challenge of the buying situation is that ABCD, a chemical raw material, is not readily available for sale on the market.

Advances in Business Marketing and Purchasing, Volume 5, pages 217-237.
ISBN: 1-55938-364-X

This fact initiated the formation of a purchasing team to closely assist the new product development team. The case follows the thorough examination of four possible solutions to the procurement problem. The success of Company Z can largely be attributed to its willingness to apply equal emphasis on innovation in purchasing management, as it does in all of its other functional areas.

SITUATION ANALYSIS

This case deals with the purchase of a new raw material in a previously uninvestigated market. This situation, in which a maximum of creativity must be exercised by the buyers and purchasing managers, is one of "Purchasing Development." This situation is shown in the lower right hand corner of a product market matrix, as indicated in Figure 1.

A case study within Company Z highlights this strategic situation in the pharmaceutical industry. Company Z is consistently at the center of new developments in markets. Since its founding in 1953, 70 new drugs have been developed in its research laboratories. Company Z employs 6,000 people worldwide and has 34 overseas subsidiaries. In 1961, the company was incorporated into a large American pharmaceutical group referred to as the "sister company." Purchasing in Company Z is recognized as a "strategic business function" (Lee and Dobler 1977), and this recognition is reflected by the fact that purchasing is administered by a vice-president who reports directly to the Board of Directors. This is illustrated in Figure 2. The internal structure of the company's purchasing department is illustrated in Figure 3.

SUPPLIER MARKET

PRODUCT

	Existing:	New:
Existing:	Straight Rebuy	Supplier Development
New:	Value Analysis Value Engineering	Purchasing Development

Figure 1.   Product/Supplier Market Matrix

Board of Directors				
Finance	Research	Purchasing	Sales	Production
	Process Development	Quality Control	Production	Production Planning

Figure 2. Company Z Organization

Purchasing Vice President	
Purchasing Manager A	Purchasing Manager B
—2 buyers for indirect production materials	—1 buyer raw material
—1 buyer diverse materials	—1 buyer capital goods
—1 buyer traffic	—1 buyer MRO-items

Figure 3. Structure of the Purchasing Department in the Selected Company (Z)

The 24 people employed by the purchasing department process approximately 33,000 orders each year, amounting to a total spending of 3.5 billion Belgian Francs (L3.6m). In Company Z, there is a very close working relationship between the new product development and purchasing departments. This is evident in the following case study and its buy-flow diagram.

A DESCRIPTIVE ANALYSIS OF THE PURCHASING PROCESS FOR RAW MATERIAL ABCD

The buying process for raw material ABCD (see Figure 4) was initiated when the sister company in the United States developed a new drug.

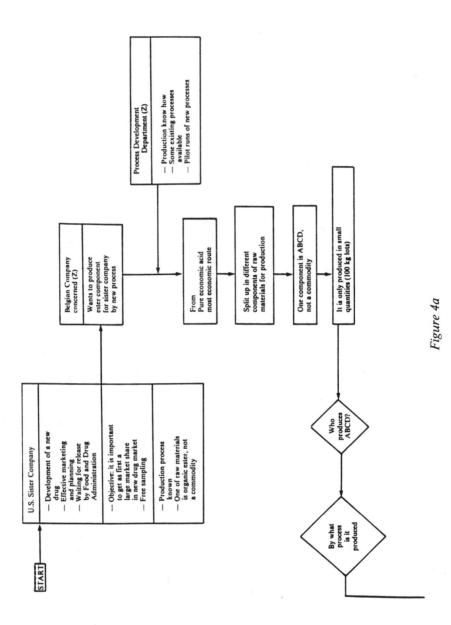

Figure 4a

220

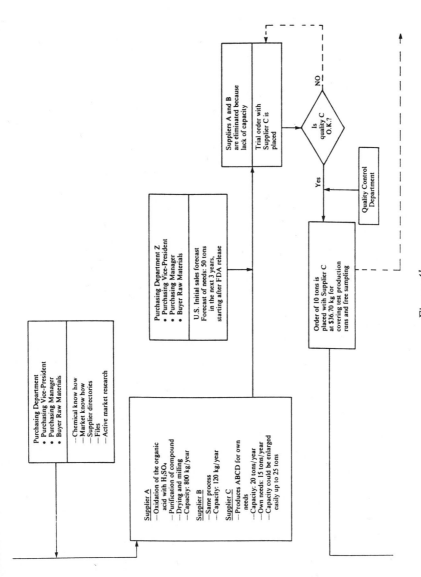

Purchasing Department
• Purchasing Vice-President
• Purchasing Manager
• Buyer Raw Materials

—Chemical know how
—Market know how
—Supplier directories
—Files
—Active market research

Supplier A
—Oxidation of the organic acid with H_2SO_4
—Purification of compound
—Drying and milling
—Capacity: 800 kg/year

Supplier B
—Same process
—Capacity: 120 kg/year

Supplier C
—Produces ABCD for own needs
—Capacity: 20 tons/year
—Own needs: 15 tons/year
—Capacity could be enlarged easily up to 25 tons

Purchasing Department Z
• Purchasing Vice-President
• Purchasing Manager
• Buyer Raw Materials

U.S. Initial sales forecast
Forecast of needs: 50 tons in the next 3 years, starting after FDA release

Suppliers A and B are eliminated because lack of capacity

Trial order with Supplier C is placed

Is quality C O.K.?

Yes   NO

Order of 10 tons is placed with Supplier C at $36.70 kg for covering test production runs and free sampling

Quality Control Department

Figure 4b

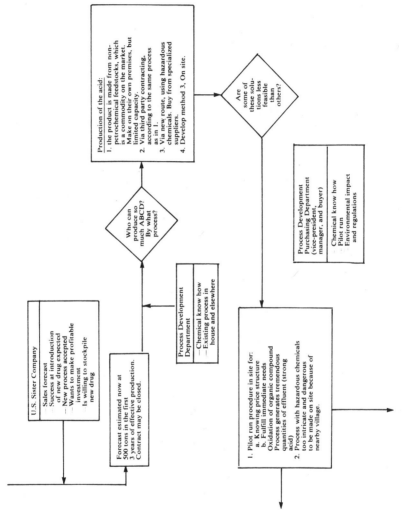

U.S. Sister Company

- Sales forecast
  - Success at introduction of new drug expected
  - New process accepted
  - Wants to make profitable investment
  - Is willing to stockpile new drug

Forecast estimated now at 500 tons in the first 3 years of effective production. Contract may be closed.

Process Development Department

- Chemical know how
- Existing process in house and elsewhere

Who can produce so much ABCD? By what process?

Production of the acid:

1. the product is made from non-petrochemical feedstocks, which is a commodity on the market. Make on their own premises, but limited capacity.
2. Via third party contracting, according to the same process as in 1.
3. Via new route, using hazardous chemicals. Buy from specialized suppliers.
4. Develop method 3, On site.

Are some of these solutions less feasible than others?

Process Development
Purchasing Department (vice-president, manager, and buyer)

- Chemical know how
- Pilot run
- Environmental impact and regulations

1. Pilot run procedure in site for:
   a. Knowing price structure
   b. Fulfill immediate needs
      Oxidation of organic compound
      Process generates tremendous quantities of effluent (strong acid)
2. Process with hazardous chemicals too intricate and dangerous to be made on site because of nearby village.

Figure 4c

222

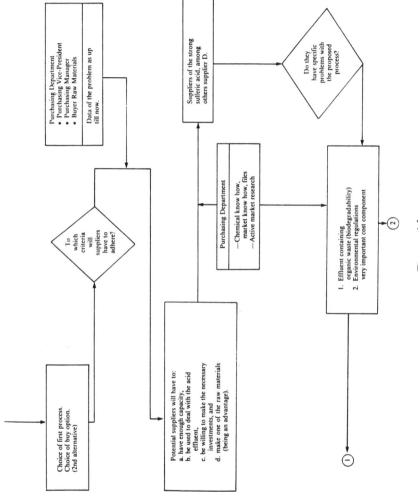

Figure 4d

Purchasing Department
• Purchasing Vice-President
• Purchasing Manager
• Buyer Raw Materials

Data of the problem as up till now.

To which criteria will suppliers have to adhere?

Choice of first process. Choice of buy option. (2nd alternative)

Potential suppliers will have to:
a. have enough capacity,
b. be used to deal with the acid effluent,
c. be willing to make the necessary investments, and
d. make one of the raw materials (being an advantage).

Suppliers of the strong sulfuric acid, among others supplier D.

Do they have specific problems with the proposed process?

Purchasing Department
—Chemical know how, market know how, files
—Active market research

1. Effluent containing organic waste (biodegradability)
2. Environmental regulations very important cost component

① ②

223

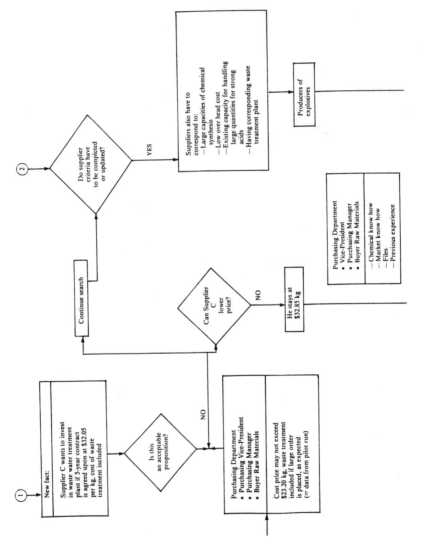

Figure 4e

224

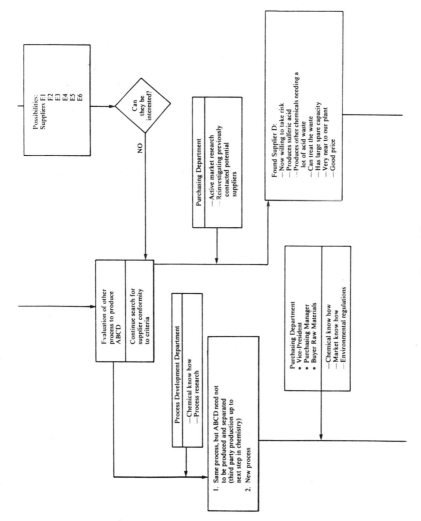

Possibilities:
Suppliers E1
E2
E3
E4
E5
E6

Can they be interested?

NO

Evaluation of other process to produce ABCD

Continue search for supplier conformity to criteria

Purchasing Department
— Active market research
— Reinvestigating previously contacted potential suppliers

Process Development Department
— Chemical know how
— Process research

1. Same process, but ABCD need not to be produced and separated (third party production up to next step in chemistry)
2. New process

Found Supplier D:
— Now willing to take risk
— Produces sulferic acid
— Produces other chemicals needing a lot of acid waste
— Can treat the waste
— Has large spare capacity
— Very near to our plant
— Good price

Purchasing Department
• Vice-President
• Purchasing Manager
• Buyer Raw Materials
— Chemical know how
— Market know how
— Environmental regulations

Figure 4f

225

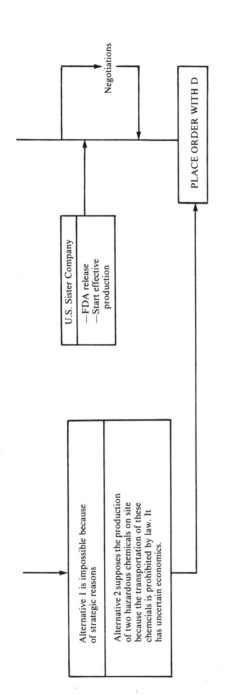

Alternative 1 is impossible because of strategic reasons

Alternative 2 supposes the production of two hazardous chemicals on site because the transportation of these chemicals is prohibited by law. It has uncertain economics.

PLACE ORDER WITH D

Negotiations

U.S. Sister Company

—FDA release
—Start effective production

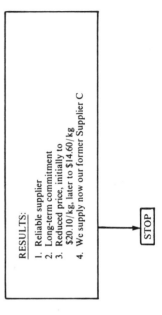

RESULTS:
1. Reliable supplier
2. Long-term commitment
3. Reduced price, initially to $20.10/kg, later to $14.60/kg
4. We supply now our former Supplier C

STOP

Figure 4g

226

The sister company predicted that the new drug, when released by the U.S. Food and Drug Administration, would be an immediate success in the market; therefore, the company was planning an effective marketing campaign for the new product. The company realized that if the drug was to be a success later in its life cycle, it needed to gain a large share of the market during its introduction. Therefore, free sampling on a large scale was a major element in the sales plan. A large quantity of the drug would have to be produced to fulfill both sampling requirements and the requirements of the market during its initial processing. The sister company was familiar with the production process for the drug and felt that it had a problem with one of the raw materials. This raw material was an organic ester not readily available as a commodity on the market. The process was then analyzed in terms of its various raw material components. One component required was ABCD, a chemical raw material not readily sold on the market.

A team was formed in the purchasing department, consisting of the purchasing vice-president, one of his purchasing managers (manager B in Figure 3), and the raw materials buyer. This team was assigned the task of sourcing ABCD and analyzing the way ABCD was currently being produced. Together, the three members of the buying team had an excellent knowledge of chemicals and this was a great asset in the search process. The search initially involved an examination of vendor files and supplier directories, but was rapidly expanded to include an active analysis of the market. The team discovered three possible suppliers, who produced ABCD in small quantities, primarily in 100 kg. lots:

- Supplier A produced ABCD through an oxidation process combining an organic acid with sulphuric acid. The compound was then purified, dried, and milled. Supplier A had a capacity of about 800 kg per year.
- Supplier B produced ABCD in the same way as A, but had a capacity of only 120 kg per year.
- Supplier C produced ABCD for its own internal needs of about 15 tons (15,000 kg) per year. Supplier C had a capacity of 20 tons (20,000 kg) per year, but this could be raised to 215 tons (25,000 kg). Therefore, the maximum spare capacity was between 5 and 10 tons (5,000 and 10,000 kg) per year.

The sister company forecasted a need for about 40 tons (50,000 kg) of ABCD over the first three years of effective production after the FDA released the drug. The buying team excluded suppliers A and B from further consideration because of their lack of capacity. A trial order placed with supplier C was tested in the quality control department and proved satisfactory. Consequently, an order for 10 tons (10,000 kg) of ABCD was placed with supplier C at the price of $36.70 per kg. This price covered trial production runs (for material tests) and the free sampling campaign requirements.

The sister company expected sales of the drug in the United States to be unusually high. Therefore, once it had approved the production process, it was willing to stockpile the new drug. Because the sales forecast for the drug was so promising, the sister company increased the amount of ABCD ordered to 500 tons (500,000 kg) for the first three years of effective production. This revised estimate was a tenfold increase over the original one.

Company Z was now faced with a dramatic and strategic problem: Who could produce such massive amounts of ABCD? To solve this problem, the process development and purchasing teams would have to be creative. They needed a relatively new product from a supplier who would not yet have the necessary technical expertise for ABCD production (= purchasing development). Company Z's process development department began by compiling a list of possible solutions. The list was based in the department's knowledge of chemicals and its familiarity with both internal and external processes. Four solutions emerged.

First, the product could be made by Company Z from food-stuffs available as commodities on the market; or alternatively, this process could be contracted out to a third party. A second set of alternatives would be to produce the product using hazardous chemicals purchased from specialized suppliers. Finally, ABCD could be manufactured using this same process, but with the hazardous chemicals manufactured on-site.

The new product development department worked with the purchasing team on a pilot run of the first solution, on-site. The text run had two main objectives: to fulfill immediate requirements and to gain insight into the costs associated with the production of ABCD. Unfortunately, the pilot run was unsuccessful. The capacity of the process was limited and large quantities of strongly acidic effluent were generated.

The second process involving hazardous chemicals was quickly eliminated because it was too dangerous, if carried out on-site. In particular, environmental dangers would increase if the chemicals were produced on-site. A village was situated nearby and chemical regulations were very stringent.

Faced with the choice between the two sets of alternatives, Company Z opted for the first alternative, with the work contracted out to a third party.

The purchasing team drew up a list of characteristics for potential suppliers. They should:

1. have sufficient spare capacity,
2. have experience in dealing with the strongly acidic effluent generated during the production process, and
3. be willing to make any necessary investment.

If the supplier was already manufacturing one of the other raw materials for the process, they would have an additional advantage.

The purchasing team thought that suppliers of strong sulphuric acid would be able to deal with the manufacturing problems of compound ABCD. However, the suppliers encountered several unique problems with the process. First, the strongly acidic effluent that was generated had a low biodegradability rate, and if they decided to initiate the process, environmental regulations would force the suppliers to assume extra costs in order to bring the effluent up to an acceptable biodegradability range. Supplier D, for example, was not willing to invest time and money into research on eliminating this problem.

At this point, discussions with Supplier C revealed that the company was willing to invest in a new water waste treatment plant, which would raise the biodegradability of the effluent to an acceptable range if Company Z agreed to a five-year purchasing contract at the price of $32.85 per kg. This price included the cost of waste treatment.

The purchasing team had gained insight into the cost/price structure of ABCD during the pilot runs and felt that this offer was not acceptable. Company Z hoped to place large orders later on and felt that $23.20 per kg was a more reasonable price. The purchasing team tried to resolve the situation in two ways. They encouraged Supplier C to reduce its price; at the same time, they continued searching for other potential suppliers with the essential capabilities, namely:

- large capacities for chemical synthesis,
- low overhead costs,

- an existing capacity for handling large quantities of strong acids, and
- a corresponding water waste treatment plant, so that new investments were not necessary (this was not available with Supplier C).

These new criteria were updated from the previous list of characteristics. They were selected by the purchasing team on the basis of previous experience, chemical expertise, files and active market research. The first solution was not feasible; Supplier C refused to lower its price of $32.85 per kg. The second solution appeared to favor producers of explosives. There were six in existence, but none were currently producing or could be persuaded to produce ABCD.

Faced with these problems, the purchasing team asked the process development department to investigate new potential production processes for ABCD. At the same time, it continued its active market research to locate possible suppliers producing ABCD via the newly proposed route, matching the previously mentioned characteristics. Process development proposed two new alternatives:

1. The production process could be moved one stage back in chemical terms, so that ABCD would no longer be needed.
2. A new process could be developed.

Company Z now had to choose between the alternatives. The first one was dismissed for strategic reasons. The second one required that two hazardous chemicals be produced on-site because their transportation was prohibited by law. Further, costs were difficult to estimate.

The purchasing team carried out active market research and reinvestigated all previously contacted suppliers. It was discovered that Supplier D was now willing to take the risk involved in research and to produce ABCD in accordance with the previously proposed process. Supplier D had sufficient spare capacity and also had a waste treatment plant, which was used in the production of sulphuric acid and other related chemicals to deal with acid waste. The supplier was also situated nearby. After completing negotiations, Company Z placed an order for production at an initial price of $20.10 per kg.

The extensive search process carried out by the purchasing and process development department lasted almost two years, and led to the development of a reliable source for ABCD, with long-term commitment. Today, Supplier C also supplies Company Z with ABCD at a price of $14.60 per kg. Compared to the original price of $36.70 per kg, this represents a savings of 60% over the initial price, amounting to total savings of L4,293,000 for purchases of 500 tons in three years. This process is described in Figure 5.

STRATEGIC IMPLICATIONS

From a detailed analysis of the purchasing process, some tentative theoretical remarks can be made. Note that the research only covered one purchase in a company that emphasizes innovation in purchasing management as well as in other functional areas. Therefore, the importance of the purchasing function may be overstated. The following conclusions are most relevant to the search and evaluation phase of the buying process.

The first conclusion is that the sooner the purchasing department becomes involved in a new product team, the better the cost control of materials will be. Purchasing must be able to perform its role as a gatekeeper for market information in innovation processes freely and actively, if reduced purchasing costs for a new product (in this case, drug) are to be realized. This confirms earlier research done by Mogee and Bean (1976), and highlights the negative implications which evolve if purchasing is not involved in the innovation process.

Gatekeeper roles were formerly attributed to all groups positioned at the boundaries between the organization and its environment by Allen and Cohen (1969), Ozanne and Churchill (1971), and Douds (1971). From a positive point of view, the situation supports the thesis presented by Gronhaug (1979), that is, in organizational buying behavior, effective cost reduction can be achieved only if coalitions are formed between purchasing and product development people (in this case, the new product development department). This can be achieved only when two conditions hold.

1. More individuals (especially from purchasing) are included in innovative and strategic decisions, and the resources of people who have different orientations are pooled. This results in a broader range of decision possibilities and can enhance results.
2. Joint decision making in purchasing has a positive correlation with the amount of purchasing research undertaken to find more acceptable alternatives.

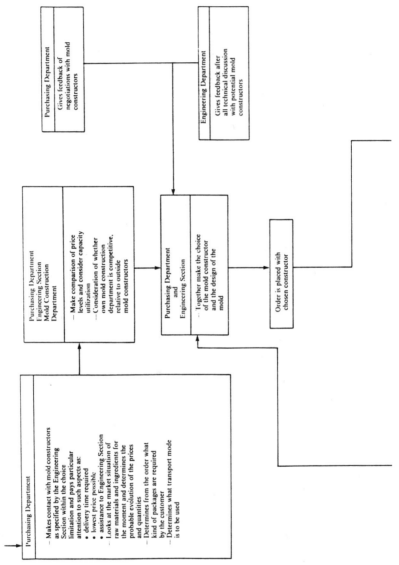

Figure 5a

232

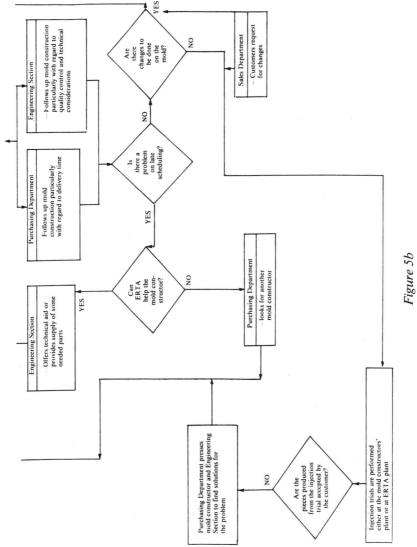

Figure 5b

233

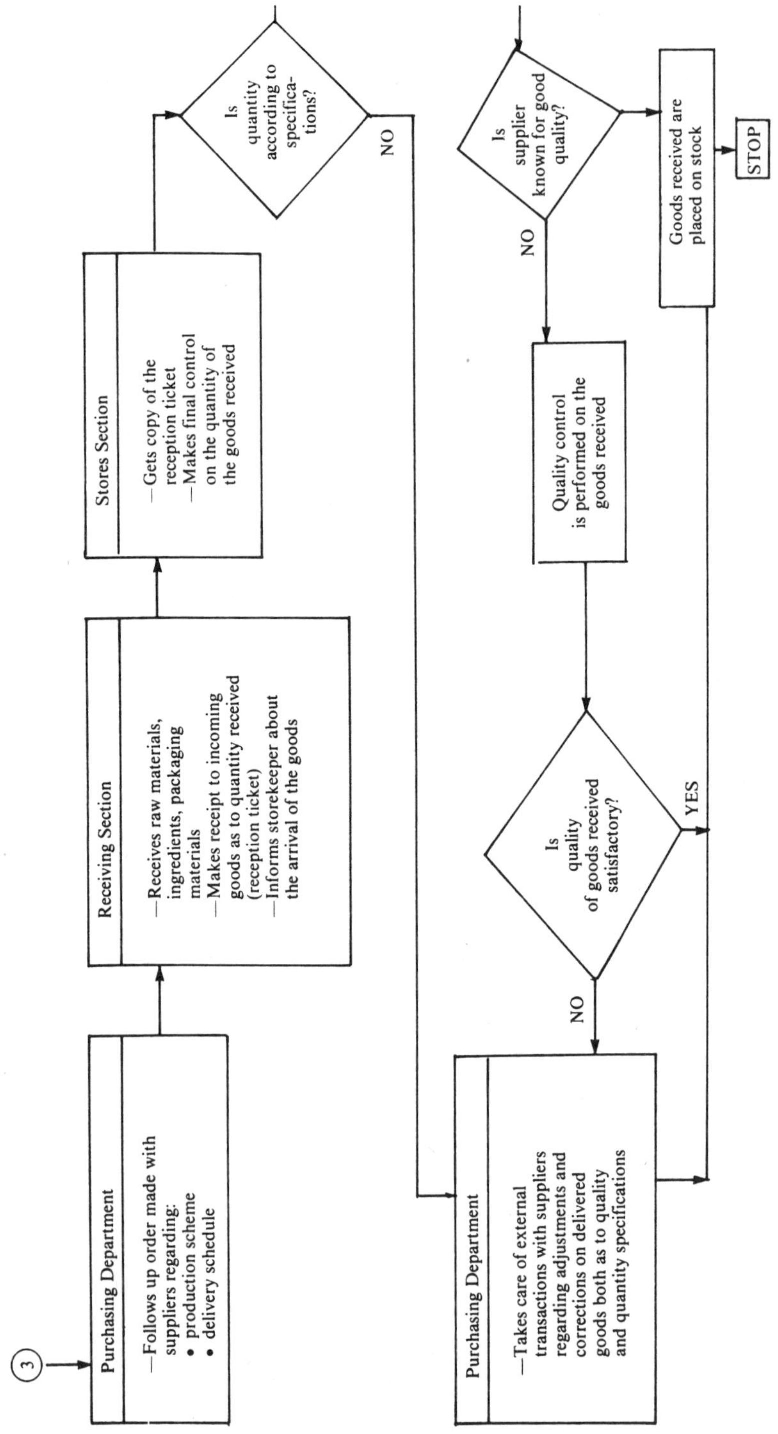
3
Purchasing Department
—Follows up order made with suppliers regarding:
• production scheme
• delivery schedule
Receiving Section
—Receives raw materials, ingredients, packaging materials
—Makes receipt to incoming goods as to quantity received (reception ticket)
—Informs storekeeper about the arrival of the goods
Stores Section
—Gets copy of the reception ticket
—Makes final control on the quantity of the goods received
Is quantity according to specifica- tions?
NO
Is supplier known for good quality?
NO
Goods received are placed on stock
STOP
Quality control is performed on the goods received
Is quality of goods received satisfactory?
YES
NO
Purchasing Department
—Takes care of external transactions with suppliers regarding adjustments and corrections on delivered goods both as to quality and quantity specifications

Figure 5c

The positive effects of close cooperation between purchasing and process development will increase if purchasing is considered to be a full partner during the early stages of the purchasing process and during the process specification stage. According to Kraljic (1981), such close cooperation is only possible if the purchasing people have both the sound commercial knowledge and sufficient technical knowledge to be respected by the R&D people. In this case study, the three people involved in the purchasing team had sufficient knowledge of chemicals to be accepted.

The organizational buying process appears to evolve over time, as indicated by Webster and Wind (1973) and Nicosia and Wind (1977). The composition of the decision-making unit was unstable from stage to stage, complicating the task of industrial marketers. The continuous interdepartmental consultation and harmony between the new product development and purchasing departments during specific buy phases (especially in the second part of Figure 4) support this hypothesis. The hypothesis was tested previously by Spekman (1977), Bradley (1977), and Kelly (1974).

A third set of conclusions are possible about the strategic decision making process, as this case concerns a purchasing development situation. According to the typology of Mintzberg, Raisinghani, and Theoret (1976) the buy process provides an excellent example of a basic design decision process on the purchasing side. Complex and innovative solutions to the problem of producing ABCD were implemented with little interruption or delay in the process. Furthermore, the process was initiated by marketing opportunities rather than by problems—a characteristic typical of this situation. Problems became the primary stimulus for repetitive phases of search, screen, and selection of alternatives only in the later stages.

Throughout the various stages of the purchasing process in this case study, individual theories have been validated. For example, active search was triggered principally by a combination of opportunities and problems. A screening routine was used to reduce the number of possible alternatives to a number of actual possibilities. Cyert and March (1963) and Soelberg (1967) described this as an intricate part of the search process, thus supporting the theory proposed by the authors that search and evaluation are performed simultaneously.

Most of the time was devoted to the selection stage. During this stage, evaluative procedures such as pilot or test runs were carried out. Dynamic decision processes were used.

The repetitive process of searching, evaluating and selecting is typical of the basic decision process; the normal limitations of linear decision processes were thus avoided. As Kennedy (1982) observed, separate decisions in the buy flow appear to be incremental in nature. Each major decision constitutes the basis for later decisions.

Consequently, decisions made at an earlier stage in the process limit the possibilities for those at the next stage of the process. By repeating the search process several times, the limitations are eliminated because the discussion is reopened at one of the first stages of the decision flow.

This phenomenon occurred in the case study at the end of the flow chart, where the processes assumed a more administrative nature. Concerning the general model, the stages cannot be delineated as easily as proposed. This is particularly apparent during the early stages (before RFQs are sent out), which may be repeated several times before a satisfactory result is achieved. This problem is central to strategic new buy situations, where the search process continues until the final evaluation of the supplier has taken place and their first delivery has been completed. This problem, occurring in new buy situations, may be solved by increasing the number of feedback loops. In rebuy situations, feedback loops are less frequent.

REFERENCES

Allen, T., and S. Cohen. (1969). "Information Flow in an R&D Laboratory." *Administrative Science Quarterly* 14(March): 12-19.

Bradley, M.F. (1977). "Buying Behavior in Ireland's Public Sector." *Industrial Marketing Management* 6(August): 251-258.

Capon, N., J.U. Farley, and J. Hulbert. (1975). "Pricing and Forecasting in an Oligopoly Firm." *Journal of Management Studies* 12(May): 133-136.

Cyert, T.M. and J.G. March. (1963). *Behavioral Theory of the Firm*. Englewood Cliffs, NJ: Prentice-Hall.

Douds, D.F. (1971). "The State of the Art in the Study of Technology Transfer—A Brief Survey." *R&D Management* (January):125-131.

Gronhaug, D. (1979). "Power in Organizational Buying." *Human Relations* 32:159-180.

Gronhaug, K. (1975). "Search Behavior in Organizational Buying." *Industrial Marketing Management* 4:15-23.

Howard, J.A., J.M. Hulbert, and J.V. Farley. (1975). "Organizational Analysis and Information System Design: A Decision Process Perspective." *Journal of Business Research* (April): 21-38.

Kelly, P. (1974). "Functions Performed in Industrial Purchase Decisions with Implications for Marketing Strategy." *Journal of Business Research* 2(October): 421-433.

Kennedy, A.K. (1982). "The Complex Decision to Select A Supplier: A Case Study." *Industrial Marketing Management* 12: 45-56.

Kraljic, P. (1981). *Strategic Purchasing Management: A Must*. The Netherlands: Discussion Buunderkamp (June).

Lee, L. and D.W. Dobler. (1977). *Purchasing and Materials Management Text and Cases*. Englewood Cliffs, NJ: Prentice-Hall.

Mintzberg, H., D. Raisinghani, and A. Theoret. (1976). "The Structure of Unstructured Decision Processes." *Administrative Science Quarterly* 21(June): 246-275.

Mogee, M.E. and A.S. Bean. (1976). "The Role of the Purchasing Agent in Industrial Innovation." *Industrial Marketing Management* 5: 221-229.

Nicosia, F.M. and J. Wind. (1977). "Emerging Models of Organizational Buying Processes." *Industrial Marketing Management* 6: 353-369.

Ozanne, U., and W. Churchill. (1971). "Adoption Research: Information Sources in the Industrial Purchasing Decision." *Journal of Marketing Research* 8(August): 322-328.

Robey, D. and W.J. Johnson. (1977). "Lateral Influences and Vertical Authority in Organizational Buying." *Industrial Marketing Management* 6: 451-462.

Soelberg, P.O. (1967). "Unprogrammed Decision Making." *Industrial Management Review* 8(Spring): 19-29.

Spekman, R.E. (1977). "A Contingency Approach to Power Relationships Within the Industrial Buying Task Group." Unpublished Ph.D. thesis, Northwestern University, Evanston, IL.

Starbuk, W.H. (1976). "Organizations and Their Environments." In *Handbook of Industrial and Organizational Psychology*, edited by M.D. Dunnette. Chicago, IL: Rand McNally.

Webster, F.E. and Y. Wind. (1973). *Organizational Buying Behavior*. Englewood Cliffs, NJ: Prentice-Hall.

ERTA PLASTICS CUSTOMER
SPECIFIED TOOLING EQUIPMENT:
THE CASE FOR INJECTION—MOLDING

Wouter Faes and T. Ireneo

ABSTRACT

This case study concentrates on a recent injection-molding buying decision by ERTA Plastics, a leading Belgian manufacturer of engineering plastics. Generally, customer requests for quotations initiate the company production to order process. Thus, ERTA often acts as a subcontractor, and to win a contract must offer a competitive bid. Clearly, if a purchasing department is notified immediately of the goals, and timing of a particular marketing project, it will have optimal flexibility in negotiating price and delivery specifications with potential suppliers. Unfortunately, as the case illustrates, a failure to involve purchasing from the beginning of a project can result in poor interorganizational relations. The organizational buying process for ERTA is complex, and involves two distinct stages: (1) design and planning and (2) the executional stage. In the first stage, several feedback

Advances in Business Marketing and Purchasing, Volume 5, pages 239-260.
ISBN: 1-55938-364-X

loops between departments are evident, and the purchasing department acts strictly as a gatekeeper to the external supply market. It is in the executional stage that purchasing becomes the primary participant. The actual purchasing process was rather structured, thus the case reflects the significance of previous buy stages.

SITUATION ANALYSIS

ERTA Plastics N.V. is located in Tielt, Belgium. The firm was founded in 1933, and has been a member of the Dutch Group D.S.M. (Dutch State Mines) since 1978. The company specializes in the production of engineering plastics and is ranked among the world's leading manufacturers.

Their current product range reflects 45 years of experience and research. They currently have six different product lines:

1. the production of semi-finished products, such as polyamide (Ectalon), polyathylene (Ertolene), acetal (Ertacetal), and polyathylene-terraphtalate (Ertalyte) in the form of rods, round blocks, rectangular bars, plates, tubular bars, and so forth (these semi-finished products are produced by the production processes of extrusion);
2. the production of machine finished products, such as bearings, gears, rollers and fittings, starting with their own semi-finished products;
3. the production of castings of polyamide, such as industrial wheels and casters;
4. the production of extruded industrial profiles, of engineering plastics in the machining department;
5. the production of molds and precision tools for the injection molding department; and
6. the injection molding department, which produces a variety of technical parts. The company's organizational chart is presented in Figure 1.

The internal organization of the purchasing department is presented in Figure 2. The purchasing manager, Mr. Van Steenkiste, deals with raw materials and all large equipment purchases. Buyer A, Mrs. Large, is responsible for raw material repeat purchases. Buyer B, Mr. De La Fontaine, carries out any technical buying, as well as the purchase of

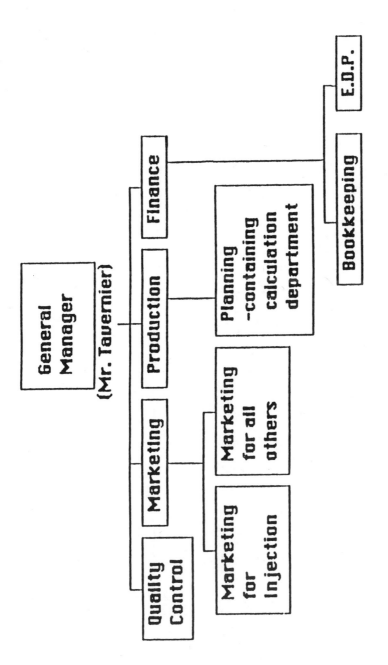

Figure 1. Organization Chart: ERTA Plastics N.V.

241

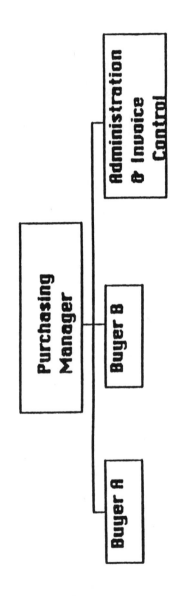

Figure 2. Purchasing Organization at ERTA Plastics N.V.

242

packaging materials. Mr. De La Fontaine is currently working with Mrs. Van Dierdonck (invoice control) on a computerized system for administering the purchasing function. At ERTA Plastics there are two different buying situations for injection-molded products: production to order and other items produced for stock.

Production to Order

Production to order is initiated by requests from customers for quotations for specific contracts. In this case, ERTA acts as a subcontractor and must quote a competitive price to get the contract. This bid price includes raw material costs, mold costs, packaging, and other costs.

The raw material may be specified by the customer, or the customer may ask ERTA to suggest materials for specific applications. ERTA will then test these in a trial run. Raw material costs may include the additional costs of material coloring or additives.

The calculation of mold costs is based on information provided by the customer. Critical factors include the estimated production quantity per year and the performance specifications. There are a variety of ways in which the molds may be produced. In some situations, it is appropriate to design a mold to produce single items; in others, the mold is more effective if it is designed to produce more than one item at a time. The design of the mold depends upon the expected volume of output over the life of the mold.

Once calculations have been completed, the sales department sends a quotation to the customer specifying the time period of the quotation. If the initial bid is rejected, internal discussion may develop on ways to reduce costs and bid a lower price. If this happens, purchasing has less time to procure the necessary raw materials before final delivery is due.

The purchasing planning process is complex, and the ERTA staff is fully aware that winning the contract depends primarily on the initial bid price and delivery date. Negotiation of the bid price internally between marketing, purchasing, and production reduces the flexibility of purchasing in the "real" buying phase. Planning for delivering on time becomes more complicated, and it has been said that buying in the injection molding business calls for "miracle buyers." ERTA must often work according to customer specifications, and this creates additional problems. The stock of raw materials which is held for injection molding currently turns over four times per year, compared to the company average of turning over six times per year.

Production for Stock (for Other Production Processes)

When producing for stock, Mr. Van Steenkiste contends that ERTA can be reasonably accurate in forecasting the company's raw material requirements. This forecast is based on the company's production plan and frequency of use; quantity of use and time of use are known variables. In producing for stock, there are maximum and minimum stock levels. These lead to a more effectively planned purchasing process, less hectic negotiations with outside suppliers, and increased flexibility for the purchasing department. Stock turnover is about ten or eleven times per year, so costs are lower than those for subcontract business.

This case study concentrates on a recent injection molding buying decision. The case involved a complex buy flow, including internal negotiations, because of the peculiar nature of the subcontract.

STAGE 1: ANALYSIS OF THE BUY FLOW FOR PLASTIC MOLDING PURCHASE OF RAW MATERIALS AND MOLDS

Recognition of Need to Purchase (Inquiry from Customer)

The purchase of raw materials by ERTA is generally motivated by events external to the firm. The stimulus comes from the sales department when they receive an inquiry from a customer for a particular product (e.g., kidney dialysis filters). The customer provides the specifications for the product—drawings with the required dimensions and tolerances and the material specification. The customer may define precisely the raw materials to be used (e.g., SAN 368F), or may allow ERTA to use substitute materials with performances similar to those specified (e.g., SAN or "equal").

Based on their past experience with raw materials from specific suppliers and material tests, the engineering section of the production department, and the purchasing department work together to determine the optimum specification of raw materials. Potential substitutes are compared regarding price, and the sales department comments on the customer's probable response to alternative quotations which could be made.

The finance section of the production department then predicts the unit cost. This calculation is based on the price of raw materials (provided by the purchasing department), the costs of any additives, packaging costs, and transportation costs. This calculation provides the basis for the offer made to the customer through the sales department.

If the customer accepts the initial offer, the order is received. If he does not, the sales department requests a re-examination of the costs. At the same time, they try to determine whether there were other reasons that the order was lost.

After costs are reviewed, the purchasing department negotiates with suppliers in an attempt to obtain better raw material prices. At the same time, the production department considers the possibility of adjusting any internally absorbed costs. If it is not possible to reduce prices after both external and internal negotiations are completed, no further offer is made to the customer. If price reductions are possible, a new offer is sent to the customer through the sales department. The number of adjustments of the offer depends on the firm's ability to negotiate better prices for its own raw materials. This may vary from two to seven adjustments, depending on the complexity of the product manufactured (see Figure 3).

STAGE 2: THE PURCHASE OF MOLDS AND RAW MATERIALS, AND THE NECESSARY PACKAGING AND TRANSPORTATION REQUIREMENTS

Buying After the Contract Is Awarded

Once an order has been placed, the sales department is responsible for ensuring that the order continues to match the customer's needs in terms of payment, delivery, quality, and so forth. The E.D.P. section prepared the necessary documentation, including the order acknowledgement.

Upon receipt of the order document prepared by the E.D.P. section, the planning section of the production department provides the purchasing department with the appropriate information. In the case of the mold itself, the engineering section specifies a delivery date and a restricted number of mold manufacturers who are considered to be suitable. The purchasing department also receives details of the raw material requirements, packaging materials, and transportation needs.

When the purchasing department receives this information, contact is made with the mold manufacturers specified by engineering. Particular attention is paid to delivery time, low prices, and engineering support. Purchasing also studies the current market situation for raw materials and other factors, to estimate the eventual probable costs. Finally, the department considers packaging and transportation requirements.

The ERTA company is then faced with the choice of sourcing the mold externally or internally. If it sources internally, then its own mold construction department must be competitive in order to be included on the list of bidders. The final selection of mold constructor and mold design is made by the purchasing department in conjunction with the engineering section. This decision is based on information accumulated by purchasing during its negotiations with the mold constructors and information from engineering gained through technical discussions with mold manufacturers. Once the choice has been made, an order is placed with the mold manufacturer.

During the mold construction phase, purchasing monitors delivery performance, while engineering monitors quality control, offering assistance to the mold manufacturer if a problem which would delay completion is encountered. If the customer needs to make any changes, these are made on the condition that the customer pays for any adjustments to the price.

When the mold is ready for delivery, it is inspected. Inspection trials determine whether the final component produced by the mold for the customer is acceptable. This process is repeated until the customer is satisfied. At this point, the mold is delivered to ERTA.

A pilot series of parts are then produced so that the customer can make the first prototype of his finished product (in this case, the kidney dialysis apparatus). Tests on the pilot series are conducted in the customer's factory and, if the results are satisfactory, then the first order schedule of the customer is completed.

At this time, purchasing is reviewing the final details concerning prices of raw materials with the supplier in an effort to come to a "gentleman's agreement." Where possible, orders from different customers are combined so that orders of larger quantities may be placed; this results in greater opportunities for negotiation of prices and longer production runs.

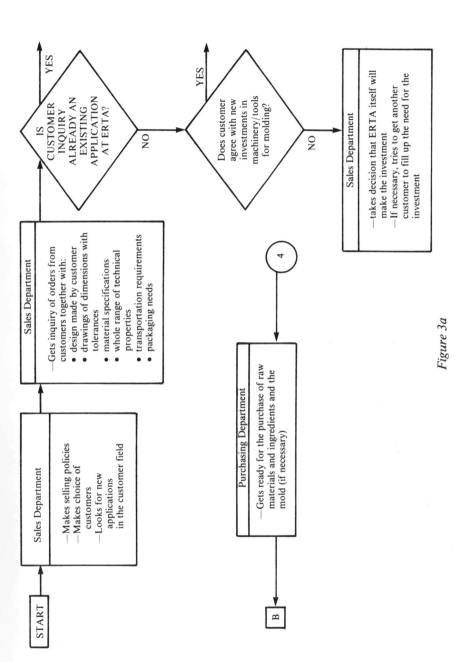

START

Sales Department

—Makes selling policies
—Makes choice of customers
—Looks for new applications in the customer field

Sales Department

—Gets inquiry of orders from customers together with:
  • design made by customer
  • drawings of dimensions with tolerances
  • material specifications
  • whole range of technical properties
  • transportation requirements
  • packaging needs

IS CUSTOMER INQUIRY ALREADY AN EXISTING APPLICATION AT ERTA?

YES

NO

Does customer agree with new investments in machinery/tools for molding?

YES

NO

Sales Department

—takes decision that ERTA itself will make the investment
—If necessary, tries to get another customer to fill up the need for the investment

Purchasing Department

—Gets ready for the purchase of raw materials and ingredients and the mold (if necessary)

4

B

Figure 3a

247

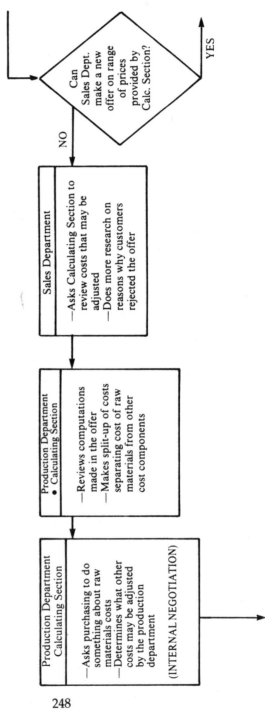

Can Sales Dept. make a new offer on range of prices provided by Calc. Section?

NO

YES

Sales Department

—Asks Calculating Section to review costs that may be adjusted
—Does more research on reasons why customers rejected the offer

---

Production Department
• Calculating Section

—Reviews computations made in the offer
—Makes split-up of costs separating cost of raw materials from other cost components

---

Production Department
Calculating Section

—Asks purchasing to do something about raw materials costs
—Determines what other costs may be adjusted by the production department

(INTERNAL NEGOTIATION)

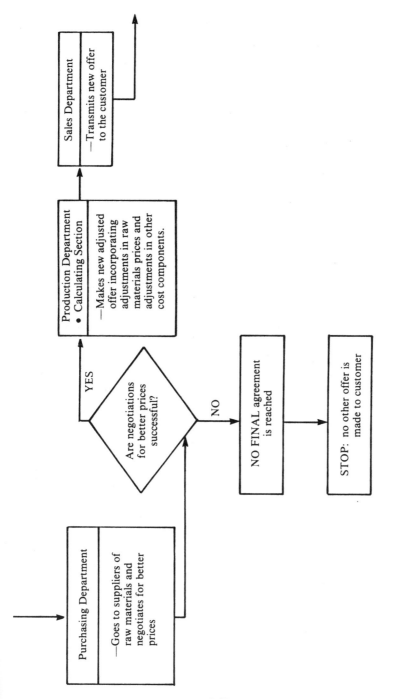

Sales Department
—Transmits new offer to the customer

Production Department
• Calculating Section
—Makes new adjusted offer incorporating adjustments in raw materials prices and adjustments in other cost components.

YES

Are negotiations for better prices successful?

NO

NO FINAL agreement is reached

STOP: no other offer is made to customer

Purchasing Department
—Goes to suppliers of raw materials and negotiates for better prices

Figure 3b

249

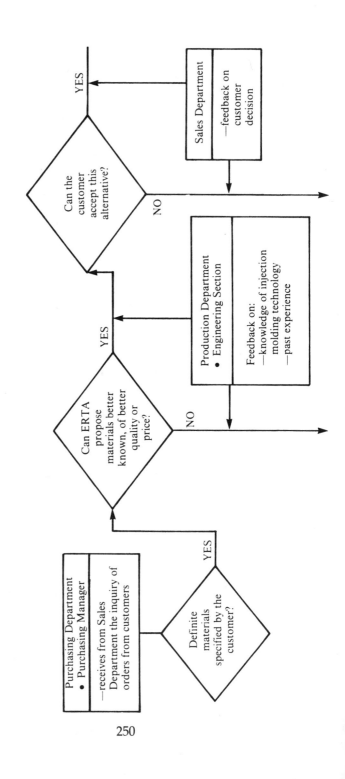

250

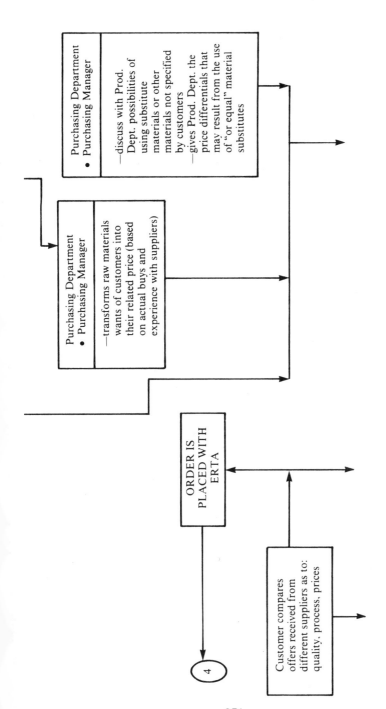

Purchasing Department
• Purchasing Manager

—discuss with Prod. Dept. possibilities of using substitute materials or other materials not specified by customers
—gives Prod. Dept. the price differentials that may result from the use of "or equal" material substitutes

Purchasing Department
• Purchasing Manager

—transforms raw materials wants of customers into their related price (based on actual buys and experience with suppliers)

ORDER IS PLACED WITH ERTA

4

Customer compares offers received from different suppliers as to: quality, process, prices

Figure 3c

251

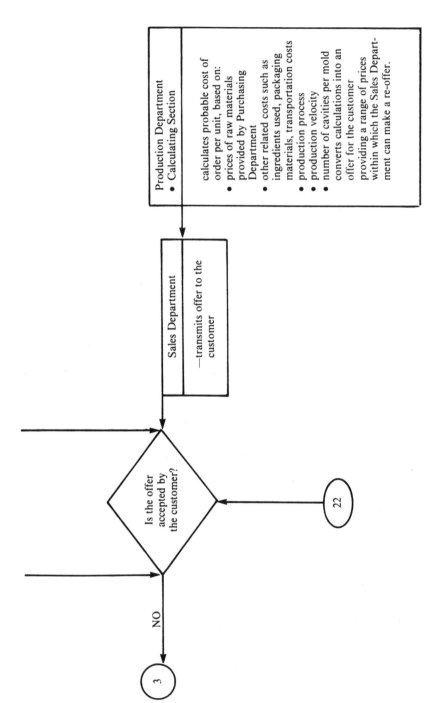

Production Department
• Calculating Section

calculates probable cost of
order per unit, based on:
• prices of raw materials
  provided by Purchasing
  Department
• other related costs such as
  ingredients used, packaging
  materials, transportation costs
• production process
• production velocity
• number of cavities per mold
converts calculations into an
offer for the customer
providing a range of prices
within which the Sales Department can make a re-offer.

Sales Department

—transmits offer to the
customer

Is the offer
accepted by
the customer?

22

NO

3

Figure 3d

252

Concerning packaging materials, purchasing first tries to determine the packaging requirement of the customer. If the packaging requirement is standard, then a fixed quantity is ordered, based on the storekeeper's inventory records. If the packaging requirement is specific to a particular order, then the quantity ordered will match production planning estimates.

When the receiving section at ERTA receives the goods (raw materials/ingredients/ packaging materials), the quantity is checked through a reception ticket. The storekeeper is then informed about the arrival of the goods and, after receiving a copy of the reception ticket, he checks the quantity of the goods again as a means of final control. The goods are subject to quality control inspections only if the supplier is not reputed to have good quality performance. After the goods have been checked for quantity and quality, they are placed in stock. If the goods fail either check, purchasing is responsible for all external transactions with the supplier regarding adjustments to the delivered goods (see Figure 4).

STRATEGIC CONCLUSIONS

A more detailed analysis of the purchasing process for components leads to some conclusions about the role of the purchasing function and of the purchasing decision process in many companies. The situation described is typical of any situation of production to order, not just in injection-molding situations.

The sooner a purchasing department is informed about the goals, scope, and timing of a certain sales or marketing project, then the greater will be the flexibility of its employees in dealing with potential suppliers and obtaining a reasonable price and delivery offer. This is not always the case as Godiwalla, Meinhart, and Warde (1978), Farmer (1981), and Woodside and Vyas (1982) have observed. In many instances, purchasing seems to play only a minor role in the purchasing decision process. Mogee and Bean (1976) have observed the negative consequences of this attitude in the relationship between purchasing and product development. In this case study, the negative impact resulted from the relationship between marketing and purchasing, and was exemplified in the statement: "Miracle buyers are needed."

Positively, effective cost reduction is possible if purchasing is fully integrated in strategic decision making, a point previously made by

```
┌─────────────┐     ┌──────────────────────┐     ┌──────────────────────────────────────────┐
│ B           │     │ Sales Department     │     │ Electronic Data      │     │ Production Department         │
│ START       │────▶│                      │────▶│ Processing Section   │────▶│ ● Planning Section            │
│             │     │                      │     │                      │     │                               │
└─────────────┘     │ —controls the order  │     │ —prepares all        │     │ —provides Purchasing Dept. with
                    │  and sees to it that │     │  necessary kinds of  │     │  information concerning the following:
                    │  it corresponds with │     │  documents for       │     │ ● Purchase of mold, together with:
                    │  all the details     │     │  internal departments│     │   delivery time
                    │  discussed with the  │     │ —prepares            │     │   range of mold constructors as
                    │  customer regarding: │     │  specifically the    │     │   specified by the Engineering Section
                    │ ● terms of payment   │     │  order acknowledgment│     │   These choices are based on known
                    │ ● delivery           │     │  to be sent to the   │     │   constructors and those who are
                    │ ● all other details  │     │  customer, indicating│     │   supposed to be able to manufacture
                    │                      │     │  that ERTA agrees    │     │   molds as required by ERTA in this
                    │                      │     │  with the order      │     │   specific case
                    │                      │     │                      │     │ ● Purchase of raw materials and other
                    │                      │     │                      │     │   ingredients (such as coloring,
                    │                      │     │        │             │     │   additives, and metal inserts)
                    │                      │     │        ▼ Customer     │     │ ● Packaging Materials Needed
                    │                      │     │                      │     │ ● Transportation Requirements
                    └──────────────────────┘     └──────────────────────┘     └──────────────────────────────────────────┘
```

Figure 4a

254

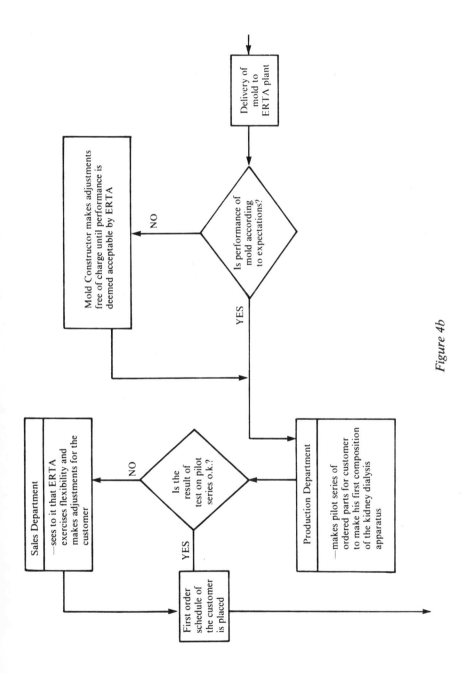

Figure 4b

255

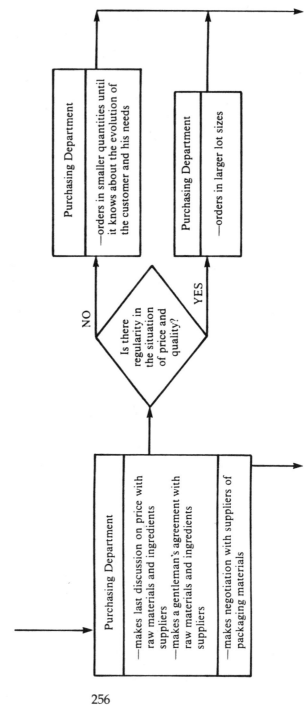

Purchasing Department

—orders in smaller quantities until it knows about the evolution of the customer and his needs

Purchasing Department

—orders in larger lot sizes

Is there regularity in the situation of price and quality?

NO

YES

Purchasing Department

—makes last discussion on price with raw materials and ingredients suppliers
—makes a gentleman's agreement with raw materials and ingredients suppliers

—makes negotiation with suppliers of packaging materials

256

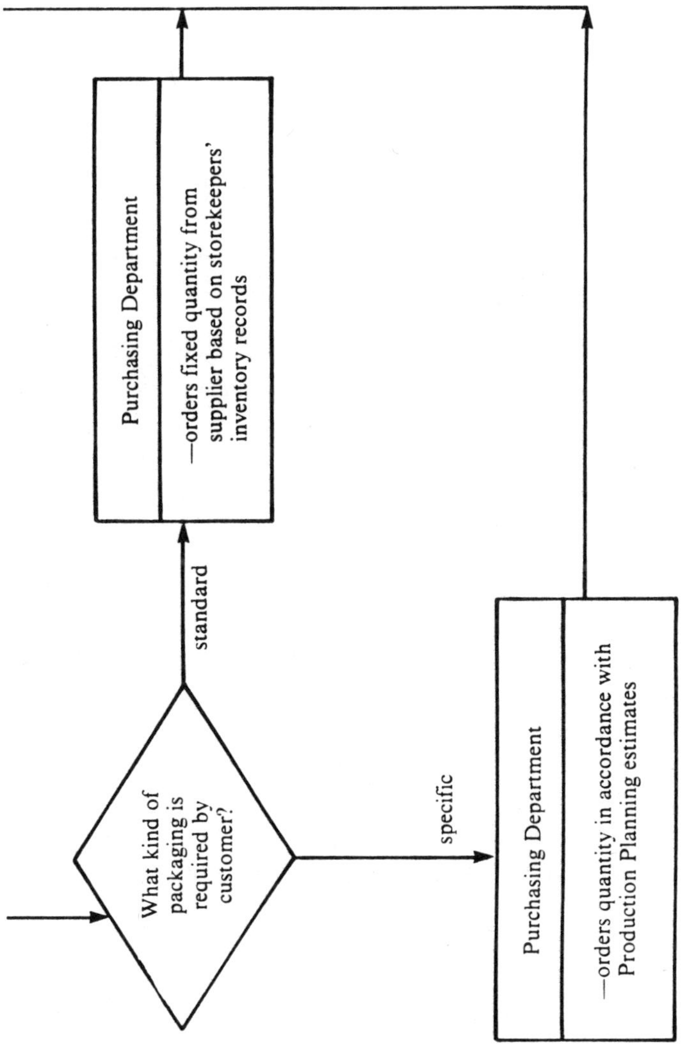
What kind of packaging is required by customer?
standard
specific
Purchasing Department
—orders fixed quantity from supplier based on storekeepers' inventory records
Purchasing Department
—orders quantity in accordance with Production Planning estimates

Figure 4c

Gronhaug (1979) and De Rijcke, Faes, and Van Weele (1982), Starbuck (1976), and Robey and Johnson (1977). This process is beneficial because the incorporation of diverse people in decision making actively pools their capabilities and gives broader scope to the decision process itself.

The organizational buying phenomenon is complex in nature because different people are playing important roles throughout the process. Two diverse stages can be observed: (1) the design and planning stage and (2) the executional stage; in these stages different phenomena were observed.

In the initial design and planning stage, several feedback loops were evident between the production, purchasing, marketing, and accounting departments in which the internal facilities offered by ERTA were compared with the customer's requirements, considering his production schedule. This process was repeated until a satisfactory design could be offered to the customer at a reasonable cost. Throughout the process, the marketing department played the most important role; purchasing acted as gatekeeper to the external supply market, particularly in terms of cost and delivery information. Different alternatives were evaluated on their individual merits. This confirms Witte's (1972) view that information-gathering and the development of alternatives is an ongoing and simultaneous process with no clear distinction between these two phases. In terms of the strategic model depicting the structure of "unstructured" decision making by Mintzberg, Raisinghani, and Theoret (1976), this stage adheres to the strict rules of a basic design and planning decision process with complex and innovative solutions tested.

The process was initiated by external opportunities, although at a later stage internal planning problems became most important. The process involved an active search triggered by a combination of opportunities and problems (similar to Soelberg 1967). The screening subroutine was an intricate part of this process, taking place at the same time, (Cyert and March 1963; Pounds 1969).

After the initial screening, agreement with the customer was reached on molding design and cost. The process then changed considerably. The agreed-upon solutions were implemented in a linear manner, involving fewer feedback loops in comparison with the previous stage. New feedback loops did not appear unless unexpected problems arose. In these situations, feedback loops were observed between purchasing-marketing-production and finance. The process became stable, linear, and incremental (Kennedy 1981) and followed the pattern of the general model.

The role of the purchasing department was to establish an ideal price/quality relationship through continuous contact with potential suppliers, to participate in the final selection of a supplier, and to execute the purchase order.

At the execution stage, purchasing no longer performs a gatekeeper role; they are now the primary participants in the process. The process itself was relatively structured and formal. Every decision was itself irreversible. This peculiar phenomenon, involving examining every conceivable failure in product delivery in order to possibly change suppliers, even when it is no longer possible to change suppliers, was also observed by Lambert, Dornoff, and Kernan (1977).

In fact, this case clearly exemplified the importance of the previous buy stages, which are only briefly mentioned in this model. The search/evaluation/selection routine of the product, especially for complex modified rebuy and new buy situations, is fundamental in terms of further stages and cannot be depicted in one simple model.

REFERENCES

Cyert, T.M. and J.G. March. (1963). *Behavioral Theory of the Firm*. Englewood Cliffs, NJ: Prentice-Hall.

De Rijcke, J., W. Faes, and A. Van Weele. (1982). "Developments in Purchasing Management in the United States." Report based on interviews with professors of universities and the purchasing executives of ten leading American multinational companies.

Farmer, D. (1981). "Input Management." 3rd World Congress I.F.P.M.M., Stockholm (June 3-6).

Godiwalla, J.M., Meinhart, W.A. and W.D. Warde. (1978). "Corporate Planning—A Functional Approach." *Long Range Planning* 11(October): 47-54.

Gronhaug, K. (1979). "Power in Organizational Buying." *Human Relations* 32: 159-180.

Kennedy, A. (1981). "Analyzing Industrial Buyer Behavior: A Descriptive Model of the Purchase Decision for a Specific Raw Material: Steel Plate." Department of Marketing, University of Strathclyde, Glasgow (October).

Lambert, D.R., R.J. Dornoff, and J.B. Kernan. (1979). "The Industrial Buyer and the Postchoice Evaluation Process." *Journal of Marketing Research* 14(May): 246-251.

Mintzberg, H., D. Raisinghani, and A. Theoret. (1976). "The Structure of Unstructured Decision Processes." *Administrative Science Quarterly* 21(June): 246-275.

Mogee, M.E. and A.S. Bean. (1976). "The Role of the Purchasing Agent in Industrial Innovation." *Industrial Marketing Management* 5: 221-229.

Pounds, W.J. (1969). "The Process of Problem Finding." *Industrial Management Review* 11(Fall): 1-19.

Robey and Johnson. (1977). "Lateral Influences and Vertical Authority in Organizational Buying." *Industrial Marketing Management* 6: 451-462.

Soelberg, P.O. (1967). "Unprogrammed Decision Making." *Industrial Management Review* 8(Spring): 19-22.

Starbuck, W.H. (1976). "Organizations and Their Environments." In *Handbook of Industrial and Organizational Psychology*, edited by M.D. Dunette. Chicago, IL: Rand McNally.

Witte, E. (1972). "Field Research on Complex Decision Making Processes—The Phase Theorem." *International Studies of Management and Organizations*. Pp. 156-182.

Woodside, A., and N. Vyas. (1982). "A Generalized Inductive Model of Industrial Buying Behavior." College of Business Administration, University of South Carolina, Columbia, South Carolina.

BUYING STEEL PLATE:
THE COMPLEX DECISION
TO SELECT A SUPPLIER

Anita M. Kennedy

ABSTRACT

This paper reports the results of a case history analysis of the J. Hampden & Company Ltd's decision to purchase a specific raw material—steel plate. James Hampden & Co., Ltd. is a Glasgow-based manufacturer of large, heavy-duty, high performance air and gas handling equipment. The case carefully documents the various buying problems, activities, and persons involved throughout the course of the steel plate purchasing process. The flow-chart method is used as a method of documenting the activities and events involved in the purchase process. An analysis of the composition of the buying group is also presented for each stage in the decision-making process. The purchasing decision process for James Hampden & Co., Ltd. is primarily decentralized and plant-based, providing a great deal of autonomy. The exact purchasing process for steel plate is dependent on the nature of the product required; whether

Advances in Business Marketing and Purchasing, Volume 5, pages 261-282.

it arises from the needs of a specific contract, or from the ongoing company review of the Material Requirements Program. It is worth noting that due to increased company emphasis on quality performance, the purchasing department is given ultimate control over and responsibility for the quality function.

INTRODUCTION

The objective of the present case study is to report the results of an empirical study that attempted to describe the buying problems, activities, and persons in organizational buying centers for steel plate. The case study presents an examination of the applicability of conceptualizing organizational buyer behavior as a problem-solving process that extends over time and across many individuals and organizational departments.

During the data collection period, a multiple method approach was used to permit a triangulation of information that provided valid observations of coordinated purchasing activities and decisions. Data were collected from direct observation, a review of company records, and personal interviews with those involved in the purchasing of the product—steel plate. Flow diagrams of decision-making processes were then developed according to the system described by Capon and Hulbert (1975) and Hulbert (1980). The prepared flow charts (Figures 1 and 2) were subsequently revised according to staff and plant managers and verified through correspondence, published reports, and staff personnel records, and by a series of reinterviews with the respective personnel. The flow-chart method is recognized as being particularly valuable in the analysis of the purchasing process.

SITUATION ANALYSIS: THE COMPANY, ITS PRODUCT RANGE AND PURCHASING BEHAVIOR

Hampden Group Ltd. is a holding company with six main operating units, two in Britain and one each in Australia, Canada, the United States, and South Africa. The group specializes in the manufacturing and installation of equipment for air, gas, and fluid handling. Its products include fans, gas circulators, blowers, air preheaters, heat exchangers, pumps, compressors, dust collectors, and fabric filters.

Applications for the group's products include inert gas systems for oil tanker explosion protection, industrial refrigeration for cold stores, mine and tunnel ventilation, and aircraft and military vehicle ventilation. The major industries that the company supplies world-wide include electricity generation, steel production, petrochemical and hydrocarbon processing, and mining.

James Hampden & Co., Ltd.
(a Member of the Hampden Group of Companies)

Based in Glasgow, James Hampden & Co., Ltd. is engaged in the research, development, design, and manufacture of large, heavy duty, high performance air and gas handling equipment. The major industries for these specialized products are power generation, iron and steel, mining, petrochemical, and marine. The company serves an international market and exports a major part of its production. The major products are: axial, centrifugal and mixed flow fans, blowers, rotary regenerative heat exchangers, dust collectors for power stations, steel works and oil refineries, and circulators for gas cooled nuclear reactors.

Specific Applications of Company Products

The total product range of the company encompasses a wide range of applications. However, the company's products are principally air and gas handling machines for power station and industrial plant installations. Each of these products can be supplied as a "tailor-made" unit or certain standard "packs" are manufactured. The company has experienced a drop in orders for smaller marine fan applications.

Organization of the Purchasing Function

Figure 1 gives details of the overall organization of the company's Scottish plant. However, a more detailed examination of the organization of the purchasing function is required. Figure 2 details the formal organizational chart of the purchasing department. It is the responsibility of the purchasing department to order all material required for use in production, for plant and equipment, and also any general materials.

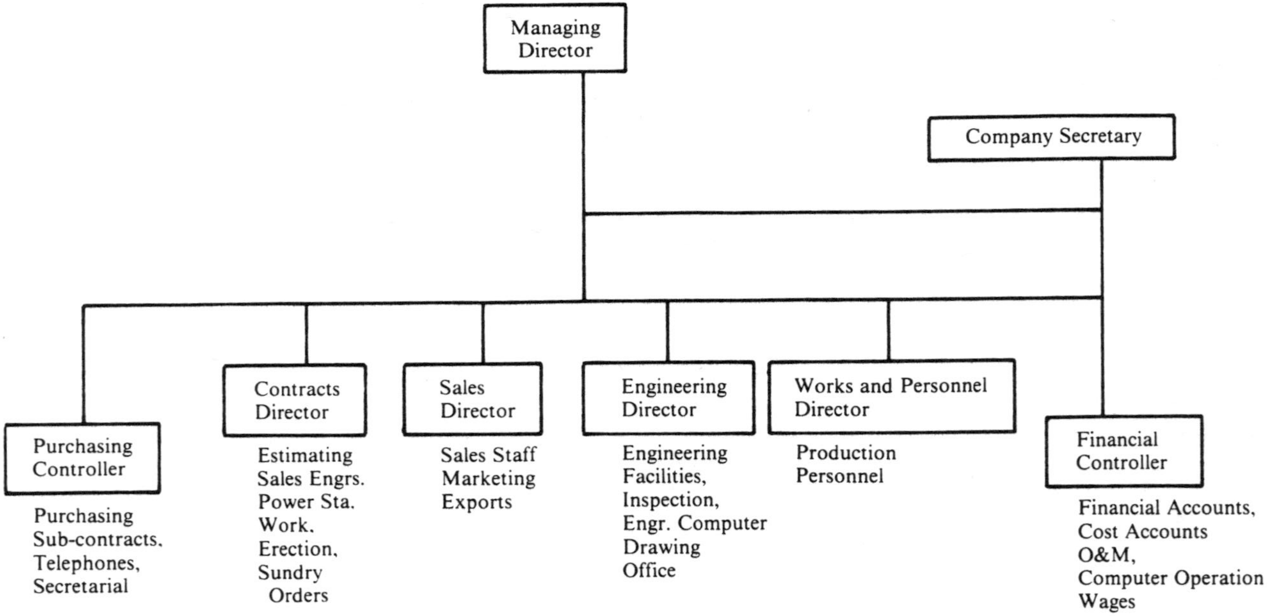

Managing Director

Company Secretary

Purchasing Controller

Purchasing
Sub-contracts.
Telephones,
Secretarial

Contracts Director

Estimating
Sales Engrs.
Power Sta.
Work.
Erection.
Sundry
Orders

Sales Director

Sales Staff
Marketing
Exports

Engineering Director

Engineering
Facilities,
Inspection,
Engr. Computer
Drawing
Office

Works and Personnel Director

Production
Personnel

Financial Controller

Financial Accounts,
Cost Accounts
O&M,
Computer Operation
Wages

Figure 1. Basic Organization Chart

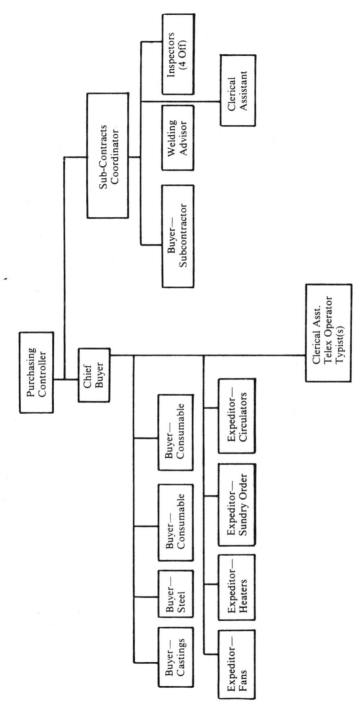

Figure 2. Purchasing Department Organization Chart

265

As this case study concentrates essentially on the purchasing of steel plate—a particular raw material—an overview of the purchasing function for raw materials as a whole is presented. Raw material purchasing includes steel plates, angles, coil, and so forth, nonferrous metals, and forgings, such as large shafts for fans and castings—both iron and aluminum. Raw materials purchasing accounts for 17 percent of the total company expenditures on purchase goods per annum. Steel plate purchases account for approximately 33 percent of raw materials purchases—consequently in the region of £1 million or $1.8 million per annum. The book price for steel plate has remained fairly static over the past 5 years, although alternative sources of supply have been sought by the company due to inconsistency of supply from British producers (e.g., the British Steel Company strike in the winter of 1979/1980 caused considerable panic throughout the industry at large and the company in particular). The raw materials purchasing expenditure is currently the largest item of expenditure in the company, slightly ahead of wages and salaries.

The company is very engineering-oriented. The board and general company policy is dictated solely by engineers. This emphasis on engineering has obvious implications for the responsibility of the purchasing function, particularly in relation to the composition of the buying center, as will be shown in the following section.

THE PURCHASING PROCESS FOR STEEL PLATE

This section gives details of the sequence of activities performed in the purchase of the raw material—steel plate. It analyzes the contribution of various departments of the company to the purchasing decision and enumerates the roles of individuals in the buying center.

STAGE 1:   THE RAW MATERIALS
REQUIREMENTS PLANNING

The purchasing department has virtually no control or influence over the initiation of a purchase requirement. The purchasing function is mainly concerned with the continuous review of supplier and product evaluation, the placement of the purchase order, and the progress of the order. The purchasing controller, himself, considers that the responsibility of the purchasing department is to give advice and coordinate the communication taking place between purchasing and production control, in order to provide forward estimates based on known and anticipated sales, inventory, and purchasing policy.

It is the objective of purchasing to obtain materials and outside services necessary for production. The department obtains and progresses the materials required by production and manufacturing management. The purchasing department has the responsibility to choose suppliers, consider prices, delivery dates, offer alternative supplies where appropriate, and generally offer service by evaluating suppliers, new products, and managerial and technical capabilities.

During the purchasing process for raw materials, forecasts of materials requirements are projected in terms of man-hours. On this basis, the company extrapolates trends and estimates capacity requirements. The volume forecast systems are "planning" systems, triggered as regular components of a fixed planning cycle and often influenced by perceived changes in market conditions. Purchasing does become very involved in the planning operations.

At the initial stage of requirements planning, the process of purchasing steel plate becomes increasingly complex due to the nature of the product. In general, two types of steel plate are purchased by the department. Special steel plate is often purchased for a *specific contract* and is chargeable to that contract. Under these circumstances, the purchase requisition is prepared by the initiating department (e.g., the drawing office, production management, or contract engineering). The requisition states the quantity, specification of goods, date when required, delivery instructions, and the contract number. The materials requisition form is then progressed to the purchasing department, which assumes responsibility for the placement of the order. (This process is documented in later stages of the descriptive analysis.)

For ordinary mild steel plate, a *material requirements program* is prepared by the senior stock controller and the purchasing controller. This is updated on a continuing basis and is formulated on an analysis of current stock and estimated usage. Previously, this was the function of the production Manager, but it has now become the joint responsibility of purchasing and stock control. Ideally, the purchasing department would like to move the emphasis of decision making to the buying function from the stock control department. This is regarded as a potential means of increasing the profitability of the operation, because purchasing is more concerned with increasing profit levels, whereas the bias of the stock control office is to maintain available stock levels at all times. The senior steel buyer and the senior stock controller meet twice a month to discuss price increases and give new steel suggestions to the engineers. Changes in lead time and negotiation of new terms with suppliers are also discussed.

In general, approximately 70 percent of steel plate is bought directly from the steel mill, which tends to be local and state-owned. The balance of requirements is purchased from steel stockholders. Usage of steel can be erratic, for example, the previous year's usage was the largest single year amount recorded by the purchasing department. It is a further responsibility of purchasing to maintain a supply of spare parts, and to oversee levels of steel plate that may be exported. The decision on the level of stock is made by the stock controller for steel and the purchasing controller.

When an order of steel plate is required to maintain existing stock levels, or to accommodate an expected upsurge in demand, the stock control department, operating as part of the production control section, is responsible for initiating a purchase requirement order. The document used is not a Purchase Requisition, but is a card retained in the stock control department and passed to the buyer as a request for authorization for certain goods. The card details the quantity, specification, stock number, date of delivery, and details of recent orders for that material. Authorization for the issue of the card is always required by either the production manager or the production control manager. The purchasing department is then responsible for the recording and preparing of computer inputs for each order sent out to the supplier. Company codes are also entered, based on specific material.

At the end of "Stint 7" (the last order period), in each year, a complete analysis of all stock held at that date will be made. Usage for the previous six stints will be prepared as input data for the computer to determine an obsolescence value.

To summarize, at this stage, the following personnel are involved in the process of making the decisions to initiate a purchase: the buyer, the stock controller, the production control manager, the planning and scheduling manager, and draftsmen. The stock controller, when recording issues of material from store to production, will check the balance left and compare this with a previously determined reorder level (determined by the senior stock controller and the purchasing controller at the beginning of the financial year). He will then inform the production control manager that this material should be repurchased. The production control manager will decide to purchase after considering alternative materials, known or possible future production requirements, and changes in supply lead times. This decision involves close collaboration and advice from the purchasing controller. Once the purchase has been decided upon, the information is passed to the buyer.

The planning and scheduling manager is responsible for initiating purchases of steel coil used in the manufacture of elements in the company's power station heater products. Steel coil must be ordered well in advance from the producer, generally on a quarter-by-quarter basis through the year. The drawing office is regularly searching for material for specific contracts—material normally maintained in stock. For this type of product, discussion takes place between steel buyer and draftsman relating to alternative specifications, sizes, and general availability.

Thus, while decisions to initiate a purchase are made, for the most part, by technical staff, the purchasing controller and the senior steel buyer are able to provide information which can aid in the reduction of certain risk factors (comparable, in a sense, to the role of gatekeeper).

The principal sources of information used by the purchasing department in the decision to initiate the order for steel plate tend to be past experience and, on occasion, trade journals. Search for information is generally stimulated by a particular problem and directed toward the solution of that problem. Therefore, one could argue that a search is motivated, biased, and follows the most simple route. On a general level, however, the steel buyer tended to rely on past experiences with the supplier.

STAGE 2: PREPARATION OF REQUEST FOR TENDER (QUOTATION)

The nature of steel plate buying is probably somewhat different from other raw material purchases. Since the most important requirement is that an adequate level of steel plate stock is maintained, RFQs are not usually issued for each specific order—the order is merely placed with the most suitable supplier.

The criteria for selection of a supplier are rather complex. The company performs a vendor assessment of the supplier performance on a continuing basis. This is mainly concerned with the steel supplier's quality inspection techniques, since a Test Certificate must be issued to satisfy quality requirements for steel plate. The supplier's financial circumstances are considered, the supplier's own sources of supply, its management structure and, most importantly, its quality and quarantine area for steel supplies. James Hampden & Co., Ltd. also conducts a commercial survey for both steel stockists and steel mills. The survey covers an analysis of such factors as market position, financial position, condition of premises, activity and order level, industrial relations, plant and equipment condition, inspection facilities, supplier performance (previous experience on price, delivery, quality, current order commitment, intended capacity allocated), and an overall rating grade for the company.

Furthermore, specific data are collected on raw materials preparation both in steel mills and in stockists. Quality assurance surveys and evaluations are undertaken that examine the supplier's quality procedures, inspection controls, and test certificate status. The steel stockists also come under very severe scrutiny—particularly in relation to quarantine areas and the level of technical services that are available, for example, metallurgical laboratory services, NDT, (including radiography and ultrasonics), and storage facilities control. Examples of such vendor assessment techniques are included as Figures 3 and 4: vendor assessment—commercial survey and vendor assessment—product capability for both steel mills and steel stockists.

When it is deemed to be necessary to prepare RFQs, however, these are sent out by the purchasing department. In general, the number requested tends to vary—usually two or three to a maximum of four. The number is limited generally because of both time and financial restraints. The RFQs are mailed to both steel stockholders and steel mills—all of which are usually local. The company trades with, on the whole, four steel stockholders and three steel mills.

In general, the key criterion for inclusion on the RFQ list is generally reliable service. Without a change in the company or supplier circumstances, there tends to be inertia in the relationship with the steel supplier. Unless there is adequate reason to change, the company will place the order with an existing supplier. On the other hand, the purchasing controller has commented on the fact that the visitation by a supplier salesman on a particular day may precipitate the placement of that order with that particular supplier. At this stage in the decision-making process, it is the sole responsibility of the purchasing department to make the decision as to the choice of supplier.

STAGE 3:   EVALUATION OF RFQs

A subsequent stage to the request for quotation is the evaluation of the specific tenders that have been returned to the customer. At this stage, however, the RFQs are not offered for each specific order. Most frequently, the purchasing department will issue a definite order for a specific quantity of steel plate. The terms of this order are based on the stock control department's description of type of steel plate and of projected usage patterns.

However, in some instances, RFQs are prepared in order to maintain evaluation of stockholder versus steel mill performance. Under such circumstances, it is the sole responsibility of the purchasing department to evaluate quotations. The process essentially involves relating price to quality and delivery to quantity. The purchasing department also monitors potential changes and improvements in both supplier performance and material availability. If after evaluation of the RFQ the steel buyer recommends a purchase from a different supplying organization than has previously taken place, a period of trial and material testing may take place.

STAGE 4:   TRIAL AND EVALUATION OF
MATERIAL PERFORMANCE

Under some circumstances, the steel buyer may make the decision to switch suppliers. For example, if the past rejection rate is high, the supplier may be disqualified from the "approved supplier list." This decision would be made by the purchasing and inspection departments. In other situations, for example during the British Steel Company strike, James Hampden & Co., Ltd. has considered international sources of supply. Information on additional supplier performance is obtained through trade directories, previous knowledge of the industry, and often through other member companies of the Hampden Group. Unsolicited visits from supplier salesmen are not encouraged. However, purchasing personnel do consider that supplier salesmen can be a useful source of information on new sources of supply.

In summary, suppliers may be added to the list of vendors who are sent RFQs under certain circumstances. These may take the form of a change in the current performance of a supplier in terms of delivery,

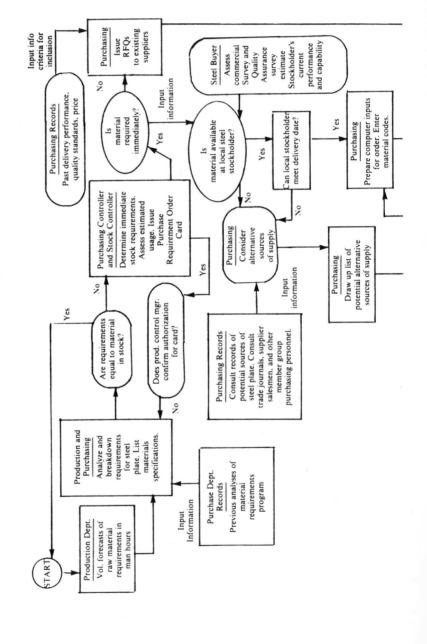

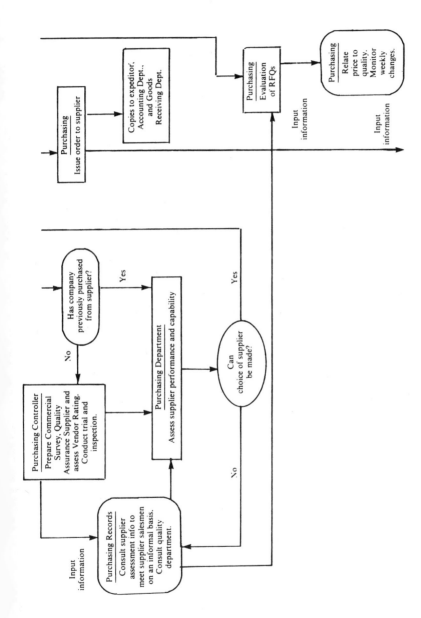

Figure 3a: Flow-Chart: The Purchase of Mild Steel Plate

273

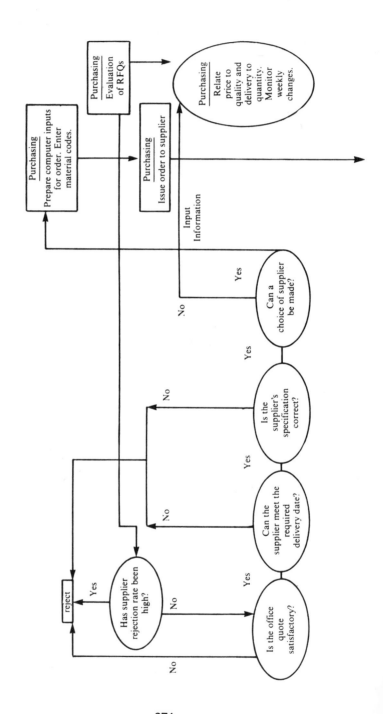

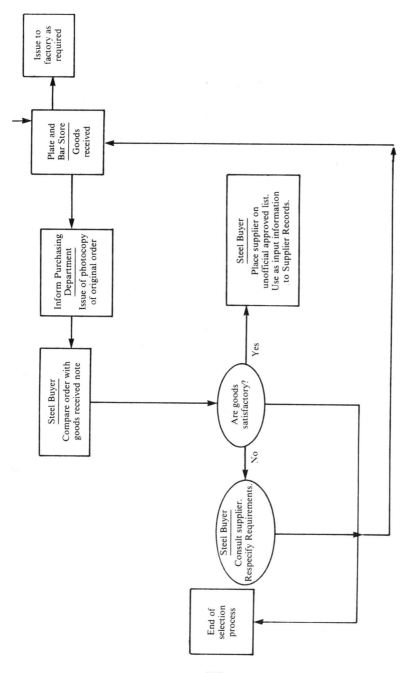

Figure 3b: Flow-Chart: The Purchase of Mild Steel Plate (continued)

275

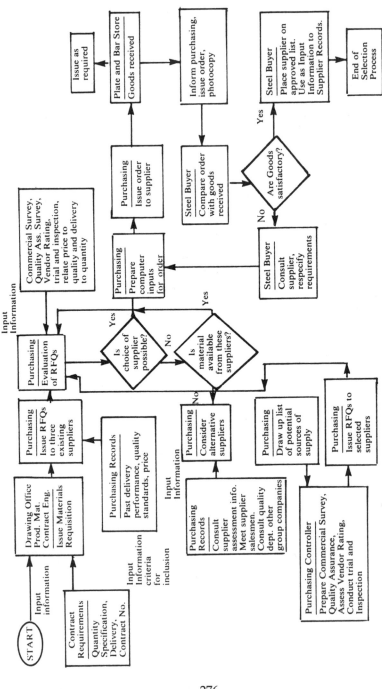

Figure 4: Flow-Chart: The Purchase of Special Steel Plate

276

quality, and price. If the steel is being bought for a specific contract, RFQs will be sought from special steel plate suppliers.

When a change of supplier is imminent, the supplier's material will be subject to a series of inspection and quality tests. The persons involved in this period of trial and approval will include members of the quality control, purchasing, and inspection departments. Purchasing is essentially and, in the final analysis, ultimately responsible for quality performance. The criteria that are used during the trial evaluation process include proof of reliability and inspection quality checks—the assessment of the supplier company's Test Certificate. Quality and delivery performance are evaluated in respect to the price tendered. The results of the trial period are documented in the forms that comprise the Quality Assurance Survey and that are related to the specific data tendered. Once the quality control data are prepared and documented, it is the responsibility of the purchasing department to determine whether or not the supplier will receive the contract or order and, moreover, whether or not the supplier will be placed on the company's unofficial approved list of suppliers.

STAGE 5:   CHOICE OF SUPPLIER AND PLACEMENT OF ORDER/CONTRACT

Essentially, it is the function of the purchasing department to make the decision as to the final selection of supplier. In general, the steel buyer will rely on past experience with a supplier as the main basis for selection. He may discuss product price quotations and manufacturer delivery and quality capabilities informally with the supplier. The buyer will also consider whether or not the supplier's quotation matches the specification demanded by either stock control or by engineering.

Once the process of evaluation has taken place, the sequence of events is as follows. The steel buyer registers the name and address of the supplying company on the requisition form. He also notes the agreed price, total value, order number, delivery date, and material code number. Once this has been formally prepared, the requisition is forwarded to the supplier. The steel buyer may sometimes, informally, negotiate discounts on a volume basis. In general, however, the steel mill publishes a list price that must be adhered to. Stockholders, on the other hand, may add £1 ($1 million) per ton or more to the estimated price. Contracts and orders are always placed on a fixed price basis.

A copy of the requisition order is then filed and one copy is retained by the buyer or passed to the expeditor to process the order. Several other departments also receive requisition copies, including the accounting department and the goods receiving department.

STAGE 6:   RECEIPT OF GOODS

Generally, a greater number of departments are involved during this stage of the purchasing process. The Plate and Bar Stockyard/Store and the stock control department are involved in receiving, storing, handling, and generally documenting raw material purchases. These sections notify all appropriate purchase orders for the purchasing department, handling steel in the form of plate sections and coil. They are also responsible for recording and reporting all goods received and goods issued to the factory and in undertaking stock checks.

On receipt of goods, the storeman issues a photocopy of the original purchasing order, together with details of the quantity that has been received and the date of delivery. The steel buyer will then compare this with his original order requirements.

STAGE 7:   CONSOLIDATION OF BUYER/SUPPLIER RELATIONSHIP

Once a supplier has been approved, the relationship is usually long standing. It can take two or three years to make a decision on a new steel or a new supplier. However, once this process is complete, the supplier is placed on the unofficial supplier "approved list" of the company.

The steel buyer will visit the supplier on an ongoing basis in order to assess the potential of possible new sources of supply or to examine and inspect new equipment or systems that have been developed by an existing supplier. He will also discuss future arrangements and capabilities or check on the progress of existing orders (e.g., for shipbuilding contracts where the steel buyers will spend one day per week in discussion with the British Steel Corporation). The company will stay with a supplier who can meet proven efficiency levels. In such circumstances, there is no written company policy to issue a fresh RFQ for each order.

Multiple source purchasing is commonly used—mainly from the British Steel Corporation and from steel stockholders—to maintain continuity of delivery. The volume split of orders is formulated on an assessment of the material requirements program. The company tends to place 70 percent of its orders with steel mills. The balance of raw materials requirements is obtained from the stocklist in order to minimize inventory costs. Estimates of past demand are important, although there may be a greater number of orders placed with stockholders at times of a sudden upsurge in demand. A change in the order split may occur as a result of an assessment of the level of business that James Hampden & Co., Ltd. have at any one time. The order split may vary depending on the performance of the supplier. If the supplying company has exhibited a certain degree of failure, the company will operate a restricted purchasing situation until performance comes up to standard. In such situations, James Hampden & Co., Ltd. will tend to place more emphasis on an examination of the supplying company's financial accounts and credit rating. In practice, however, the volume of business is never really substantially reduced at any one time. Any decision regarding a change in order split would be made by the purchasing controller and the senior stock controller. There are generally no differences or conflicts between departments.

Specific circumstances exist within the steel industry that tend to foster inertia in buyer/seller relationships. There has tended to be contraction among the supplying industry, which has resulted in a reduced number of steel manufacturers. Many of the traditional "mill" sources are now uncompetitive and are consequently closing their plants. Moreover, there has been a regrouping of supply facilities within the nationalized steel industry. This has tended to reduce the number of supply locations and thus reduce the number of potential suppliers. The principal effect of this situation on the purchasing function at James Hampden & Co., Ltd. has been a stabilization and consolidation of existing sources of supply, together with a change in attitude toward the rest of Europe and the world in more general terms.

There are fears among the supplying companies, however, that their customers are not contributing in any significant manner to the continued profitable existence of the steel industry. As one supplier has commented:

> I am not critical of buyers who are twisting the arms of suppliers—good luck to them. I am not asking buyers to buy at my price because I have

invested in the future. But, buyers who are dealing with foundries now
and forcing them to cut prices cannot expect those foundries to exist in
the long-term—they must be kidding.

Consequently, it is generally recognized throughout the industry that
steel customers will have a considerable role to play in the future
development of the industry itself. Such a close, almost incestuous,
relationship between supplier and buyer tends to reinforce inertia in
purchasing within the industry and favors the continuation of long-term
relationships between buyer and supplier.

EVALUATION OF THE DECISION PROCESS FOR THE PURCHASE OF STEEL PLATE

Detailed diagrammatic descriptions of the decision process are
presented in Figures 3 and 4. However, a brief summary of the
purchasing procedure for steel plate is worthwhile at this stage.

The purchasing process for steel plate tends to be dependent on the
nature of the product required. If the steel plate desired is *special* or
to be bought for a *specific contract*, then the material requirements order
is developed by engineering and production staff. The purchasing
department assumes full responsibility for the selection of supplier and
the progressing of the order. The impetus to precipitate a purchase may
result from the ongoing review of the *Material Requirements Program*
that is undertaken by the purchasing controller and the stock controller.
In this case, material is purchased to maintain optimum inventory levels.

At no time during the purchasing process does top management become
particularly active in decision making. The DMU tends to be decentralized
and plant-based. Hence, materials are purchased essentially for use in a
specific plant. The purchasing function tends to have a high degree of
autonomy in decision making, although it is ultimately answerable to the
Board of Directors. The emphasis within the company is tending to shift
(partly as a consequence of the personality and attitude of the purchasing
controller himself) from an engineering-biased purchasing function
toward greater control and administration of this activity by the
purchasing department itself. However, purchasing has traditionally had
more responsibility for supplier selection, while the more technical aspects
of material specification have come within the dominion of production
and engineering.

An interesting point to note, however, is that purchasing has ultimate control over and responsibility for the quality function. Perhaps this has acted as a precedent to the increased emphasis on quality performance that the company now shows.

The case study would appear to confirm the work of a number of scholars in that the buying center does change over time. As Wind (1978) has pointed out: "the basic concept of a buying center suggests that it is a temporary organization unit, which may change in components and function from one purchase to another." Spekman and Stern (1979) and Spekman (1977) confirm this and suggest that, unlike a formal structural subunit (i.e., a marketing or purchasing department), the buying group is a more nebulous construct that permeates diverse functions of the organization. They suggest that the buying unit's composition, hierarchical levels, lines of communication, and so forth are not strictly prescribed by an organizational chart or official document:

> The buying group evolves as an informal communication network which does not derive its structural configuration from the formal organization per se, but rather from the regularized patterning of interpersonal communication flows among the various group members.

One of the most significant conclusions that can be drawn from the steel plate case study is that buying group membership appears to evolve during the procurement process and is a function of the information requirements and needs of a particular buying context.

A study by Doyle, Woodside, and Michell (1979) has also attempted to locate the participants in the buying decision. Their study has suggested that the number of participants in the buying center was smaller in size for firms operating in straight rebuy situations. The steel plate case study would appear to confirm this contention. When the purchase decision involved is concerned with a reorder to maintain stock levels, the buying group is relatively small. However, when the purchasing decision is concerned with the purchase of special steel plate, the buying group dilates to include members of the engineering, production, and quality control departments.

By analyzing the specific decision process for steel plate, purchase decisions appear to be done incrementally. Hence, each major decision consists of several corollaries and does itself constitute the basis for further decisions. If this concept is applied generally to purchasing decisions, it can be seen that the precipitating decisions will form the basis for the confirmed commitment decisions. At each stage, there is a buying center and the focus of responsibility varies from one stage to another. The decisions that are made by members of the buying center in the early part of the buying process inevitably limit and shape the decision-making activities for buying centers involved in the later stages of the process. The formality of the decision-making activities increases as the process progresses toward the formal placement of the order.

REFERENCES

Capon, N., J.U. Farley, and J. Hulbert. (1975). "Pricing and Forecasting in an Oligopoly Firm." *Journal of Management Studies* 12(May): 133-136.

Doyle, P., A.G. Woodside, and P. Michell. (1979). "Organizations Buying in New Task and Rebuy Situations." *Industrial Marketing Management* 8: 7-11.

Farley, J.U., J.M. Hulbert, and D. Weinstein. (1980). "Price Setting and Volume Planning by Two European Industrial Companies: A Study and Comparison of Decision Processes." *Journal of Marketing* 44(Winter): 46-54.

Spekman, R.E. (1977). "A Contingency Approach to Power Relationships Within the Industrial Buying Task Group." Unpublished Ph.D. dissertation, Northwestern University, Evanston, Illinois.

Spekman, R.E. and L.W. Stern. "Environmental Uncertainty and Buying Group Structure: An Empirical Investigation." *Journal of Marketing* 43(Spring): 54-64.

Wind, Y. (1978). "Organizational Buying Center: A Research Agenda." *Organizational Buying Behavior*, edited by G. Zaltman and T.B. Bonoma. Chicago: American Marketing Association.

CONCLUSIONS ON MAPPING HOW INDUSTRY BUYS

Arch G. Woodside

The contributors of this volume have presented many maps of the streams of activities, decisions, and interactions of persons participating in organizational buying processes. The principle method used for such mapping has been decision systems analysis (DSA), that is, the design and confirmation of the activities-decisions-interactions in such processes using multiple data collection methods and flow diagrams.

The old saw, "God is in the details," is relevant for mapping of both buying and marketing strategies of organizations. Learning the concrete details of what actually is happening—who did what, why, where, when, and with what outcomes?—is very useful for gaining the insights necessary for making small adjustments that lead to strategic improvements in how decision processes are designed and implemented. Japanese managers at Toyota have referred to this process as "inching ahead rapidly."

The following example of mapping the process of two persons playing basketball provides another useful illustration of recording the details

Advances in Business Marketing and Purchasing, Volume 5, pages 283-300.
ISBN: 1-55938-364-X

of the process, gaining insights, and making strategic improvements in the process. Analogous to DSA flow diagrams, video tapes were used for recording and examining the details.

In 1986 Kareem Abdul-Jabbar reflected on playing basketball against Moses Malone, "He's very physical and very smart. In 1983, the 76ers blew us out of the finals in four straight games, and Moses was just relentless. I had to appraise what I was doing wrong insofar as the way I played him, so I went to Pete Newell, who has a summer camp for teaching pros the fundamentals of whatever it is they're not doing right. Newell's the professor—about 25 years ago, when he coached the University of California, his team won the N.C.A.A. championship. Anyway, I took Pete some video tapes of our '83 play-off game against the 76ers and asked him to critique my performance against Moses."

What was Abdul-Jabbar doing wrong? "Specifically, I was holding my hands at my sides and, just before a rebound, Moses would lean against me and pin one of my arms to my side. He'd knock me off balance enough to let him get the rebound. Moses makes his living doing things like that. Newell showed me that I had to keep my hands and arms up higher and use my butt to knock people's weight off me so that I didn't get thrown off balance. The next two years—'84 and '85— my rebound average went up."

This case illustrates several points about the value of analyzing the flow of activities, decisions, and interactions among people. Many basketball experts consider Abdul-Jabbar the "greatest basketball player of all time," yet even the greatest benefitted from a detailed analysis of the flow of events involving his own behavior and the behavior of a competitor as the behavior occurred in its natural setting. Abdul-Jabbar avoided the "GM fallacy," that is, superiority leading to a belief of infallibility (cf. Wright 1979).

Second, detailed information was collected on the dynamics of the events, decisions, and interactions, that is, the video tapes. While video tapes are rarely available of industrial purchasing strategies, the need to *collect data through time* to increase understanding of what is occurring and to decide on corrective measures, if needed, is apparent for all research on the dynamics of decisions, activities, and interactions of people.

Third, Abdul-Jabbar sought help from an outside expert; the outside expert analyzed the data and offered concrete recommendations. Thus, the value of objective, outside, reviews of decision processes is illustrated; even the greatest among us needs to be coached from time to time. Recognizing the need for coaching may be unique, especially if you carry the label, "the greatest player."

One aim of the papers in this volume has been to demonstrate that DSA is a useful research procedure for systematically developing flowchart descriptions of the decisions, activities, and interactions of people through time that are related to specific management strategies, for example, the purchasing decision process for fuel oil in plant purchasing agreements among two to four possible suppliers. The field studies reported in this volume of *Advances in Business Marketing* are applications of DSA.

DSA was first used in describing industrial purchasing strategies by Howard and his associates (cf. Howard 1965; Hulbert, Farley, and Howard 1972). Wind (1966) provided flow diagrams of the industrial purchasing decision processes in-use in one firm, and related the descriptive models to the behavioral theory of the firm (Cyert and March 1963). The procedure of how to apply DSA in field settings has been described in some detail by Hulbert, Farley, and Howard (1972).

THE RESEARCH METHOD

The research method includes a series of steps starting with establishing cooperation with a key interviewee in the firm and ending with a detailed flow-diagram, written narrative, and summary evaluation of the strengths and weaknesses of the decision process.

Establishing Contact with Key Interviewee

The key interviewee provides an entree into the organization, and his/her insight can greatly assist the research group. The key interviewee is asked to identify the major phases in the decision process and the personnel who were involved in each phase. These personnel constitute the first round of interviews. Each interviewee in the first round is interviewed face-to-face, one at a time, to learn the actions and decisions each was involved in for each phase of the decision process. Each interviewee is asked to identify other persons who were involved in the decision phase; if additional persons are named, these additional persons are interviewed in a second series of interviews. This is an example of the "snowballing" research technique, that is, interviewing persons identified by interviewees who were, in turn, identified by the key interviewee as involved in one or more phases of the decision process. The snowball technique continues until no additional persons are mentioned by the interviewees as being involved in one or more phases of the decision process.

The key interviewee provides access and credibility to the other persons to be interviewed in the study. Members of the IBB Group provided examples of previous research reports (Woodside and Sherrell 1980; Woodside and Samuel 1981) to the key interviewee in each organization participating in the study to help explain the importance of the research method.

Initial Interviews, Observations, and Document Analyses

The initial round of interviews was done on an individual basis, one-on-one, to decrease the tendency of one member of the buying committee taking special care not to offend other members of the buying committee. The research team believed that less biased, more valid descriptions of buying processes are learned when interviewees are interviewed separately; their descriptions were compared, followed by second and third rounds of interviews to resolve conflicts and confusion.

In one case a plant buyer recommended that senior corporate buyers be fired: "Can them all—that's what I would do." This response would be unlikely if the plant buyer was interviewed in a room with other buyers, especially the Purchasing Director from corporate headquarters.

At least three persons were interviewed for each buying process analysis. The number of interviews completed in the first round among all the buying processes analyzed ranged from 3 to 17.

The initial interviews were semi-structured with all answers being open-ended responses. The respondents were encouraged to expand on their answers as they believed necessary for completeness. For each interview, the interviewer recorded answers in detail on a note pad. Electrical tape recordings of the interviews were not used; members of the IBB research team believed that tape recording the interviews would inhibit the interviewees from responding openly and completely.

The interviewees were asked to describe the actual history of the identified buying process for a specific product, usually involving a plant purchasing agreement (PPA). The PPAs studied most often were annual agreements between a buyer and supplier that specified price, product features, delivery schedules, and other terms and conditions.

The specific buying processes studied were current or recently completed PPAs or capital purchases. Purchases of capital items involved major manufacturing machinery. Initially, the key interviewee in each firm was asked to identify "an important purchasing process that would likely involve or affect more than one department in the firm. The purchasing process could be for a raw materials, component production part, capital good, maintenance-repair-operations (MRO) product, or non-production item (packaging materials, wood pallets)."

The key interviewee was asked to identify an active purchasing process—a buying process that first comes-to-mind that has received some attention during the past few days. This procedure was used to decrease problems in recalling details about the buying process and the activities and interactions of participants in the buying center.

The major research problem in using this research methods was that interviews often had to be scheduled two to three times per month with the same persons for one to four months to learn how the buying process actually occurred. This method had the advantage of allowing for direct observation of meetings and interactions among members of the buying center, and, in several cases, between members of the buying center and vendor representatives.

The members of the research team asked to read the written documents related to each buying process (e.g., user requirement survey, request for quotations, vendor bids, contract awards, memos sent/received among members of the buying center, correspondence with vendors, engineering specifications, vendor plant surveys by buying center members, and buying committee reports). In all the cases studied, these written documents were provided, if requested. However, such documentation was not often volunteered before being requested.

Research on current buying processes resulted in data rich descriptions of the detailed steps and learning of situational factors influencing different phases of the processes. Seemingly, small but important events are unlikely to be reported if data on buying strategies are collected only after the buying processes have been completed.

The interviewing of all members of the buying process was focused on the specific behavior, interactions, and decisions that each member participated in during the process. The participation of the buying center members overlapped in all the buying strategies studied. The use of multiple initial interviews increased the IBB research team's ability to confirm specific activities, temporal sequences of activities, and heuristics used in making choices (decisions) occurring during the buying strategies.

An operating research rule-of-thumb by members of the IBB research team was that two sources of information were necessary to confirm specific behaviors, events, decisions, conversations, and temporal orderings of activities provided by one source. Each written document, initial interview, or direct observation was counted as one data source.

The result of the initial interviews, observations, and document analyses was a series of descriptions or protocols which comprised the basic building blocks of the DSA method. The protocols were then converted into flowcharts which effectively summarize the sequence of key events, interactions of people, and both the decision criteria and choice rules used in making decisions.

The Second and Third Rounds of Interviews

At least two persons involved in two or more phases of the buying process are selected for a second round of interviews. In these second, in-depth, face-to-face interviews, the initial flow diagrams are shown and described individually to the interviewees. Each interviewee is requested to make recommendations for correcting mistakes in sequencing activities, to add important steps overlooked, and to note additional criteria and decision rules used in the turning points within the diagram. Thus, the two or more respondents selected for the second round of interviews becomes part of the research team. In all the reported cases, the depth of knowledge and understanding of the buying processes were increased substantially by the additions and corrections coming out of the second interviews.

The improved drafts of the flow-diagrams are shown to two persons in the third round of interviews. Two respondents are interviewed independently in the third round: one person from the second round and an additional person who participated in the first round but not the second. Both sets of diagrams are shown to each respondent in the third round of interviews. Expressed differences of opinions about the actual behavior, decision criteria, and decision rules noted from the second interviews are discussed and resolved in the third round. Following the third round of interviews, the flow-diagrams of the buying process are revised a final time.

Thus, research applications of decision systems analysis reflects time-consuming work analogous to a reporter trying to solve a mystery. By using multiple interviews of the same person through time, and confirming the gathered information by interviewing other persons, a rich depth of details and understanding emerge about the buying processes. The contributors to this volume believe that such depth and understanding are necessary for creating useful strategic insights— nuggets of wisdoms for improving purchasing and marketing strategies.

TEN MAJOR CONCLUSIONS AND INSIGHTS OF MAPPING HOW INDUSTRY BUYS

What major conclusions and insights might be drawn from the case research studies reported in this volume? Ten conclusions and insights for improving marketing-purchasing strategies and for theory-building are offered here.

1. Mapping Real-Life Decision Processes Is a Useful Research Method

The single, most important conclusion from this volume is that building more relevant theories of how industry buys and improving organizational buying strategies can be done by mapping the details of real-life buying decisions. Mapping decision processing allows us to examine the actual strategies used by firms in making acceptable choices. Such maps of realized strategies will likely be useful for building effective decision support systems (cf. Merten 1991) and lead to improvements in future implemented strategies.

Insights

The informational complexity which is typical of strategic decisions, combined with the computational limitations of human decisionmakers, makes it normally impossible to find an optimal strategy for a company that interacts with other companies. Strategic decisionmakers, therefore, do not look for optimal strategies but for acceptable ones (Merten 1991, p. 372). Similar to process engineering, strategic decision making is so complex that no one person is likely to follow what is happening and to make improvements in strategy without a blueprint, a map of implemented strategy. By constructing and validating such maps, we are on firmer ground for offering recommendations for both improving the buying processes and for creating more effective marketing decisions to influence such processes.

2. The Two and More Persons from Different Functional
    Areas Involved Directly in Organizational Buying
    Processes Prefer to Avoid versus Resolve Conflicts

The inductive models offered in the papers in this volume confirm Sheth's (1973) deductive observation that two or more persons are usually included in organizational buying processes. Some implications from this finding include the following: (1) no one actor in the buying process is likely to be able to provide all the details useful for really understanding the process—several persons need to be interviewed; (2) the perceptions and relative importance of attributes and benefits sought by the different actors involved in the buying process are likely to differ; and (3) some mechanism is likely to be incorporated in the buying processes to solve conflicts, or at least, to manage conflicts.

Insights

From a reading of the case studies examined in this volume, none of the four methods proposed by Sheth (1973) appear to be used most often to resolve buying conflicts, that is, problem solving, persuasion, bargaining, or politicking. The prevalent method appears to be conflict avoidance by dividing up phases in the buying process and assigning each phase to persons in different functional areas. Thus, purchasing handles the "commercial relationship" with suppliers and engineering designs the specifications. While this approach often achieves the goal of conflict avoidance, the approach reduces the likelihood of team-building and inching ahead rapidly in making continual improvements.

3. The "Revised Phase Theorem" Proposed by Witte (1972)
    Does Reflect Reality

Witte's (1972) findings and insights from field observations of business decisions in Germany are supported by the findings reported in the papers in the present volume: distinct phases in organizational decision processes can be observed but these phases do not follow a pre-specified sequence. For example, evaluation criteria, and even written specifications, often change after information search and such changes often lead to more information search followed by more changes in evaluation criteria.

Insights

The reality in decision processes summarized in the Revised Phase Theorem suggests the importance of recognizing that, "It's not over, until its over." A more apt observation is that, "It's never over." The implication for both purchasing and marketing strategy is the need to be there, that is, to be continually involved in relationship-building and maintenance by using face-to-face interactions before, during, and after all phases in the buying process.

4. The Membership in a Buying Center Changes for Different Phases in the Buying Process

We can expect some persons to remain in a buying center for two or more decision phases and some persons to be active in only the first and final phase of the buying process. Thus, membership in a buying center is unstable and not always clear-cut.

By using decision systems analysis we may be able to identify the specific persons included in the buying center and the roles played by each person. For example, in the paper titled "Gum Rosin" by Vollering the interactions of persons between three levels of management are identified for the buying process of gum rosin. No one person or department was involved in every phase of the buying process. A relatively obscure member of a buying center may play a big role in affecting the outcome of the buying process. Remember the computer terminal operator in the case reported in the paper by Woodside and Sherrell. This order processor continually changed the order split between two suppliers from 60-40 to 80-20, without authorization or approval from other persons in the buying process. In fact, the order processor was not even recognized to be a member of the buying center involved in purchasing the required equipment.

Hill and Hillier (1977) have emphasized that senior managers are often involved in sanctioning, giving formal recognition of a buying problem and the creation of a buying center to solve the problem. Then, these senior managers may not be involved in the buying process until a recommended solution is presented to them for "ratification." Thus, the role of senior management in such processes is limited to only two phases in the buying process.

Middle-managers may act as information gate-keepers between senior and junior management members within the same buying process (cf. Pettigrew 1975)—gate-keepers who manipulate the information flow to bias the knowledge and insights of others, and ultimately, the outcome of the buying process.

Insights

Buying centers are a fact of life. The quality of organizational buying decisions is likely to be low and abuses are more likely to occur in the absence of creating a recognized "buying team" versus vaguely recognized and understood "buying centers." Such buying teams should consist of persons from several functional areas and all three levels of management. Face-to-face meetings of the buying team are necessary to reach consensus and commitment to each of the small steps that occur during a buying process, and to help minimize abuses.

5. Real-life Buying Decision Processes are Simplified into Taking a Series of Related Steps that Are Often Not Pre-specified

The reality of organizational buying processes often include a lack of knowledge by the participants of where the process will lead. Members of the buying center often focus on solving the immediate step before them and the solution leads to a new step that was not initially intended.

Thus, in the tufted carpet case by Parkinson and Baker, the initial phase of the buying process was a study of potential internal solutions to the problem of developing a less expensive carpet; only when no solution was found did the company search external solutions. The members of the buying center did not initially realize that the initial steps in the buying process would result in a purchasing decision.

Insights

Predicting what will happen in organizational buying processes might best include a network of related contingency statements. Marketing's focus on the issue of "will the customer buy from us" is likely often to be a premature issue. More useful questions and thinking by both marketing and purchasing include issues that occur early in the buying process, such as, "What is the customer's next step if an internal solution is not found? What will the customer do next? How can we influence the series of steps taken by the customer in the buying process?"

6. The Creeping Commitment Proposition (CCP) is Supported in the Realized Buying Decisions Reported in the Case Studies

The CCP proposes that decision making actually involves a sequence of incremental choices, each of which eliminates certain alternative solutions from further consideration. The examples in the fifth paper by Parkinson and Baker of creating "short lists" of approved vendors in the crawler-loader buying processes illustrates the CCP.

Insights

Reality in organizational buying processes includes option-narrowing subroutines to allow easy handling of information and simplified evaluations of competing alternatives. While not necessarily recognizing the CCP or their preference for conjunctive decision rules, a natural tendency appears to occur for buying center members to mentally use conjunctive decision rules (i.e., each alternative must meet or surpass specified levels of performance of 5 to 9 evaluative attributes) to eliminate options down to two to four alternatives.

How does the CCP relate to improving purchasing strategies? Creeping commitment may lead to buying mistakes in two ways. First, options may be eliminated quickly that would provide superior performance if they were included in more extensive evaluations.

Second, the option not-to-buy from any vendor may not receive the consideration it warrants because of the belief that the costs of time, effort, and money in the vendor search and evaluation process would be lost—the feeling is created that the organization is committed to buying, when it actually is not. A noteworthy case study of backing-out of the purchase process and reversing creeping commitment is reported by Cyert, Simon, and Trow (1956).

7. Compensatory Decision Rules Are Used in Organizational Buying Processes for Ranking the Vendors Making the "Short List"

A compensatory decision rule includes selecting a few (usually 5 to 9) attributes for evaluating the performance of each option in a set of competing alternatives, for example, each vendor making the "short list." An alternative's low performance score on one attribute can be compensated by a high performance score on another attribute. For example, each vendor might be evaluated using a 0 to 10 performance scale for each of four attributes. A vendor's scores are summed; the vendor receiving the highest summed score is chosen to be the principal supplier.

In reality, several of the case studies reported in this volume indicate that a performance scoring system of a 0 to 10 scale is not used by buying centers to evaluate competing vendors. The actual compensatory decision rule used by the buying center often includes adjusting the prices quoted by each of the vendors on the organization's short list to reflect higher or lower costs associated with transportation costs, testing and reliability costs associated with deliveries of each vendor, and product quality levels. Examples of such adjustments are reported for purchasing cases for steel castings reported in the paper by Nielsen.

Insights

Quoted prices are often transformed into total purchase and use costs by buyers and others included in buying centers. Thus, the lowest quoted price vendor often is not the vendor submitting the lowest total cost bid. For marketing strategists, research to learn the compensatory rules used by buying centers in adjusting quoted prices to reflect performance levels for other evaluative attributes may lead to better responses to requests for quotations and successful negotiations with customers.

8.   For the Buying Center, Market Acceptance of Product Components May Dominate Final Vendor and Component Selection Decisions

The conclusion that customer acceptance and other marketing issues in the buying organization may dominate product specifications and vendor selection decisions is illustrated by the in-depth shampoo bottle redesign case reported in Vollering's paper. In this case the marketing department estimated the type and size of market response to different bottle restyling configurations based on field studies. The estimates were used to guide the final selection of chemical make-up of the bottle.

Insights

How much knowledge do vendor's acquire of the behavior of business customers' customers? Given that the preferences and buying behavior of customers buying the end products of business customers influence product designs and raw material components, vendors marketing to business customers are likely to benefit from detailed knowledge about the customers being served by these vendors' immediate business customers.

Thus, business marketing and purchasing strategies always include three enterprise links: X marketing to Y marketing to Z. Proposition: the more enterprise X knows about Z, the better X can serve Y. Very little knowledge is available in the published literature of X's behavior in gathering information about Z and how X uses such information to ultimately influence Y.

9. Greater Commercial Knowledge and Technical Skills for
    Members of the Purchasing Department Are Likely
    Outcomes from Innovations in Purchasing Management
    That Are Required by New Product Development

Purchasing managers, buyers, and assistant buyers in many manufacturing enterprises in the United States, United Kingdom, Belgium, Denmark, Finland, and likely other industrial countries are not receiving the technical and commercial training necessary to gain the respect and acceptance by members of the buying centers in their own enterprises—members involved in the buying process from engineering, production, and marketing. In such firms, purchasing people are told that they are not to involve themselves in the technical issues of design specifications or to propose new technologies found in their supplier search process—technologies representing major breakthroughs in the performances of required components. Purchasing is to stick to decisions related only to commercial aspects of the buying process.

The buying process by the pharmaceutical firm for a new production material reported in the paper by Faes and de Rijcke illustrates the benefits and necessity of purchasing gaining equal status with members of the buying center from other departments. Technical skills for purchasing, team-building, and the elimination of the old rule of attempting to separate the buying decision into commercial and technical subroutines were necessary for achieving success in creating a new drug by the pharmaceutical company.

Insights

Given the enormous impact of purchasing on profits, and the need for speed in successful launches of new product, a purchasing management revolution is needed in manufacturing enterprises to change all levels of management's views and relationships with the purchasing function. The continued lower salary levels for comparable job responsibilities and impact of firm performance experienced often by purchasing versus engineering, production, financial controlling, and marketing reflects the lower status, lack of full acceptance, and less technical and people training received often by purchasing people.

Purchasing management solutions to this continuing problem has been to gain professional status among themselves through such programs as the Certified Purchasing Manager education programs offered in the United States by the National Association of Purchasing Management. While such training is meaningful in improving some of the commercial aspects of the buying process, dramatically greater improvements in purchasing are likely to occur from technical training for purchasing people and team-building organizational designs that include the offer of full membership to purchasing by the members in the buying centers involved in the organizational buying process.

Similar to the marketing revolution experienced by manufacturing enterprises in the 1950s and 1960s (cf. Keith 1960), a new purchasing philosophy needs to be embraced by senior management before one can observe the organizational changes, team-building, and the technical training needed by purchasing that will lead to dramatic improvements in the effectiveness of purchasing decisions.

10.   A Paradigm Shift in Relationships between Vendors and Customers from Focusing on Exchanges to Focusing on "Partnering" is Not Found in Most of the Cases in This Volume

Most of the data for the case research studies reported in this volume were collected during the 1980s. The relationships described usually reflect "arms-length" interactions between vendors and buyers, with a strong purchasing bias in favor of promoting competition among vendors to secure low price bids.

In the buying processes reported in this volume, the new philosophical paradigm of supplier-buyer partnering advocated in the late 1980s and early 1990s (cf. Kotler 1990), and practiced since the 1950s in Japan, is less evident. Partnering, or "relationship marketing," includes building and maintaining close working interactions that usually lead to single-sourcing, just-in-time delivery systems, elimination of inventories, and substantial improvements in product quality and reliability.

Insights

Several short case research studies have reported in the early 1990s to illustrate the benefits of partnering. More detailed mapping of such relationships are needed for learning both the strengths and limitations in implementing this relatively new paradigm.

The vendors' fear of being forced by customers into unprofitable pricing, as illustrated in the steel plate buying case in the paper by Kennedy, is one illustration of the need for a paradigm shift from focusing on exchanges to focusing on partnering. The shampoo bottle innovation case (Vollering's paper) illustrates the potential for gaining fast and effective technical assistance from a long-term supplier to assist the buying enterprise's product innovation process; even without a formal recognition in a paradigm shift to partnering, the case demonstrates that the special, felt relationship between the supplier and buyer may be required to reach innovation objectives and, possibly, long-term survival for both enterprises.

RECOMMENDATIONS FOR THEORY-BUILDING AND RESEARCH

Case research studies, such as the studies reported in this volume, are useful for both theory-building and theory-testing. Theory-building and testing from case research includes the development of a series of related binary choice predictions (true-false, present-absent) based on the propositions of the theory. The propositions of the theory are derived from inductive model building—insights and observations from the interactions of people, decision rules used in making choices, and linkages of events through time for a strategic decision. *A Behavioral Theory of the Firm* (Cyert and March 1963) is an early and classic attempt at such inductive theory building. The development of a series of related binary choice predictions based on the theory is an attempt

Table 1. Prediction Matrix

Operating Mechanism	Bounded Rational Model	Theoretical Prediction for Models Bounded Rationality	Bounded Political Process	Garbage Can
1. Problem Definition				
A. Do the participants view the problem in the same way?	Y	P	N	P
B. Does the problem definition represent the goals of the organization?	Y	Y	N	Y
2. Search for Alternative Solutions				
A. Is search limited to a few familiar alternatives?	N	Y	P	P
B. Are potential solutions considered simultaneously and compared to one another?	Y	P	N	N
3. Data Collection Analysis and Use				
A. Is information collected so that an optimal decision can be made?	Y	N	N	N
B. Is control over data and analysis used as a source of power?	N	N	Y	N
4. Information Exchange				
A. Is information biased so as to conform to the preference (position) of the person transmitting it?	N	Y	Y	N
B. Is information exchange negatively affected by people entering and leaving the decision process, and changing their focus of attention?	N	P	N	Y
5. Individual Preferences				
A. Do preferences change as problems become attached to or detached from the decision?	N	P	N	Y
B. Are individual preferences a function of personal goals and limited information about the alternative?	N	Y	P	P
6. Evaluation Criteria/Tradeoffs				
A. Are criteria for a solution agreed on a priori?	Y	P	P	N
B. Do tradeoffs across solution criteria occur?	Y	N	P	N
7. Final Choice				
A. Is the first alternative that exceeds the cutoff level(s) selected?	N	Y	P	N
B. Is the alternative chosen one which is expected to maximally benefit the organization, compared to other alternatives?	Y	P	N	P

Notes: Y = Yes; N = No; P = Partially Supported.

Source: Wilson and Wilson (1988, p. 590).

298

to build in degrees of freedom (Campbell 1966) for testing the theory. The number of hits, that is, correct predictions of the theory within a given case research study, indicates how much the theory is supported by the implemented process depicted in the case.

Table 1 is a prediction matrix of such a series of predictions expected to be supported based on the propositions of a given theory. The predictions of four theories are presented in the table. The "operating mechanisms" in the table are the diagnostic tests of each theory.

Thus, for the first operating mechanism, the Rational Model of decision making predicts that the participants do view the problem in the same way; the opposite prediction for the same issue reflects the Political Process Model of decision making.

The development of such prediction matrices permit the testing of validity of competing theories of implemented strategy. Thus, a "critical test" (Carlsmith, Ellsworth, and Aronson 1976) can be made of the relatively ability of each theory to reflect reality.

Using such a testing procedure is akin to conducting an experiment to test each theory. Statistical tests can be applied of how well the theory matches reality and the case can be generalized to support one theory to a greater extent than another. Thus, the criticism that case research is not scientific, because generalizing to a population is impossible, is a misapplication of sampling logic to access the incidence of phenomena (cf. Yin 1989, p. 55). At the individual case level, the scientific contribution of case research is in generalizing to a theory, and in critical testing among a set of competing theories (e.g., Wilson and Wilson 1988).

Full-blown inductive theories of partnering strategies and exchange strategies need to be developed and tested based on case research studies. The case studies reported in this volume provide the raw materials necessary for such theory-building for exchange strategies. We do not yet have the thick descriptions of partnering strategies needed for theory building of such strategies. We must await additional case research reports in the 1990s on partnering strategies.

REFERENCES

Campbell, D. (1966). "'Degrees of Freedom' and the Case Study." *Comparative Political Studies* 8(July): 178-193.

Cyert, R.M., and J.G. March. (1963). *A Behavioral Theory of the Firm*. Englewood Cliffs, NJ: Prentice-Hall.

Howard, J.A. (1965). *Marketing Theory*. Boston: Allyn and Bacon.

Hulbert, J., J.U. Farley, and J.A. Howard. (1972). "Information Processing and Decision Making in Marketing Organizations." *Journal of Marketing Research* 9(February): 75-77.

Kotler, P. (1990). *Marketing Management*, 7th ed., Englewood Cliffs, NJ: Prentice-Hall.

Keith, R.J. (1960). "The Marketing Revolution." *Journal of Marketing* 24(January): 35-38.

Merten, P.P. (1991). "Loop-Based Strategic Decision Support Systems." *Strategic Management Journal* 12: 371-386.

Pettigrew, A. (1975). "The Industrial Purchasing Decision as a Political Process." *European Journal of Marketing* 9: 4-21.

Sheth, J.N. (1973). "A Model of Industrial Buyer Behavior." *Journal of Marketing* 37: 50-56.

Wilson, E.J., and D.T. Wilson. (1988). "'Degrees of Freedom' in Case Research of Behavioral Theories of Group Buying." *Advances in Consumer Research* 15: 587-592.

Wind, Y. (1966). "Industrial Buying Behavior: Source Loyalty in the Purchase of Industrial Components." Ph.D. dissertation, Stanford University.

Woodside, A.G., and D.M. Samuel. (1981). "Observation of Centralized Corporate Procurement." *Industrial Marketing Management*." 10: 191-205.

Woodside, A.G., and D.L. Sherrell. (1980). "New Replacement Part Buying." *Industrial Marketing Management* 9: 123-132.

Wright, P.J. (1979). *On a Clear Day You Can See General Motors*. Grosse Pointe, MI: Wright Enterprises.

Yin, R.K. (1989). *Case Study Research: Design and Methods*. Newbury Park, CA: Sage.

Advances in Business Marketing and Purchasing

Edited by **Arch G. Woodside,** *A.B. Freeman School, ulane University*

REVIEW: ". . . a valuable reference source in the field and an important forum for research in business marketing."
— *Journal of Marketing*

James W. Dean, Jr., Pennsylvania State University. **A Theory to Generate New Products that Incorporates Supplier Advantages and Market Segmentation,** Dennis H. Gensch, University of Wisconsin-Milwaukee. **Leadership in Sales Management,** Robert E. Hite, Kansas State University. **Maximizing Response Rates in Industrial Mail Surveys: A Review of the Evidence,** David Jobber, University of Bradford, England. **A Sales Forecasting Model for Firms Selling Projects "To Order",** William Rudelius, University of Minnesota, Steven M. Hartley, University of Denver, and Raymond E. Willis, University of Minnesota. **Strategic Issues for Hi-Tech Marketing,** A. Coskun Samli, University of North Florida and James Wills, University of Hawaii. **Is Long Copy Effective For Industrial Advertisements?,** Lawrence C. Soley, University of Minnesota. **Examining Salespeople's Performance: The Impact of Job Environment Variables and the Need for Achievement,** Nicholas C. Williamson, University of North Carolina, Greensboro and Alan J. Dubinsky, St. Cloud State University.

JAI PRESS INC.

55 Old Post Road - No. 2   P.O. Box 1678
Greenwich, Connecticut 06836-1678
Tel: (203) 661-7602   Fax: (203)661-0792

J A I   P R E S S

JAI PRESS

Advances in Nonprofit Marketing

Edited by **Russell W. Belk,** *Department of Marketing, University of Utah*

Volume 3, 1990, 260 pp. $63.50
ISBN 0-89232-825-8

CONTENTS: A Framework For Managing Synergy in Planned Change-Systems, *Christine Moorman, Brian Uzzi, and Karen Russo France.* **Matching Material Cultures: Person-Object Relations Inside and Outside the Ethnographic Museum,** *Grant McCracken.* **Developing a Research-Based Communication Campaign to Increase Financial Contributions to a University Library: An Application of the Theory of Reasoned Action,** *Susan E. Middlestadt.* **Nouveaux Riches As Quintessential Americans: Case Studies of Consumption in an Extended Family,** *Janeed Arnold Costa and Russell W. Belk.* **Campus Culture as a Consumer Benefit for Institutions of Higher Education: Initial Explorations,** *John A. McCarty.* **Nonprofit Marketing for Development Planning,** *Anil Pandya.* **Commercial Activities for Not-for-Profit Organizations: Review, Problems, and Recommendations,** *Priscilla A. LaBarbera.*

EDITORIAL NOTE: Starting with Volume 4 — Advances in Nonprofit Marketing will be edited by Gary Bamosey, Vrije University and Richard J. Semenik, , University of Utah

Also Available:
Volumes 1-2 (1985-1987) $63.50 each

JAI PRESS INC.

55 Old Post Road - No. 2   P.O. Box 1678
Greenwich, Connecticut 06836-1678
Tel: (203) 661-7602   Fax: (203)661-0792

Advances in Distribution Channel Rsearch

Edited by **Gary L. Frazier,** *Department of Marketing, University of Southern California, Los Angeles*

Advances in Distribution Channel Research is dedicated to promoting knowledge about the operation and functioning of distribution channels for products and services. More specifically, thought-provoking, scholarly research articles will be sought and published dealing with (1) distribution channel strategy, (2) the design and organization of distribution channels, (3) the initiation, coordination, and review of inter-firm channel relationships, and (4) interactions between other elements of the firm's marketing mix and its distribution channel strategy and management. Given the lack of adequate theory development in the channels area at this, primary emphasis in the annual will be given to theoretical articles. However, articles that center on either problems that exist in doing channels research and ways to solve them or empirical tests of underlying theory will also receive high priority.

Volume 1, 1992, 275 pp. $63.50
ISBN 0-89232-821-5

JAI PRESS

J
A
I

P
R
E
S
S

Research in Consumer Behavior

Edited by **Elizabeth Hirschman,** *School of Business, Rutgers University*

Volume 5, 1991, 213 pp. $63.50
ISBN 1-55938-338-0

CONTENTS: Consumer Panic: A Perspective on the Relevance of Collective Behavior for Consumer Behavior, *William Strahle and E. H. Bonfield.* **An Asian Approach to the Understanding of Consumer Energy, Drives and States,** *Stephen J. Gould.* **Romanticism and Sentimentality in Consumer Behavior: A Literary Approach to the Joys and Sorrows of Consumption,** *Morris B. Holbrook.* **Mass Media Communication of Sacred and Secular Values: A Semiotic Analysis of Mister Rogers and Johnny Carson,** *Elizabeth C. Hirschman.* **Effects of Sudden Income Loss on Consumption and Related Aspects of Life: A Study of Unemployed Steel Workers,** *Scott D. Roberts.* **Escape from the Tyranny of Time: Temporal Themes and Consumer Values in Advertising,** *Barbara B. Stern.* **The Impact of Subculture on Black Spousal Decision Making,** *Judy Cohen and Carol Kaufman.*

EDITORIAL NOTE: Starting with Volume 6 — Research in Consumer Behavior will be edited by Russell W. Belk, Department of Marketing, University of Utah

Also Available:
Volumes 1-4 (1986-1990) $63.50 each

JAI PRESS INC.
55 Old Post Road - No. 2   P.O. Box 1678
Greenwich, Connecticut 06836-1678
Tel: (203) 661-7602   Fax: (203)661-0792